Changing Boundaries in the Americas

U.S.-Mexico Contemporary Perspectives Series, 3
Center for U.S.-Mexican Studies
University of California, San Diego

Printed with the Assistance
of the Tinker Foundation

Changing Boundaries in the Americas

New Perspectives on the U.S.-Mexican, Central American, and South American Borders

edited by
Lawrence A. Herzog

Center for U.S.-Mexican Studies, UCSD

Printed in the United States of America by
the Center for U.S.-Mexican Studies
University of California, San Diego

1992

Cover design by Leah Hewitt

ISBN 1-878367-08-0

Contents

List of Tables   vii

Abstract   ix

INTRODUCTION

1 Changing Boundaries in the Americas: An Overview   3
Lawrence A. Herzog

2 Historical Frontier Imagery in the Americas   25
Richard W. Slatta

THE UNITED STATES-MEXICO BORDER

3 Urbanization and Development of the United States-Mexico Border   49
Rebecca Morales and Jesús Tamayo-Sánchez

4 The Maquila Industry and the Creation of a Transnational Capitalist Class in the United States-Mexico Border Region   69
Leslie Sklair

5 The Mexican-Origin Population of the United States as a Political Force in the Borderlands: From Paisanos to Pochos to Potential Political Allies   89
Rodolfo O. de la Garza and Claudio Vargas

6 The Emerging Environmental Crisis along the United States-Mexico Border   113
C. Richard Bath

CENTRAL AMERICA

7 Managing Resources across Borders: The Case of the 133
United States-Mexico and Mexico-Guatemala Boundaries
Stephen P. Mumme

8 The Integration and Disintegration of Regionalism in 151
Central America, 1950–1990
Mitchell A. Seligson and Ricardo Córdova Macías

SOUTH AMERICA

9 The Transformation of South America's Borderlands 169
William H. Bolin

10 National Security and Politics: The Colombia-Venezuela 185
Border
John D. Martz

11 Pendulum Politics: Paraguay's National Borders, 1940–1975 203
Melissa H. Birch

12 National Borders and Foreign Policy: The Case of Argentina 229
Freeman J. Wright

About the Contributors 247

Tables

3.1	Chronology of Border Cities	52
3.2	Growth of the Labor Force by Sector in Five Mexican Border Municipalities, 1930–1940	58
3.3	Number of Braceros by Origin for Selected Years	60
3.4	Profile of Mexico's In-Bond Industry, 1983	64
3.5	Nonagricultural Employment in Selected Texas SMSAs, 1982, 1983	65
8.1	Central America: Intra-Regional Exports, 1960–1986	154
8.2	Summits of Central American Presidents	162
10.1	Venezuelan Public Opinion on Foreign Policy	197
10.2	Venezuelan Attitudes toward Illegal Immigration	198
11.1	Paraguay's Foreign Investment	223
11.2	Paraguay's Real GNP Growth, 1938–1975	223
12.1	South American Nations Ranked by the Percentage of Total Trade Conducted with Bordering Nations, 1986	234
12.2	Comparison of Trade between Argentina, Bordering Nations, the United States, and the World, 1980–1986	235
12.3	Absolute Value of Goods Traded between Argentina and Its Bordering Nations, 1980–1986	236
12.4	Argentine Trade with Neighboring Nations by Type of Commodity, 1986	237
12.5	Distribution of Foreigners from Bordering Countries by Argentine Region, 1960–1980	238
12.6	Argentines Born in Bolivia, Chile, and Paraguay by Province of Residence	239

Abstract

In the final decade of the twentieth century, walls between nations are falling and new patterns of trade, travel, communications, and cross-boundary decision making are taking shape. In the new global order, boundaries between nation-states assume different roles. Traditionally viewed as buffer zones protecting the critical cores of nation-states, or as fortifications against intrusions on national sovereignty, boundaries and boundary regions have suddenly taken on strategic and dramatically different functions. As a result, cross-border relations are entering a period of severe change.

The essays in this book view individual cases of changing border relations as part of a vast regional phenomenon: the transformation of the Americas. As these nations discover the new and varied kinds of cross-border interactions now open to them, some are transforming their border areas into industrial corridors to attract foreign investment, a change that is accompanied by population growth, urbanization, and, all too frequently, environmental degradation. In other cases, border regions offer a proving ground for cross-frontier decision making, coalitions among cross-border interest groups, and even informal political alliances. In still others, we find binational collaborative efforts in economic and infrastructure development. But the study of changing cross-boundary relations is not merely about new land use patterns in border areas, coalitions and interest group politics, or the joint exploitation and management of natural resources that span political demarcations. The larger issue of how to share and manage a nation's borders helps shape all countries' domestic and foreign policies to a considerable degree, and as border relations change, these nations' policies need to be modified as well.

The chapters in this book represent some of the leading work on changing geopolitical and territorial conditions sweeping the Americas, from the U.S.-Mexico border to points south. Taken together, these essays offer an incisive commentary on economic integration and the new regional dynamics that will very likely take hold in the Americas in the twenty-first century.

Specific topics addressed in this discussion of changing North, Central, and South American borders include: urbanization and industrial development, the creation of a transnational capitalist class, the growing influence of border populations in setting national policy, cross-border political alliances, changing trade orientations and the possibilities for regional trade blocs, environmental and natural resource concerns, regionalism, national security, and foreign policy, all situated within two contexts: first, the meaning of borders in historical perspective, and, second, the implications of new patterns in terms of regionalism and international politics. Finally, discussions also touch upon some of the constraints on enhanced cross-border relations, including drug trafficking, political unrest, undocumented immigration, unequal development, and territorial disputes.

INTRODUCTION

1

Changing Boundaries in the Americas: An Overview

Lawrence A. Herzog

The final decade of the twentieth century marks an important moment in which to contemplate the transformation of the world political map and, in particular, its implications for the Western Hemisphere. While the first half of the twentieth century witnessed two world wars fought to consolidate territorial rights among nation-states, the second half of this century has seen the evolution of a new global order, one in which technological and economic processes—from communication systems to marketing and manufacturing—transcend nation-state boundaries. In effect, the nation-state's role as the dominant unit of international political and economic behavior is eroding as it becomes integrated within an economy and ecology that is increasingly global in scale. We are truly in a transnational era.

One important result of this new geopolitical arrangement is that the functions and perceptions of international boundaries have changed. National governments are beginning to dismantle military infrastructure along their boundaries, as they realize that border regions can have strategic economic value. Thus, in various parts of the world, nations have begun to include boundary regions in national investment strategies. Some border regions, notably the China/Hong Kong zone and the U.S.-Mexico border, have been converted into export-processing zones, where foreign firms set up cooperative manufacturing programs with the host countries. Other boundary areas are being transformed by investments in tourism activities, commercial expansion, and natural resource development projects. In places where the physical boundary regions have remained undeveloped, other changes such as free trade agreements are opening the borders to increased transboundary exchange, setting up the possibility of border development in the near future.

All of this signals new roles and meanings for boundaries, a logical outcome of the broad reorganization of global territory. No more appropriate location for the study of boundary transformation can be found than in the Americas. This is the only place in the world where a land border joins a developing Third World nation with a post-industrial First World country. Despite the enormous differences between the United States and its southern neighbors, there is no question that Latin America and North America are becoming more integrated. For example, recent discussions about a common market between the United States, Mexico, and Canada have accelerated. Trade relations between these nations continue to grow; estimates suggest that some 225 billion dollars was exchanged between these nations in 1989 (*Business Week* 1990). Latin America is also strongly tied to the United States through huge national debts owed largely to U.S. banks. A less pleasant example of U.S.-Latin American integration lies in the growing linkage between the supply of narcotics in Mexico and Central and South America, and the demand for these illegal substances in the United States.

Given these expanding interdependencies in the region and the global trends that are changing boundaries throughout the world, it is time to take stock of international borders in the Americas. This chapter introduces a number of the important themes underlying the transformation of boundaries in the Americas. It begins with a brief discussion of changing boundaries in general, and then moves on to the case of the Americas. It should be noted that the focus of this book is on the U.S.-Mexico border, Central America, and South America. Obviously the Canada-United States boundary could also be included under the rubric "Americas," but because the concern of this book lies with the interface between the United States and Latin America, we have chosen not to include this boundary in the discussion.

One must acknowledge that the U.S.-Mexico border and its transformation sets the tone for the remainder of the Americas. Do changes along this border reflect a pattern that may take hold in other parts of the Americas? To what extent can the transformation of the U.S.-Mexico border be compared to other borders in the Americas? This chapter seeks to establish a context for answering these important concerns about boundary development and international relations in the Western Hemisphere.

THE ROLE OF BOUNDARIES AND THE NEW TERRITORIAL ORGANIZATION OF THE WORLD SYSTEM

In understanding the role of international boundaries in world territorial organization, one might, for the sake of illustration, consider two general historic periods: first, the pre-1950 period of nation-state formation and rigidly defined territorial boundaries; and second, the post-1950 era of porous borders and transnational territorial reorganization.

Only a century ago, most of the world's borderland regions were sparsely populated and largely undeveloped. Not only were border zones peripheral by virtue of their physical location at the edges of nation-states, in a deeper sense they were marginal to national economic and political life. Most nations concentrated resources and political power in the interior. International boundaries mainly served an administrative function: to mark where the defense of a nation's sovereignty began (or ended) in a territorially based world.

Scholars writing in the pre-1950 period (Boggs 1940; Spykman 1942) found border regions to be unstable. Both world wars involved conflicts over land-based territorial sovereignty. Boundary zones often were the places where nation-states resolved territorial disputes and other interstate conflicts. Land invasions logically began at a nation's border; thus it was here that nations located military fortifications.

Because national governments traditionally viewed frontier regions as unsuitable for economic development, policymakers proposed cautious border development strategies: valuable infrastructure, such as factories, major banks, and other investments, were to be located away from the border territory, while defensive facilities (forts, fences), border checkpoints, customs houses, and monitoring stations could locate at the border. Boundary zones would remain as protective spaces between nation-states. French political geographer Jean Gottman would later term this arrangement the "shelter function" of borders (Gottman 1973). Economists and economic geographers (Losch 1954; Christaller 1966; Hoover 1948) argued that border regions were inherently destabilizing to economic development and trade. National boundaries created distortions in regular marketing patterns over space (Christaller 1966) as well as uncertainties for consumers and retailers (Losch 1954).

Following the Second World War, the world system began to take on a new shape. New technological developments—air power, rocketry, nuclear power—shifted the scales of military confrontation and power. The possibility of global warfare, either real or imagined, overshadowed traditional land-based forms of territorial conflict. Nor were innovations in military technology the only new development contributing to a shift in the scale of inter-state relations. Other technologies, such as satellite communication and air transport, gradually made human activity on a transnational scale more commonplace. A world market evolved—products and people roamed the globe freely in search of opportunity.

Thus, in the last four decades, the functions of international boundaries have been redefined. The internationalization of the world economy—the evolution of transnational markets, production-sharing strategies, labor migration, and banking systems—has led to an inevitable reshaping of boundary functions. The most obvious change has been the shift from boundaries that are heavily protected and militarized to those that are more porous, permitting cross-border social and economic interaction.

One result of these changing boundary functions is that, for the first time in history, border regions are beginning to house large populations and vital national economic facilities. The U.S.-Mexico border region, for example, will hold ten million urban dwellers by the end of the century, while twice that number will live within daily commuting distance. Industries and other prominent economic activities have relocated here. Investors increasingly find the border location attractive, as the tourism, high technology, and trade sectors grow. Political power is gradually shifting toward this region (Sale 1975; Ugalde 1978). Such changes did not occur whimsically; indeed, they are clear manifestations of global economic, technological, and geographic processes. Multinational corporations are relocating their assembly operations to this border because of the attractions of cheap labor combined with proximity to large markets for assembled products. Tourism development along this border has been fueled in part by the increased mobility of North Americans and by the growing integration of the U.S. and Mexican cultures and economies. The same can be said for expanding trade relations along the border. These are local examples of the gradual emergence of an interdependent world system in the late twentieth century.

These kinds of changes have also implied that international land boundaries shed their primary function as "buffers" between nation-states—defended corridors of national sovereignty. Duchacek (1986) has called this new territorial development a case of "percolated sovereignties." As nations softened their military postures toward boundaries, the use of frontier territory changed as well. For example, where the French-German boundary was heavily fortified during World War II (the so-named Maginot and Siegfried lines) today there is increasing cooperation in economic and infrastructure development. In essence, a new territorial order emerged in the post-World War II period, one in which boundaries are no longer simply militarized, isolated wastelands at the edge of nation-states; boundary regions have developed autonomous and viable economies; permanent boundary population centers are no longer the exception but the rule.

A third important result of changing international boundary functions is that frontier regions can now spawn their own dynamic and autonomous economies. Several factors have contributed to this pattern of change. First, growing populations living along international borders are generating large markets for retail and other service economies. Second, some economic activities in the high-technology and the defense industries find the cheap land costs and availability of large lots locationally attractive. Third, new technologies have eliminated the cost of transportation as the primary factor in traditional industrial location decisions, replacing them with concerns over cheap labor costs (Storper and Walker 1984). Many border regions have become a prime target for the location of cheap-labor assembly operations tied to larger strategies of global production (Sklair 1989).

In a more global sense, the second half of this century has been marked by the development of a transnational economic system superseding the earlier organization of the world into relatively autonomous national markets. Wallerstein (1974), one of the first scholars to speak of a capitalist world economy, argued that the origins of world capitalism can be traced to class formation in fifteenth-, sixteenth-, and seventeenth-century Europe. While for many centuries, the principal unit of global economic interaction remained the nation-state, by the late twentieth century the nation-state's role in international marketing was gradually eclipsed by new forces—banking systems, multinational corporations, production-sharing techniques and marketing structures—that operated outside the logic of nation-states. Today, an analysis of border regions, or any national region for that matter, can no longer be carried out solely at the level of the nation-state; one must account for new patterns of global economic and technological structure (Henderson and Castells 1987).

A fourth outcome of the new economic and technological ordering of the world system is visible in the ecological arena. Advanced production schemes generate spillover effects that are geographically more far reaching than ever before. High-technology disasters in industries such as pharmaceutical and chemical plants or nuclear production, are capable of spreading quickly over thousands of miles and do not recognize political demarcations. Innovative technologies carry new costs by raising the ecological stakes in a global production system. In 1986, for example, a chemical fire at a pharmaceutical plant in the trinational (Swiss-French-German) border city of Basel, Switzerland, caused a spillage of some thirty tons of toxic chemicals into the Rhine River; the ecological damage would impact a water system affecting millions of residents in France, Germany, Switzerland, and the Netherlands. Boundary regions are especially sensitive to the new territorial-ecological order; the growing relocation of economic activities and population to border regions means that more environmental problems are likely to occur near international boundaries and spill into neighboring nations. Such transborder flows of pollutants could create explosive international incidents and raise long-term problems in relations between neighboring nation-states.

BOUNDARY TRANSFORMATION IN THE AMERICAS

In speaking of boundary transformation in the Americas, one cannot forget that the origins of national boundaries in the nineteenth and the first half of the twentieth centuries were preceded by explorations of frontier regions. While scholars have acknowledged the differences between "linear" boundaries and "zonal" frontiers (Prescott 1965), the terms are sometimes used interchangeably. But historically the distinction is an important one, as Slatta reminds us in his essay in this book. Slatta offers a detailed historical analysis of the image of the frontier for many of the important borderland regions of the Americas—the Spanish borderlands (U.S.-Mexico border), the Venezuelan and Colombian llanos, the Argentine pampas, the Chilean southland, and the Brazilian frontier. These frontiers were settled prior to or during the period of nineteenth-century nation-state formation. One question that historians have asked is whether the process of frontier settlement can be linked to nation-state formation. A highly popular scholarly interpretation of this issue came from Turner (1953), who, based on an analysis of the North American frontier, concluded that the frontier was a zone of opportunity and a stimulus to democratic processes. Slatta shows that the Turner thesis is not replicated in other parts of the Americas. In most of the frontier regions from the Spanish borderlands to the south of Chile, indigenous populations were driven off their lands by European settlers; thus the frontier expansion that preceded the drawing of national boundaries was characterized by the eclipse of an indigenous people by a conquering one.

As the landscape of nineteenth-century frontiers gave way to twentieth-century nation-state boundaries, new territorial patterns have taken shape. The Americas, two vast continents that once separated distant and distinct cultures and societies, are "shrinking." Technology is gradually removing physical distance as a barrier to trade, human transport, and communication. Increasingly, capital and labor freely cross boundaries, while ecological processes become more globalized. North America and South America grow ever more integrated, and, in general, nation-states find their destinies intertwined.

The organization of the hemispheric system is slowly transforming, and a new social fabric is emerging in the Americas. Production is becoming globalized, and scholars speak of a "new international division of labor." Multinational conglomerates' searches for cheap labor transcend nation-states, and workers migrate to those world subregions where a demand for labor is created (Petras 1980; Sassen Koob 1983).

An important case of labor relocation is the emergence of "export-processing zones," cheap labor locations in Third World settings like Mexico or in newly industrializing countries (NICs) like Korea, Singapore, and Taiwan. The idea is that certain stages of industrial production controlled by transnational corporations can be transferred to cheap labor sites in or near the Third World. The most important site in the Americas has, of course, been the U.S.-Mexico border region (see Sklair 1989).

Export-processing zones represent one thread in the fabric of the new global social order. The most powerful global mechanism in reordering regions and communities has been labor migration, particularly from the less developed nations in the south to the industrialized ones in the north. Portes and Walton (1981) and others have noted that labor has become more mobile and flexible as quickly as multinational structures have created strategies to make the labor market more globally interdependent.

Another important concern for students of boundary transformation in the Americas is the question of transnational natural resources and ecology. The U.S.-Mexico border now faces severe ecological problems in the areas of toxic-waste dumping, air pollution, and sewage contamination (Bath 1986; Herzog 1986). As other border regions in the Americas continue to develop and urbanize, problems of transborder environmental pollution will materialize; this is sure to be on the agendas of international organizations in the next century.

The effects of boundary transformation in the Americas vary according to geographic context. Three subregions of the Americas deserve separate consideration: (1) the U.S.-Mexico border; (2) Central America; and (3) South America.

THE U.S.-MEXICO BORDER

The U.S.-Mexico border region has undergone perhaps the greatest demographic and economic transformation of any border zone in the world, and certainly in the Americas (Herzog 1990). By 1980 on this border lay some of the fastest-growing cities on the continent: San Diego-Tijuana (over 3.0 million); El Paso-Ciudad Juárez (1.2 million); Brownsville-Matamoros (450,000); McAllen-Reynosa (604,000); Calexico-Mexicali (460,000). Growth rates on the U.S. side of the border hovered between 3.7 and 5.1 percent per year, while the national figure was 1.0 percent (1970–1980). In Mexico, border city growth rates ranged between 4.1 and 8.9 percent per year, while the national average was about 3.0 percent (1970–1983).

Explanations for the border's demographic transformation are numerous and complex, as Morales and Tamayo assert in their chapter on the economic history of U.S.-Mexico border urban growth. The range of factors that contributed to border urbanization is extensive. Historically, events such as the Mexican Revolution in the second decade of this century and World War II in the fourth contributed in different ways to the border's transformation. The Mexican Revolution created economic and political chaos, causing many citizens to flee toward the border and the United States. World War II created labor shortages in the United States, triggering that government to author a formal program of labor exchange with Mexico. The Bracero Program eventually brought millions of Mexican workers to the border and the southwestern United States.

But, as Morales and Tamayo surmise, the border's transformation was primarily fueled by technological developments and continued economic integration between the United States and Mexico, both forces accelerated within the common geographic space of the border region. In the first half of this century, Mexican labor became firmly enmeshed in the U.S. economy; its flow across the border was dictated by cycles of growth and decline in the North American economy. For example, during the depression era (1924–1939) the northward flow of Mexican workers slowed to a trickle and many workers were deported back to Mexico. Yet at other times (the first and fourth decades, for example) labor moved freely north.

After 1960, the evolution of global systems of assembly and manufacturing led to the conversion of the border into an international assembly zone. A series of currency devaluations in Mexico in the 1970s and 1980s lowered wage structures, making it even more attractive for multinational companies to locate their assembly plants in northern Mexico. At the same time, other economies—such as trade, tourism, and services—in northern Mexico and the southwestern United States were expanding their base in line with demographic growth (see Dillman 1970; Hansen 1981; House 1982; Sale 1975). Thus the border is no longer merely a line; it has become an economic zone that reaches into both Mexico and the United States.

The results of the border's growth have not gone unnoticed either among scholars or in the media. In fact, the increase of scholarly attention to the border led to the formation of an academic subfield of "border studies," highlighted by the organization of a national scholarly Association of Borderland Scholars, border studies professional journals on both sides of the boundary, and major research centers in universities on or near the border. This recognition has extended to Washington, D.C. and Mexico City. In Washington, a special branch of the Fulbright Scholar Program has been set up along the U.S.-Mexico border, and there is increasing recognition among high-level policymakers of the importance of the U.S.-Mexico border for foreign policy. For example, a recent study of U.S.-Mexican relations included border questions under its umbrella of binational policy concerns (Bilateral Commission on the Future of United States-Mexico Relations 1989).

The rapid transformation of the U.S.-Mexico border region suggests one boundary region prototype against which other border areas of the Americas might be compared. The elements of the U.S.-Mexico border model are: first, urbanization, the gradual population shift toward permanent urban centers on or near the boundary; second, industrialization, or the relocation of industry (mainly assembly-plant manufacturing operations) toward the border zone;[1] and third, new social formations.

---

[1] U.S.-Mexico border industrialization has brought numerous side effects with it, including the growth of multiplier effects on the U.S. side (in services, finance, etc.), and positive spillover effects in Mexico (especially in retail trade, finance, services, and the growth of a border bourgeoisie (see Sklair 1989).

Speaking of social formations, as Sklair points out in his chapter in this volume, a new social class is emerging in the borderlands, one that is tied to the assembly-plant industry. Sklair calls this the "transnational capitalist class." This social group, he argues, has evolved as a regional response to the border area's role as an export-processing zone for global manufacturing systems. Unlike traditional arrangements where a local bourgeoisie served multinational interests, the U.S.-Mexico border transnational capitalist class has a certain degree of autonomy. So long as cheap labor in Mexico serves to attract an unwavering influx of foreign investment in assembly plants along the border and in northern Mexico, the "border bourgeoisie"—factory managers, lawyers, accountants, consultants, financial experts, and investors—will continue to wield considerable power in this region.

Yet another form of power is found building among another social class in the U.S.-Mexico border region: the power of the growing Latino population living north of the border. The Latino populations of California and Texas, the two most heavily populated Mexican American states in the United States, are increasingly significant sources of political power both at the state and national levels. As de la Garza and Vargas point out in their chapter in this book, the evolution of the Mexican population in the borderlands is a fascinating kaleidoscope of an ethnic population filtering between two nation-states. The Mexican-origin population in the United States was strongly linked to Mexico in its first phase of residence in the United States (1848–1928); even the original Treaty of Guadalupe Hidalgo (1848), which created the current international boundary, included language that called for the protection of the rights of Mexican citizens who remained in the United States. But as de la Garza and Vargas demonstrate, the Mexican immigrant population in the United States gradually severed its ties with Mexico during the remainder of this century. Between 1929 and 1970, many Mexican Americans actually came to oppose Mexican immigration into the United States. Yet in the most recent era, 1970 to the present, relations between Mexican Americans and Mexico have been revitalized. Mexican American leaders recognize the importance of their ties to Mexico in building cultural pride among Latinos in the United States. At the same time, the Mexican government has discovered that Latinos have power north of the border, and that an alliance with Latinos in the United States could serve their interests in their relationship with the U.S. government and also yield political gains within Mexico. Thus, the borderlands have become strongly integrated into national politics both north and south of the boundary line.

A fourth element of the U.S.-Mexico boundary region prototype is the range of transborder ecological concerns generated by the region's rapid development. As Bath outlines in his essay, the environmental problems arising in certain subregions of the borderlands have reached crisis proportions, particularly in the areas of water supply and quality, sewage contamination, air quality, hazardous-waste disposal, and pesticide dumping. The desert ecology of the borderlands is a fragile geographic setting, posing the probability that these problems will have a severe impact on the region and its vital resources, especially water. Bath also notes in his chapter that the problems are exacerbated by the poverty prevalent along most of the border on both sides (California is an exception). There is a temptation to favor economic development over environmental regulation, both in Mexico, where public funds for environmental programs are limited, and in the United States, where poor border counties favor economic growth over preservation. The prospects for greater government involvement in protecting these fragile ecologies from environmental degradation are dim, partly because in the United States the federal government has distanced itself from involvement and placed the burden on local governments, and in Mexico the government has simply not had the resources to create effective border region environmental policy. Still, some agreements have been reached on environmental matters, including one signed by the U.S. and Mexican presidents in 1983, which created ongoing binational cooperation efforts in the areas of water, air, and hazardous-waste management. There is still hope that institutional agreements can be reached that allow cooperative U.S.-Mexico border planning programs (see Herzog 1986; Martínez 1986; Hansen 1983).

CENTRAL AMERICAN BOUNDARIES

The Central American region contrasts dramatically with the U.S.-Mexico border zone. Mumme's comparative research on the U.S.-Mexico and Mexico-Guatemala borders is instructive. As he describes in his chapter, the nearly 2,000-mile U.S.-Mexico border is an arid region experiencing substantial demographic and economic growth, with water being the most vital resource needing management. The Mexico-Guatemala boundary is about 600 miles long, traverses a humid, tropical ecology, and is sparsely populated but houses a vast array of natural resources including forests, grazing lands, and hydroelectric potential. For the U.S.-Mexico border the important management issues have been water apportionment and pollution control. For the Mexico-Guatemala boundary, the policy concerns center around flood control (because the region receives high annual rainfall) and ecological preservation (mainly of forests).

One also finds some similarities between the two boundary regions: both have international boundary commissions fashioned along similar lines—as technical and advisory agencies. Both boundary commissions are expanding to try to meet the increasing problems generated by settlement and development along the borders. While the U.S.-Mexico border is commonly understood to be an important passageway and springboard for large volumes of Mexican migrants heading north, it is less well known that the Guatemala-Mexico boundary has become an important corridor of movement for Central and South American migrants also moving toward the United States. One estimate has it that between 200,000 and 300,000 people illegally cross this border each year (Portillo 1989).

Central America as a region suffers from isolation and neglect, a pattern inherited from the period of the Spanish colonial empire, when, because it lacked both mineral wealth and a population large enough to be considered for indentured labor, it was ignored by Spain. Today the region's most striking characteristic is its territorial political fragmentation. During the colonial period, the provinces of Central America evolved into separate regional subcultures. Since it was colonial Spain's policy to discourage trade between provinces, forcing all territories to trade directly with the mother country (West and Augelli 1976), the Central American provinces developed independently early on. After the region achieved independence from Spain in 1821, what had been the Captaincy General of Guatemala quickly split into five small independent nation-states (Guatemala, El Salvador, Honduras, Nicaragua, Costa Rica). Two other states, Belize (British Honduras) and Panama, evolved later. Belize remained a British colony from 1862 until it achieved independence in 1981. Panama, once a province of Colombia, became an independent nation in 1903.

The above partially explains why the Central American isthmus remains a highly fragmented region. In the nineteenth and twentieth centuries, moreover, foreign powers like England and the United States did not encourage greater integration in Central America because it was not in their interests to do so. Keeping the Central American nations isolated and powerless allowed foreign interests to exploit Central America.

While transport development unified other parts of the hemisphere (northern Mexico, the Argentine frontier, etc.), Central American infrastructure remained limited and nations remained isolated from one another. Physical geographic barriers, especially mountainous terrain, accentuated this pattern of political separation.

In the last two decades, little has occurred in Central America to alter the pattern of political fragmentation. The legacy of past regional differences has carried over to the present-day cultural and economic landscape of the isthmus. For one, there are significant contrasts in the racial compositions of various nation-states. Guatemala is dominated by indigenous populations, while El Salvador, Nicaragua, and Honduras tend to be more mestizo and Panama and Nicaragua have large black or West Indian populations. Economies vary from canal-oriented Panama to Costa Rica's more developed industrial sector, to nations that remain heavily dependent on agriculture (Guatemala, Honduras, El Salvador), to Nicaragua's experimentation with a socialist economy.

The above is all background to Central America's environment of fragile inter-state relations and correspondingly difficult and unstable border relations. While the 1950s and 1960s were a period of economic growth, the last two decades have been distinguished by economic stagnation. The well-being of the 1960s led to the push for a Central American Common Market (CACM), an institution that it was thought might lead to economic integration among a confederation of nation-states. The idea of the CACM had several limitations. For one, many of the nations had similar economic programs; thus there were few comparative advantages to be gained from trading with each other. Also, there were inequalities between nations and considerable suspicion about opening the borders for trade and interaction.

A period of military conflict began in Central America in 1969. A recently passed land reform act in Honduras stood to expel large numbers of Salvadorans living there, putting the two countries at odds over the treatment of this substantial population. When El Salvador and Honduras faced off in a qualifying soccer match for the World Cup, riots erupted, eventually leading to the Soccer Wars of July 1969 and ushering in a period of military conflict and unstable border relations. Honduras closed its portion of the Pan American Highway to the movement of Salvadoran goods, and CACM trade was severely disrupted. Border incidents between the two nations continued into the early 1970s.

For the last decade, Central America has, more often than not, been best described as a region in crisis. Problems have included the guerrilla movement and civil war in El Salvador; territorial conflicts between Guatemala and Belize; the political and military activities of the Sandinista regime in Nicaragua; continuous violence and political uncertainty in Guatemala; and political instability in Panama, leading to a U.S. invasion and overthrow of the Noriega government. These volatile political conditions have led Central American nations to pursue conservative border policies, policies aimed at defending national security and territorial sovereignty. Some nations are concerned about being "invaded" by refugees from El Salvador, Guatemala, or Honduras. For much of the 1980s, Nicaragua was seen as a security threat because of the military buildup. At one point, the Honduran border became a virtual "armed camp" for the U.S.-funded Contras, the group trying to oust the Sandinista regime in Nicaragua. The Contras, some have argued, displaced thousands of Honduran peasants, threatened families, and generally brought instability into what was once a viable coffee-growing region (Cockcroft 1989). Costa Rica also began a policy of closer vigilance along its boundary with Nicaragua due to the location of anti-Sandinista Contra encampments in the early 1980s (*Nation* 1983).

Recently, there have been attempts to stabilize the Central American political situation. Seligson and Córdova, in this volume, see recent events such as the election of civilian governments, the winding down of the Contra War, and an easing of internal conflicts in El Salvador as cause for optimism that regional integration may be possible in Central America. In fact, they argue that such integration is essential in overcoming the severe economic problems that face the region. Not only has a climate of war been costly in political terms, it has drained struggling national economies. Integration not only offers regional peace and economic cooperation within the region; it also sets up the possibility of parlaying local stability into broader trade agreements with other world regions such as the European Economic Community.

On a more political level, the Arias Peace Plan of 1987, which sought a regional peace initiative, served to isolate the influence of the United States. This may eventually demilitarize the region and open the possibilities for more stable and permanent cross-national relations, but for the moment the region still faces many obstacles before escaping a state of instability and crisis. As a result, these boundaries will tend to fulfill the most traditional functions in all of the Americas: they will continue to serve as lines of defense and to be carefully monitored. Little development will occur along these boundaries, and cross-border cooperative ventures will remain few and far between in the immediate future.

SOUTH AMERICAN BOUNDARIES

South America's nations have a long history of engaging in territorial disputes over national boundaries. In fact, nation formation in South America in the nineteenth century was complicated by the assumption that land borders should follow the territorial limits of colonial Spanish possessions, under the legal principle of *uti possidetis, ita possideatis* (as you possess, so may you possess). These limits were often difficult to determine and thus created controversy as nations sought to define their borders (Boggs 1940). Among the salient geopolitical conflicts in South America have been the Chaco Wars, fought between Paraguay and Bolivia over the Gran Chaco, an oil-rich region; the War of the Pacific (Chile-Peru-Bolivia), fought over northern Chile's nitrate-rich Atacama Desert region; Bolivia's dispute with Chile over access to the Pacific; Ecuadorian-Peruvian conflicts over oil-producing regions along the border between the two nations; Argentina and Chile's conflict over the Beagle Channel; Paraguay's dispute with Argentina and Brazil over access to a port; and Venezuela-Colombia boundary disputes (Day 1982; Child 1985). Typically, boundary disputes amounted to negotiations over territorial resources that were seen as linked to national security or to economic development.

Despite these land boundary conflicts, the last three decades have seen an increase in levels of economic integration among South American nation-states. Numerous trade agreements and economic confederations have emerged, including the Economic Commission for Latin America (ECLA) and the United Nations Commission on Trade and Development (UNCTAD). The Inter-American Development Bank has created a separate agency, INTAL (Instituto para la Integración de América Latina), that recognizes economic integration.

The growing integration of Latin American economies has led national governments to revise traditional policies of export-oriented development where relations with immediate, nontrading neighbors were considered unimportant. Indeed, a recent survey of South American countries (Bolognesi-Drosdoff 1990) found twenty-seven examples of cooperative border development projects in various stages of planning. These included programs to jointly develop and manage natural resources, tourism development, mining, food production, and agriculture. In addition, nations are discussing the possibility of building binational border facilities such as electrical plants, bridges, highway and other transport systems, and water projects. Many of these projects will locate in the leading subregion for border cooperation, Brazil-Argentina-Uruguay (Castello 1990). There have also been attempts to form decision-making entities, called "comités de la frontera," along South American borders, especially in the Southern Cone region (Argentina-Paraguay-Brazil-Uruguay-Chile). These "comités" are informal decision-making bodies with diplomats and local officials as members (Valenciano 1990).

There have been notable increases in trade between South America's nations. As Wright outlines in his chapter, Argentina and Brazil exchanged more than $1.2 billion in 1986, while Bolivia and Argentina exchanged $450 million, and Chile and Argentina $285 million. In general, Argentina's border relations have become increasingly important to its national economy and, therefore, to the political success of the nation's leaders. While some traditional territorial disputes, such as the Beagle Channel matter with Chile, have continued in the post-1970 period, for the most part Argentina's border concerns have modernized. Such issues as cross-border trade and economic cooperation and labor migration are the boundary concerns the Argentine government must grapple with today.

The labor migration problem which now faces Argentina is also a concern in other international border zones in South America, especially labor flows from Colombia to Venezuela (see Martz's essay in this volume), and also from Bolivia to Brazil. Such movements form part of a larger pattern of economic integration which has suddenly opened the possibility of regional development in some of South America's border regions. In his chapter, Bolin uses anecdotal data and secondary information to describe the amazing transformation of some of South America's most distant, isolated border regions into zones of new settlement, resource development, and economic expansion. These areas include the Lower Orinoco Valley, the Paraná River/Itaipu zone, and the southern tip of the continent. Another important boundary that is transforming is the Colombia-Venezuela one. A brief overview of these changing boundary regions follows.

THE LOWER ORINOCO (VENEZUELA-BRAZIL BORDER) AND THE AMAZONIAN FRONTIER (BRAZIL-PERU; BRAZIL-BOLIVIA; BRAZIL-COLOMBIA). While much of the territory at the Brazil-Venezuela border—the southernmost portion of the llanos of Venezuela and the northwestern reaches of Brazil's Amazonian frontier—remains undeveloped, there are increasing hints that this region is headed toward a more developed future. In Venezuela, the efforts to create a growth pole at Ciudad Guayana-Puerto Ordaz and Ciudad Bolívar have caused a population of nearly a half million to cluster in the lower Orinoco region. According to Bolin, urban and economic infrastructure are suddenly drifting southward toward the Brazilian border. Airports are being built near steel mills and aluminum factories, and there are efforts underway to drill for oil and natural gas. These developments mirror the larger campaign in Brazil to develop the Amazon basin; developments are now pushing farther into the nation's interior, touching up against the boundaries of Peru, Colombia, and Bolivia (Smith 1989).

ITAIPU (PARAGUAY-BRAZIL; PARAGUAY-ARGENTINA BORDERS). The Paraná River system, bordering both Brazil and Argentina with Paraguay, is one of the most important sources of hydroelectric energy in the hemisphere. The region houses perhaps the largest hydroelectric project in the world. The building of a dam at Itaipu, a cooperative venture between Brazil and Paraguay, and the proposed dam at Yacyreta, a Paraguayan-Argentine cooperative development scheduled to produce electricity by 1993, have attracted highways and other economic infrastructure to this trinational border region. As Birch suggests in her chapter, these developments have been crucial to Paraguay's economic survival, as they allowed a small landlocked nation to utilize its borderland resources (mainly hydroelectric power) to leverage power in its bilateral relationship with two strong neighbors—Brazil and Argentina. By playing one neighbor off against the other, in what Birch terms "pendulum politics," Paraguay has forged a clever modern boundary policy that allows it to achieve economic integration (construction of roads, free trade agreements) while also pursuing a goal of increasing individual economic well-being.

The Paraná River projects reflect a pattern of accelerating economic cooperation among bordering South American nations. In the Itaipu region, cooperation has been directly responsible for the movement of greater populations into the area, as well as economic activities such as manufacturing and soybean cultivation.

BEAGLE CHANNEL (CHILE-ARGENTINA BOUNDARY). During the 1970s, Chile and Argentina nearly came to blows over territorial disputes in the Beagle Channel region south of the Tierra del Fuego area. The dispute centered around three islands claimed by Chile near the eastern entrance to the Beagle Channel. These disputes were eventually settled and since 1978 Chile and Argentina have moved along a path of cooperation and development of this region.

The southern regions of both Chile (Magallanes Province) and Argentina (Santa Cruz Province, Tierra del Fuego) are valuable to their respective nations. In Argentina, there has been talk about moving the national capital to the south, and there is recognition of the large number of untapped resources in the southern frontier regions. In Chile, the province of Magallanes has been one of the few noncentral provinces to experience growth in the last three decades (Blakemore 1974). This province is recognized as being one of the important zones of economic development, centered around the area's oil and natural gas resources. In fact, both Argentina and Chile are putting more resources into the development of oil and gas, coal production, fishing, and chemicals in the shared southern frontier regions of the two nations. As Bolin notes, Chile has developed a free trade zone near Punta Arenas, while Argentina is building small factories on its side of the border of Tierra del Fuego. The population in these southern frontier areas is steadily increasing (Smith 1990).

THE VENEZUELA-COLOMBIA BORDER. While the Venezuela-Colombia border area has been beset with numerous problems causing binational conflict (Llambi 1989), it is also a region that has become increasingly porous to economic interaction. According to Martz (1989 and this volume), the important transfrontier issues for Venezuela and Colombia are: boundary location disputes in petroleum-rich maritime zones, illegal Colombian migration into Venezuela, guerrilla insurgency in Colombia, and the spread of the narcotics industry. Venezuela has long been concerned about protecting its precious oil deposits in the Lake Maracaibo/Gulf of Venezuela region, an area where Colombia has made claims to oil exploration rights. Drawn by Venezuela's booming oil-export economy, more than 250,000 Colombians have gone to Venezuela as illegal migrant workers. More recently Venezuela has proved unable to escape the impact of the growth of powerful narcotics smugglers in Colombia and their alliance with political insurgent guerrilla groups. There have been attacks on Venezuelan border guards by Colombian "narco-guerrillas."

Conclusion

Boundaries in the Americas, from the U.S.-Mexico border in the north to the Chilean-Argentine boundary in the south, are experiencing a transformation without historical precedent. Such changes are not entirely unexpected in light of recent examples around the globe of changing borders: the dismantling of the Berlin Wall, the opening of borders in Eastern Europe and the former Soviet Union, the emergence of free trade pacts. Yet, changing boundaries in the Americas have only recently begun to be explored, and much remains to be understood. The essays in this book begin an important process of generating a framework for comparative analysis of boundary regions in North and South America. To date, little has been written about boundaries in Central and South America; the overwhelming thrust in the literature has been toward the study of the U.S.-Mexico border zone in isolation from the remainder of the hemisphere. Yet it can be argued that the processes that have shaped greater integration between the United States and Mexico, and transformed their common borders, are not entirely unlike those operating between other nations in the Americas. And equally, the processes that have allowed for large-scale development and urbanization of border spaces along the U.S.-Mexico frontier may be at work, albeit to different degrees, in other regions of the Americas. The moment is ripe to begin systematically to explore these other regions, placing them in a comparative framework with the U.S.-Mexico border, and ultimately with all international borders.

In the Americas one can identify various prototypes for border development. At one end of the spectrum we find the rapidly developing, urbanizing boundaries, such as the U.S.-Mexico border. We can isolate a set of conditions under which development occurred along this border: (1) sharp contrasts in levels of economic development, creating an attraction for labor and investment near a region of greater opportunity; (2) locational advantages for the siting of industry, mainly cheap labor derived from the different levels of economic development; (3) patterns of regional decentralization in nations that favor border areas over central locations; (4) emerging roles for border towns in specialized, nonindustrial economic activities, such as services and tourism.

At the other end of the spectrum we find Central American national borders. Here is a region that is politically fragmented and where, although some economic differentiation exists between nations, border development is overshadowed by strong disincentives: economic stagnation and political instability. Political unrest in nations such as Guatemala and El Salvador makes it difficult for any of the nations bordering these countries to want to participate in cooperative border development schemes, or even in cross-border trade agreements. The continued presence of the Sandinistas in Nicaragua adds additional uncertainty to the region. These conditions, combined with relatively unimpressive economic gains in the last two decades, severely limit the possibility of border cooperation. In fact, the Central American border prototype is one of boundary fortification, vigilance, and defense—in short, virtual closing of international borders. Still, recent attempts to revive the Central American Common Market hold out the possibility that economic integration may yet be possible in the future.

The case of South American boundaries falls somewhere between the two ends of this spectrum. There is evidence that in South America, particularly the Southern Cone subregion, some countries see borders as regions where cooperative programs of settlement and economic development can take place, not unlike what goes on along the U.S.-Mexico border. Of course, in other ways South American borders clearly remain different from the U.S.-Mexico case. There is far less development and urban growth along South America's borders, and they remain considerably more isolated from the economic mainstream than in the U.S.-Mexico boundary region. Two considerations surface in South America: first, the importance of resource frontiers and, second, the role of border trade. The opportunity to develop new resources has played a key role in the development of South American boundary regions. Many of the wide open spaces, the vast untapped frontiers, lie at the edges of nation-states. So it is that Brazil's developing Amazon reaches out toward Venezuela in the north and toward Peru and Bolivia in the west. Paraguay, a small nation, has strengthened its hand by using the hydroelectric potential of the Paraná River in its relations with neighboring Brazil and Argentina. Oil deposits in the Tierra del Fuego area offer incentives for cooperative development programs between Argentina and Chile. The more developed countries of the Southern Cone, especially Brazil and Argentina, are now putting greater emphasis on border cooperation and coordination of common resource development in the spirit of economic integration. On the other hand, when larger conflicts, such as drug smuggling, overshadow the development of the border, as in the Colombia-Venezuela boundary case, incentives for border cooperation quickly fall away.

In the end, the value of the study of changing boundaries in the Americas is to emphasize that boundary transformation is a universal phenomenon manifest differently in varied locations in the hemisphere. It is clear that a number of common social and economic processes operate or have operated in border regions throughout the Americas: illegal immigration (the U.S.-Mexico border, Honduras-El Salvador, Colombia-Venezuela, Paraguay-Argentina); drug smuggling (U.S.-Mexico, Colombia-Venezuela); environmental pollution and depletion of natural resources (U.S.-Mexico, Mexico-Guatemala, Chile-Argentina); the demand for water resource management (U.S.-Mexico, Mexico-Guatemala, Paraguay-Argentina-Brazil). But there are also forces that are unique to specific border regions, such as tourism development and export-processing zones along the U.S.-Mexico border. The U.S.-Mexico border, in fact, seems to represent a highly evolved example of the way global processes can transform boundaries. This is a boundary that only a few decades ago was sparsely populated and distant from the attentions of national political and economic powers. Today it is one of the most important regions for investment and policy in both Mexico and the United States.

Will the rest of the Americas' boundaries follow suit? There is already evidence that the processes operating along the U.S.-Mexico border operate in lesser magnitudes on other borders. Many South American nations, for example, have made the decision to incorporate boundary zones into the national economy. This involves at least two actions: first, to change the nature of the boundary itself, i.e., to develop and change the actual use of land around the border. This includes opening boundary and frontier areas for settlement, economic development, and resource management. Second, the nature of cross-boundary relations must be changed, especially in the areas of cross-border trade and cooperation in economic development. The results of such changes are already visible in many parts of the Americas, although obviously to far lesser degrees than along the United States-Mexico border. Still, frontier regions are expanding; more wealth-producing activities, such as agriculture, mining, and industry, are relocating to boundary zones at the same time that economic infrastructure (roads, dams, irrigation facilities) are also being located in boundary areas. These are yardsticks by which the transformation of boundaries in various parts of the Americas can be compared.

While one is hesitant to identify the U.S.-Mexico border as the standard against which all other boundaries are contrasted, much can be learned from this boundary. Here is an example of large-scale economic development leading to the evolution of new political power bases, social classes, cities, institutions, and even a culture that is increasingly less dependent on the core region of the nation-state. In a hemisphere that grows ever more interdependent, one wonders whether this kind of border regionalism could, at some point, take hold in other parts of the Americas. Obviously this is not likely to happen very soon in regions with deeply ingrained conflict, such as Central America, where territorial disputes, narcotics smuggling, and political instability have combined with economic hardship to severely limit boundary transformation. And equally obvious, the vast, still largely isolated South American frontiers and border areas are significantly different than the U.S.-Mexico border. But the transformation of the hemisphere is at least partly about the changing uses of territory; it is hoped that this book will contribute to our understanding of border territory and the role of boundary regions in the new territorial order that forms in the Americas as the next century begins.

REFERENCES

Bath, C. Richard. 1986. "Environmental Issues in the United States-Mexico Borderlands," *Journal of Borderlands Studies* 1 (Spring): 49–72.

Bilateral Commission on the Future of United States-Mexican Relations. 1989. *The Challenge of Interdependence: Mexico and the United States.* Lanham, Md.: University Press of America.

Blakemore, Harold. 1974. "Chile." In *Latin America, Geographical Perspectives*, edited by H. Blakemore and C. Smith. London: Methuen.

Boggs, Samuel W. 1940. *International Boundaries.* New York: Columbia University Press.

Bolognesi-Drosdoff, María Cecilia. 1990. "Iniciativas de integración fronteriza en América Latina," *Integración Latinoamericana* 156:14–29.

Business Week. 1990. "Mexico: A New Economic Era," November 12.

Castello, Héctor L. 1990. "Antecedentes y propuestas de integración entre las regiones CRECENEA LITORAL y FORUM SUR," *Integración Latinoamericana* 156:47–53.

Child, Jack. 1985. *Geopolitics and Conflict in South America.* New York: Praeger.

Christaller, Walter. 1966. *Central Places in Southern Germany.* Englewood Cliffs, N.J.: Prentice Hall.

Cockcroft, James. 1989. *Neighbors in Turmoil.* New York: Harper and Row.

Day, Alan. 1982. *Border and Territorial Disputes.* London: Longman.

Dillman, C. Daniel. 1970. "Urban Growth along Mexico's Northern Border and the Mexican National Border Program," *Journal of Developing Areas* 4:487–507.

Duchacek, Ivo. 1986. *The Territorial Dimension of Politics, within, between and across Boundaries.* Boulder, Colo.: Westview.

Gottman, Jean. 1973. *The Significance of Territory.* Charlottesville: University Press of Virginia.

Hansen, Niles. 1981. *The Border Economy.* Austin: University of Texas Press.

———. 1983. "European Trans-boundary Cooperation and Its Relevance to the United States-Mexico Border," *Journal of the American Institute of Planners* 49:336–43.

Henderson, Jeffrey, and Manuel Castells, eds. 1987. *Global Restructuring and Territorial Development.* Beverly Hills, Calif.: Sage.

Herzog, Lawrence A., ed. 1986. *Planning the International Border Metropolis.* Monograph Series, no. 19. La Jolla: Center for U.S.-Mexican Studies, University of California, San Diego.

———. 1990. *Where North Meets South: Cities, Space and Politics on the United States-Mexico Border.* Austin: CMAS/ILAS, University of Texas Press.

Hoover, Edgar M. 1948. *The Location of Economic Activity*. New York: McGraw Hill.

House, John. 1982. *Frontier on the Rio Grande*. New York: Oxford University Press.

Llambi, Luis. 1989. "The Venezuela-Colombia Borderlands: A Regional and Historical Perspective," *Journal of Borderland Studies* 4:1–38.

Losch, August. 1954. *The Economics of Location*. New Haven: Yale University Press.

Martínez, Oscar J. 1986. *Across Boundaries: Transborder Interaction in Comparative Perspective*. El Paso: Texas Western Press.

Martz, John D. 1989. "National Security and Politics: The Colombian-Venezuelan Border," *Journal of Interamerican Studies and World Affairs* 30:117–38.

Nation. 1983. "Costa Rica Next." May 21.

Petras, Elizabeth. 1980. "The Role of National Boundaries in a Cross-National Labor Market," *International Journal of Urban and Regional Research* 4:157–95.

Portes, Alejandro, and John Walton. 1981. *Labor, Capital, and the International System*. New York: Academic Press.

Portillo, Ernesto. 1989. "Mexico Also Has Problems along its Southern Border," *San Diego Union*, August 17.

Prescott, J.R. 1965. *The Geography of Frontiers and Boundaries*. Chicago: Aldine.

Sale, Kirkpatrick. 1975. *Power Shift*. New York: Random House.

Sassen Koob, Saskia. 1983. "Labor Migration and the New International Division of Labor." In *The New International Division of Labor*, edited by June Nash and Maria Patricia Fernandez Kelly. Albany: SUNY Press.

Sklair, Leslie. 1989. *Assembling for Development*. London: Unwin and Hyman.

Smith, James F. 1989. "Problems Flow into Amazon," *Los Angeles Times*, December 14.

———. 1990. "Chile's New Frontier," *Los Angeles Times*, April 1.

Spykman, Nicholas J. 1942. "Frontiers, Security and International Organization," *Geographical Review* 32:436–47.

Storper, Michael, and Richard Walker. 1984. "The Spatial Division of Labor: Labor and the Location of Industries." In *Sunbelt/Snowbelt: Urban Development and Regional Restructuring*, edited by L. Sawers and W. Tabb. New York: Oxford University Press.

Turner, F.J. 1953 [1920]. *The Frontier in American History*. New York: Henry Holt.

Ugalde, Antonio. 1978. "Regional Political Processes and Mexican Politics on the Border." In *Views across the Border*, edited by Stanley Ross. Albuquerque: University of New Mexico Press.

Valenciano, Eugene O. 1990. "Los Comités de Frontera: funcionamiento y experiencia," *Integración Latinoamericana* 156:40–46.

Wallerstein, Immanuel. 1974. *The Modern World System*. New York: Academic Press.

West, Robert C., and John Augelli. 1976. *Middle America*. Englewood Cliffs, N.J.: Prentice Hall.

2

Historical Frontier Imagery in the Americas

Richard W. Slatta

The literature on the frontier in the United States is as extensive as it is pervasive. Since Frederick Jackson Turner presented his frontier thesis in 1893, the frontier has become a dominant interpretive theme and political symbol. Over the decades, the definitions and role of the frontier have been debated and revised. Scholars have taken Turner's theory out of the North American context for comparative testing elsewhere.[1]

The role of the frontier has also preoccupied Latin American thinkers. We find important roles and images, often influenced by or consistent with Turner's formulation, assigned to the frontier in the region. This chapter examines the historical development of the positive and negative images associated with plains frontiers in Latin America. Examples are drawn principally from the cattle frontiers of the Spanish borderlands, Venezuelan llanos, Argentine pampas, Brazilian *sertão*, and southern Chile.[2]

Frontier definitions are as abundant as they are vague. Is a frontier a place, a process, or both? Do frontier forces modify or override the "germs" of European culture carried across the Atlantic? Do we categorize frontiers by type of economic activity; hence mining, ranching, and farming frontiers? In describing Brazilian frontiers, for example, Martin T. Katzman combines geographical and economic categories, such as the

---

[1] Frontier literature, particularly for the United States, is voluminous. See Turner 1894; Bolton 1933; Billington 1966; Webb 1951, 1957; Hennessy 1978; Forbes 1962; Paxon 1933, among others. Criticism of the Turner hypothesis has been gathered into a single convenient volume edited by Hofstadter and Lipset (1968).

[2] On Latin American frontiers, see Belaunde 1923; Bolton 1933; Zavala 1957; Bowman 1931; Morrisey 1951: 3–6, 41–42; Katzman 1975; M. Lombardi 1975; Clementi 1981; Baretta and Markoff 1978; Hennessy 1978.

São Paulo coffee frontier and the Amazonian rubber frontier. From the Latin *fronteria*, the term as used in Europe indicated a national boundary. Usage in the United States through most of the nineteenth century followed this definition. By the late nineteenth century, however, one dictionary defined a "frontiersman" as someone living "beyond the limits of a settled or civilized region." Similar definitional differences arise in Latin America.[3]

THE LLANOS

The llanos of Venezuela and Colombia are a tropical plain, crisscrossed by many rivers and shrouded by forests of dense trees and shrubs (*matas*). The prevalence of trees, almost always in sight, stands out in marked contrast to the Argentine pampas and the North American Great Plains. The llanos are bounded to the north and west by the Andes and to the south by the Amazonian jungle. Depending on the definition used, the llanos of Venezuela cover between 237,000 and 300,000 square kilometers, or up to 30 percent of the national territory.[4]

Two seasons, a dry summer (*verano*, October–March) and a rainy winter (*invierno*, April–September), divide life in the region. These seasons are extreme and inhospitable. Drought conditions, high temperatures, and lack of rain alternate with torrential downpours and mass flooding. The llanos of Venezuela average 1200 mm (47.28 inches) of rainfall per year, but it all falls within a six-month period. Some areas, such as Guanare and occasionally Barinas, receive up to 2000 mm (nearly 79 inches) of rainfall annually. Within the llanos, subregional variations exist, but the livestock industry developed throughout the tropical plains (P. Vila 1969: 236–39; also Rausch 1984).

The tropical climate of the llanos made infection and disease constant threats to riders and their animals. Travelers found themselves under constant attack by what Karl Sachs (1955: 94, 236), a German physician, termed "monstrous armies of insects." He found that "the feeling of solitude and forlornness that in these desert plains overwhelms the traveler who moves completely alone, is difficult to paint." The many rivers held their own danger. Voracious piranhas, large crocodiles, and electric eels infested the tropical streams (Landaeta Rosales 1963: 2:230–31; Iturbe 1942: 25–27).

The foreboding, fascinating plains of Venezuela hold an important position in the nation's economic and political history. They served as site of the colonial livestock industry and as a chief battleground during the independence and subsequent civil wars. As birthplace of prominent

---

[3]On the general definition of the frontier, see Lattimore 1962; Mood 1948: 78, 80–81; Febvre 1973: 208–209; Katzman 1975: 275–81.

[4]Iturbe 1942: 5, 33; J. Lombardi 1976: 22. Frederick Gerstacker (1968: 67) compares the llanos, pampas, and Great Plains.

caudillos such as José Antonio Páez, the llanos helped shape Venezuela's political destiny. Yet despite their historical significance, the tropical plains and their inhabitants remain enigmas in Venezuelan historiography. Few substantial studies exist of the horsemen, cattle ranches (*hatos*), or geopolitical and economic development of the llanos.[5]

Contradictory images of "garden" and "desert" have grown up around many frontiers. Despite vastly different climates and natural features, perceptions of the Venezuelan llanos have been very similar to those of the Argentine pampas. Writing in 1875 Manuel Tejera (1875: 247) painted a glowing portrait of the llanos, "the immense plains where, without any work by man, livestock multiply, grazing on the abundant grass." He waxed eloquent over the region's "picturesque variety of plants," the "majestic silence of the forest," and the "prodigious vegetation." Some believed that the natural bounty of the llanos, as on the pampas of Argentina, killed initiative by permitting a comfortable life without toil.

Many observers held fast to the vision of the underpopulated llanos as the key to Venezuela's future greatness. Agustin Codazzi, a French geographer, estimated in 1841 that the llanos, with only 390,000 people, could support a population of six million (Codazzi 1940: 90). About three decades later, Luis Alfonso (an apologist for Antonio Guzmán Blanco, who ruled intermittently as dictator from 1870 to 1888) stressed that with "the fertility of the land, its vast extension, varied climates" and other advantages, Venezuela needed only capital, roads, and labor to prosper (Alfonso 1872: iii).

The plains frontier of Venezuela gave rise to important novels of civilization and barbarism. Rómulo Gallegos makes the battle between these forces the central motif of his powerful *Doña Bárbara*. Santos Luzardo, a handsome young gentleman from the city, confronts the powerful, bewitching mistress of the Venezuelan llanos, Doña Bárbara. Civilization triumphs over barbarism, but at the cost of revealing the close ties between the two. As with most other Latin American writers, Gallegos (1931) presents a frontier of wild, dangerous, powerful forces that must ultimately succumb to civilizing influences.

The role of the llanos in the nation's political and military history constitutes yet another element of its negative image. Fierce *llanero* cavalrymen turned the tide of battle during the savage independence wars against the Spanish. Thereafter, the llanos continued to serve as the theater of countless military engagements. Ambitious caudillos erupted from the llanos to keep Venezuela in turmoil. To Venezuelans, the llanos came to represent political disruption and anarchy. As the writer and geographer Antonio Arraiz mused cryptically, "the llano is the enemy

---

[5] No work comparable to Rausch's *Tropical Plains Frontier* exists for Venezuela. On llanos historiography, see Slatta and Alvarez D'Armas 1985.

and the explanation of Venezuela" (in Rodríguez 1979: 5; see also Vallenilla Lanz 1930: 66).

In contrast, other politicians and thinkers conceived of the llano as bleak, backward, unchanging, and unchangeable. They emphasized its vile, extreme climate, unhealthy for man and beast. The region suffered from repeated, devastating epidemics. Periodically, wet-season rains exceeded the norm and flooded vast stretches of the llanos. Gallegos, whose writings strongly molded Venezuelan perceptions of the llanos, found many negative elements in the plains. But in his romantic optimism, he hoped that the obstacles could be overcome. In *Cantaclaro*, his novel published in 1934, he has a dying man utter the following lament: "But we're in a completely savage desert! The desert! The enemy against which we should first fight! The cause of all our problems" (Gallegos 1945: 246 [quote], 1954: 84–85; M.A. Vila 1975: 95–129).

The closing of plains frontiers in Latin America occurred for widely different reasons. For the llanos of Colombia and Venezuela, decline came during the first half of the nineteenth century as a result of generalized political violence. Ranching declined precipitously on the llanos during the independence and civil wars, lasting from 1810 through the 1850s. The warfare decimated herds, drained manpower, and interrupted market routes. Similar but shorter lived disruptions hit Chile and Uruguay. We can date the decline of the Mexican vaquero with precision to the violent revolution that swept the nation from 1910 to 1920 (Matthews 1974; Izard 1979; Machado 1981: 7–28).

The llanos of Colombia and Venezuela began experiencing Spanish exploration by the mid-sixteenth century. Cattle raising and the expansion of missions to convert the Indians quickly followed. For a variety of reasons, the llanos remained a "static, permanent" frontier into the twentieth century. The region experienced little of the modernizing changes that altered the livestock industries of Argentina, Canada, and the United States. But despite the persistence of a traditional cattle frontier over the centuries, llanos imagery has less significance in Venezuelan and Colombian national life than the Western cowboy does in the United States (see Rausch 1984).

SPANISH BORDERLANDS

Expansion of Mexican ranching began during the 1530s in the central valleys and plains of Querétaro, Michoacán, and Guanajuato. Some ranches began with grants of Indian labor (*encomiendas*) or lands given to the conquerors who accompanied Hernán Cortés on his invasion of the Aztec capital in 1521. Livestock became a significant element of conquest against the fierce Chichimec tribes of northern Mexico. Spanish soldiers drove livestock with them. Mission and presidio sites raised livestock for food and transportation. Wild and domesticated cattle thrived in the arid plains of San Luis Potosí, Sinaloa, and Zacatecas, where the craggy Sierra Maestra ranges crisscross the countryside. From the mid-sixteenth century on, a heady demand for animals from the silver-mining boom fueled north plains ranching (Brand 1961: 133).

The Mexican cattle industry required extensive grazing areas, because the native grasses were sparser and less nourishing than in the bountiful Río de la Plata. Water could also be scarce, especially during hot summer months, when thirsty cattle strayed widely. But aside from the construction of natural fences out of cactus to protect farmlands, the environment saw little change by man. The harsh environment plus the Spanish cultural and legal bias contributed to the growth of large estates in northern New Spain. Great livestock haciendas came to dominate Chihuahua, Coahuila, Durango, and Tamaulipas and persisted into the twentieth century (McBride 1971: 38, 154).

As in Venezuela, political disruptions brought disaster to the ranching frontier. All sides fighting in the Mexican Revolution helped themselves to livestock from northern Mexican haciendas. Gangs of rustlers took advantage of the chaos to steal more animals. Although some ranchers managed to ship some of their animals over the border to safety in the United States, the number of cattle in Mexico dropped 67 percent from 1910 to 1923 (Machado 1981: 9–29).

CHILE'S SOUTHERN FRONTIER

Chile, wedged tightly between the towering Andes to the east and the vast Pacific Ocean to the west, did not enjoy the wide expanses of open range available in the Río de la Plata. Suitable grasslands for livestock existed in the central valley of Chile, near Santiago, where agricultural food production and grazing developed side by side. Chile's frontier extended to the south, encompassing some 40,000 square kilometers between the Bío-Bío and Tolten rivers. Today the area includes the provinces of Arauco, Bío-Bío, Malleco, and Cautín. But the Spanish military faced stiff, successful opposition from Araucanian Indians. The southern frontier in Chile could not be opened to European settlement until nearly the twentieth century. The long period required to subdue the Indians generated a frontier ambience of violence, brutal repression, coercion, and disrespect for law (Solberg 1969: 115; Loveman 1979).

The independence wars that swept Chile in 1817 and 1818 had similar negative effects. Livestock and agricultural production suffered, particularly in the southern part of the nation. Livestock production during the 1820s fell to less than half of what it had been during the first decade of the century. Taking advantage of the turmoil, Indians in the south pushed the frontier of European settlement back further to the north. Like the llaneros, Chile's cowboys (*huasos*) found themselves fighting as cavalrymen rather than working on ranches (Loveman 1979: 142–43).

Like the Argentines, Chilean elites viewed their land as perhaps overly abundant. Landowners complained that the benign climate and fertile land permitted the shiftless rural population to subsist with little or no labor. To the jaundiced elite eye, the rural poor enjoyed a secure life of fiestas and merriment. They worked only long enough to earn a few coins to be squandered at the next celebration (Bauer 1971: 1070).

But little rancher-farmer conflict occurred in Chile. Agriculture had always coexisted with ranching in the fertile central valley around the capital of Santiago, because a few wealthy landowners controlled both grazing and farm lands. Sharecroppers worked the land, supplemented by migrant labor during the harvest and roundup seasons (Loveman 1979: 123–24).

The history and imagery of Chile's southern frontier are much like those of the Argentine pampas. Both Argentines and Chileans faced indigenous populations too strong militarily to be defeated and dislodged until the late nineteenth century. The white perception of the frontier as a barbarous region derived in part from the continued presence of the "savages." The Araucanians held fast to the lands south of the Bío-Bío River. They launched devastating attacks on white and mestizo settlements well into the nineteenth century. Chilean officials conceded the south to the Araucanians until nearly the twentieth century. Official policy encouraged Chile's growing landless labor surplus to cross the Andes and settle in the vacant lands of Argentina's Patagonia.[6]

In Chile, European immigration is closely tied to the expansion of agriculture. Chilean elites looked down on their native rural population. Leaders worked assiduously to replace it with "superior" immigrant blood. Chilean officials even evicted Chilean squatters in order to give the land over to immigrants. As a result of such policies, the Chilean rural landless ended up working for foreigners in the countryside. Southern Chile became a virtual German colony during the late nineteenth century. Marginalized ranch workers and other landless Chileans migrated over the Andes to Patagonia. Ironically, Chile's discrimination against its rural poor spurred Chilean settlement of the southern Argentine frontier in Patagonia (Solberg 1969: 125–27; Griffin 1957).

Chile's landed elite nurtured great hopes that European immigrants would improve the nation racially and culturally. The nation's elite deprecated the abilities of natives (criollos) and looked to racially superior European immigrants. Chile succeeded in attracting substantial numbers of German farmers to the southern frontier, where they prospered as farmers and sheep ranchers. But immigration did not ensure national greatness on either side of the Andes (Solberg 1970: 139–46; also Castillo 1983).

---

[6]On perceptions of Southern Cone Indians, see Jones 1986.

THE ARGENTINE PAMPAS

The pampas of the Río de la Plata are probably the world's richest natural grazing lands. A temperate climate and adequate but not excessive rainfall combine into a near-ideal environment for livestock. Ranging from flat to gently rolling, the pampas stretch nearly unbroken by hills for several hundreds of miles from the Atlantic Ocean inland. Only two ranges of hills, one in southern Buenos Aires Province and another in Córdoba Province, interrupt the vast grasslands. These rich grasslands continue northward across the Río de la Plata to Uruguay and into the Campanha of Rio Grande do Sul, Brazil.

Unlike the llanos, the pampas are nearly treeless, a condition that may have been natural or created by Amerindians. Upon their arrival, the Spanish found only an occasional twisted ombu tree. Tall coarse grasses, thistles, wildflowers, and, in swampy areas (called *pajonales*), low shrubs covered the plains. The spongy ombu is worthless as lumber or firewood. Europeans had to plant fruit, eucalyptus, and other usable trees that gradually changed the physiognomy of the pampas. But the rich, natural pastures remained the mainstay of ranching until the advent of alfalfa, wheat, and corn farming in the latter half of the nineteenth century (Slatta 1983: 18–19).

The Argentine thinker Ezequiel Martínez Estrada believed in the telluric power of the pampas. He expresses the mystical forces of the plains in his brooding, masterful, existential *X-Ray of the Pampa*:

> The vastness of horizon, which always looks the same as we advance, as if the whole plain moved along with us, gives one the impression of something illusory in this rude reality of open country. Here prairie is expanse, and expanse seems to be nothing more than the unfolding of the infinite within, a colloquy of the traveler with God. Only the knowledge that one is traveling, fatigue, and the longing to arrive gives scale to this expanse seemingly without measure. It is the pampa, the land where man is alone, like an abstract being that will begin anew the story of the species—or conclude it (1971: 6–7).

The pampas of the Río de la Plata stood as a hostile, forbidding barrier to European settlement. Spaniards had to make two determined attempts before the backwater settlement of Buenos Aires could be established in Argentina. Compared with the human and mineral riches of Upper Peru and Mexico, the Río de la Plata seemed singularly unappealing for conquistadors bent on New World glory and wealth. And once they acquired horses, the many Indian tribes of the plains became even more formidable opponents to Spanish expansion.

The image of a desert persisted long after the vast plains had been explored and become better known to Europeans. In reality, the humid pampa, radiating out in a semicircle from the Atlantic coast, had nothing in common with a true desert except for its flatness and sparse population. The dry pampa bridged the humid coastal plain, the western Andean foothills, and the stony Patagonian plains south of the Río Negro. It constituted a geographical and ideological desert. Argentines refer to the incorporation of the dry pampa into the national patrimony as the "conquest of the desert."

Argentine intellectuals and politicians developed views of the pampas similar to those expressed in Venezuela toward the llanos. Domingo F. Sarmiento best expressed Argentina's perceived struggle between "civilization and barbarism." He viewed the plains as the bastion of barbarism. The pampas sheltered disruptive caudillos who stifled progress. Yet he found the strength and skill of the gaucho strangely compelling. Argentine political development was the struggle between caudillos and gauchos of the backward pampa and civilizing, Europeanizing leaders of Buenos Aires. Only by pacifying the plains and repopulating it with "civilized" European immigrants would Argentina enjoy progress and prosperity. Some Argentines today continue to view their society through a similar lens, substituting Juan Perón for Rosas, and the "shirtless" masses of Peronism for yesterday's gaucho (Sarmiento 1971).

The concepts of "civilized" and "barbaric" have usually included a racial component. In general, white people have pronounced nonwhites to be barbarians. But this means of conceptualizing the frontier involves more than white racism. It can carry a religious component that divides people into heathens and believers. Recall that the unchurched gauchos of the Argentine plains referred to themselves as "Christians" to distinguish themselves from Indians, whom they called "savages." Europeanized elites in Argentina in turn defined themselves as civilized and the lowly gaucho as the barbarian. The construct can involve multiple levels of definition (Rodríguez Molas 1968: 136; Granada 1896; Slatta 1983: 11–13).

But we find another side to the coin of dominance and racism. Frontiersmen, those labeled "barbarians," frequently hold outsiders, even their conquerors, in contempt. One unlettered gaucho of the nineteenth century complimented a European visitor to the Argentine plains: "He is a foreigner, true, but very civilized" (in Wilde 1966: 78). To the gaucho, this meant that the man could ride a horse well—the gaucho's hallmark of civilization. It is the views of frontiersmen, including indigenous societies, that are needed to round out our social description of these regions.

Juxtaposed with disparaging views, positive images of the pampa also developed. Observers expressed amazement at the prodigious livestock wealth of the plains. Ironically, some considered the Argentine plains to be too rich. The natural bounty of the region was seen as the root cause of the gaucho's perceived indolence. On the pampa, abundance made it possible to live without labor. Henry Marie Brackenridge noted that in Uruguay in 1817, "horses are so cheap and abundant, that they best can be had for only a few dollars" (Brackenridge 1819: 1:222). Cattle remained so plentiful in Buenos Aires Province through midcentury that meat was not even sold in some areas. Anyone with a lasso could find his own dinner. After consuming a few delicacies, the gaucho left the remainder of the carcass for scavengers (Slatta 1983: 21–25).

The modernizing liberal elites of the nineteenth century viewed the pampas as an area of great potential owing to its natural abundance. But the rich land needed better people, they felt—white people. The backward mestizo population of the plains held back progress. Several administrations hatched a variety of colonization schemes to populate and cultivate the frontier. Argentine leaders, including Juan Bautista Alberdi, Sarmiento, and Julio A. Roca, all believed that large numbers of European immigrants could almost magically turn the desert into a garden. According to liberal dogma, sturdy European yeomen would push aside the racially and culturally inferior Argentine rural natives and regenerate the nation economically and socially. Alas for the immigrants and for the nation, very few success stories emerged from these quixotic dreams of agricultural paradise.[7]

The Argentine pampas showed little evidence of the freedom and democracy that Turner imputed to the frontier. From the 1820s on, elites ruling from the port city of Buenos Aires waged military and political war against the frontier gaucho population. They passed a plethora of restrictive laws. Internal passports, working papers, military conscription, and vagrancy laws curtailed the movements of gauchos. Elite policy used the gaucho to fight against another "barbarian" threat, Plains Indians. Governmental oppression, coupled with massive immigration, new technology, and rural economic changes ended the open-range form of the gaucho.[8]

The demands of ranch work as well as powerful, negative pressures from the landed elite condemned most gauchos to enforced bachelorhood or, at best, serial concubinage. Some ranchers discouraged or even prohibited women from living on their land. Women were thought to arouse jealousy and provoke fighting among the men. The requirements of ranch work and the desire to escape military conscription forced gauchos to live nomadic lives. With little hope of owning land, gauchos had few opportunities for a stable home life (Martínez Estrada 1971: 205; Slatta 1983: 58–60).

---

[7] On Argentine agriculture, see Scobie 1964; Slatta 1983: 150–60; Rock 1987: 135–40.

[8] On repressive laws, see Buenos Aires Province 1822: 69, 170, 277; Díaz 1959: 105–06, 202–03; Slatta 1983: 106–25, 141–60.

Observers have often found frontiers to be violent places. For example, cowboys and expanding livestock industry came into conflict with Indians throughout the Americas. Argentina's lengthy confrontation with various Indian groups of the pampas extended from the sixteenth century to nearly the end of the nineteenth. Only a massive military mobilization and superior technology applied by Julio A. Roca in the "Conquest of the Desert" finally defeated the Indians. Bandit gangs operated with impunity and even controlled many rural areas of Latin America well into the twentieth century. Pillage, extortion, rape, rustling, theft, murder, and kidnapping victimized inhabitants of such bandit-infested areas.[9]

Gauchos of the Río de la Plata engaged in ritualized but nevertheless bloody knife duels. The traditional goal of a gaucho duel was simply to mark an opponent's face. But drunken fights often went far beyond simple marking. One Argentine rancher suggested (with some exaggeration) that 99 percent of homicides, injuries, and disorders occurred at *pulperías*, combination general stores and taverns frequented by gauchos. Police and judicial records are full of cases in which knife duels ended in wounding or death. The perpetrator usually fled to a more remote area of the frontier. Some passed through the cultural membrane of the frontier and took up a new outcast life among Indian raiders.[10]

Officials and gauchos took very different views of such frontier violence. Gauchos considered the killing of someone in a drunken duel to be a *desgracia* — an unfortunate accident. In the eyes of his peers, the killer deserved sympathy, not blame. Police viewed the incident as murder. In many other instances, the perspectives of the frontiersman and those seeking to extend their domination over the frontier diverged widely (Slatta 1983: 12–13, 118–19).

The landed elite controlled the expansion of agriculture in the late nineteenth century by maintaining ownership of the land. Spanish and Italian immigrant farmers worked the land as sharecroppers on three- to six-year contracts. Farming only became established where it complemented or did not compete directly for land with livestock raising (Scobie 1964: 53–54, 58–60, 162).

Faced with a growing foreign population on its soil, Argentina took belated interest in developing the southern Patagonia frontier. In 1895 only 300 of 24,000 inhabitants of the border territory of Neuquén were Argentine. Argentines remembered that earlier Chilean emigration to

---

[9]On the Indian frontier, see Marfany 1940; Walther 1964; Slatta 1989. On rural banditry, see Slatta 1987.

[10]See Buenos Aires Province 1864; letter from Mauricio Díaz, Bahía Blanca, March 6, 1850, juez de paz de Azul 9-4-4; reports of juez de crimen 1872, 38-4-313; Archivo Histórico de la Provincia de Buenos Aires "Ricardo Levene" (La Plata, Argentina); police reports of March, June, July 1852, Policía 1852, Archivo Histórico Municipal de Tandil (Tandil, Argentina).

Bolivia and Peru fueled Chilean expansionism. Argentina did not wish to see the War of the Pacific (1879) repeated in Patagonia (Solberg 1970: 24; Rock 1987: 179).

Like its Brazilian neighbor, Argentina continues to view its vast hinterland as the key to future national greatness. Brazil in 1964 made such faith a matter of public policy by moving its national capital from coastal Rio de Janeiro to the new city of Brasilia in the backlands. Likewise in 1987 Argentina decided to move its national capital from the megalopolis of Buenos Aires south to the Patagonian "desert." In both cases, future progress has been equated with frontier expansion.

Brazilian Frontiers

Topographically, southern Brazil is a slightly more tropical and rolling extension of the pampas of the Río de la Plata. Summer temperatures in January and February are a mild seventy-two degrees Fahrenheit at night but soar to the mid-nineties during the day. Fresh breezes moderate the climate and blow early morning fog from the hills during the less oppressive autumn months. The rich rolling hills of the Campanha region of Rio Grande do Sul proved well suited to grazing livestock. As a result the area that later became the counties of Alegrete, Bage, Dom Pedrito, Livramento, Quarahy, Rosario, and Uruguayana developed a robust livestock economy. The southern mountains (*serra*) and coastal plain (*litoral*) bound the Campanha to the north and east.[11]

Brazil's southern plains served as an important military buffer against the Spanish in the Río de la Plata. Spain and Portugal both sought to expand and control the lush grazing lands of the Banda Oriental, modern-day Uruguay. Seesaw battling over the area persisted for decades. Brazil invaded and occupied the territory in 1817. Brazilians stole large herds of Uruguayan cattle and drove them over the border to Rio Grande do Sul. Ranchers in Rio Grande do Sul, covetous of the fertile grasslands to the south, vigorously supported the Brazilian cause. Eight years later Uruguayan exiles supported by Argentina launched an attack to oust Brazil. To preserve the regional balance of power and the profits of trade, the British denied the lands to both contenders and insisted on a new, weak, independent country as a buffer between Argentina and Brazil. In this fashion, the small nation of Uruguay was born in 1828. Like Buenos Aires in Argentina, Montevideo developed as a large, dominating city that profited from and dominated the surrounding plains (Castellanos 1975: 7, 30–33, 59–64, 82).

But the rich lands of southern Brazil did not guarantee prosperity. In political and economic development, the southern Brazilian plains had more in common with the llanos than with the pampas of nearby Argentina. Ranching areas in Argentina, the United States, and Canada

---

[11] Mulhall 1873: 24. On the colonial history of Rio Grande do Sul, see Viana 1972, vol. 2.

modernized in the late nineteenth century. The Colombian and Venezuelan llanos and the Campanha of southern Brazil remained technologically backward in comparison. A few Colombian ranchers did bring fencing, hybrid cattle, and improved pasture to their estates, but they produced for a local meat market and exported a few hides. The llanos in general did not participate in the profitable cereals and chilled beef export booms that boosted other livestock economies.[12]

Part of the diminished significance of the frontier in Brazil is attributable to its coastal settlement pattern. Exploration and settlement began in 1550 on the northeastern "hump" and crept slowly southward to Rio de Janeiro, São Paulo, and Rio Grande do Sul. The sharp escarpment that rises from the coastal plain, a dearth of navigable rivers outside the Amazonian Basin, and hostile, nomadic Indians inhibited Portuguese expansion inland. Thus Brazil developed a "hollow frontier." The inland sertão and the Amazon remained largely unpopulated by Europeans. Despite the difference in frontier development between the United States and Brazil, imagery not unlike that employed by Frederick Jackson Turner also developed in Brazil (M. Lombardi 1975: 448, 456).

The Campanha of Rio Grande do Sul, with its gauchos, would seem an ideal place for the growth of strong frontier imagery. In addition to being a traditional cattle-raising region, southern Rio Grande also constitutes a frontier in the European sense—a boundary between the nations of Brazil and Uruguay. To be sure, the gaucho becomes an important regional symbol. In terms of popular values and material life, the gauchos of Uruguay and the gauchos of southern Brazil share a common equestrian folk culture. But the national boundary did create two different political climates (see Chasteen 1988; Vellinho 1968).

Brazil's frontier seems to fit midway between the ready abundance of Spanish America and the niggardliness of North America. In the early sixteenth century, Portuguese explorers encountered only hostile Indians and stands of wood suitable for making red dye. No major mineral deposits were found until the very end of the seventeenth century. Sporadic gold and diamond strikes have occurred since, but for the colonial period, "the mining industry in Brazil never went beyond a fleeting venture." Neither did Brazilian planters subdue large numbers of Indian laborers. They had to import black slaves from Africa instead. Most remaining Indians avoided direct conquest except for those enslaved by the marauding *bandeirantes*. Plentiful herds of cattle did develop in Minas Gerais and Rio Grande do Sul, but Brazilian ranches mostly produced for local markets and did not develop the large export capacity that characterized ranching in Argentina (Prado 1971: 197, 213–41).

---

[12]LeGrand 1986: 8–9. On southern Brazil, see da Costa Franco 1963; Xavier 1963. For contemporary descriptions of Brazil, see Frances 1890; Hamilton 1960.

While not as prevalent as in the United States, frontier images have played a role in Brazilian historiography. A number of Brazilian scholars, including Caio Prado, Jr., Gilberto Freyre, and J.F. Normano, have pondered the nature of frontier characteristics and influences. First of all, in Brazil the frontier region is generally defined as the sertão, the rugged interior plains or "backlands" of the country lying between the narrow coastal plain and the Amazonian Basin. The Portuguese word *fronteira* is employed like the customary European usage of "frontier" to mean a national boundary (M. Lombardi 1975: 441–42, 447–48; Febvre 1973: 209–11).

Unlike the cowboy in the popular culture of the United States, the Brazilian cowboy becomes a regional, not a national, type. Neither the gaucho of southern Brazil nor the *vaqueiro* of the northeastern sertão becomes the archetypical frontiersman. It is rather the bandeirantes of São Paulo, mestizos who trekked into the interior in search of Indians to enslave. These slave-hunting expeditions, sometimes involving thousands of men and lasting for years, depopulated many Jesuit Indian missions of Brazil and Paraguay. But Brazilian mythology creates a figure very different from that of history. Throughout the Americas, frontier expansion is accompanied by myth making.[13]

In 1902 Euclides da Cunha cast Brazilian history in similar terms in another classic of Latin American literature, *Rebellion in the Backlands*. The author based his work on conflict between frontiersmen and government forces at Canudos in 1896–97. Followers of a messianic figure named Antonio Conselheiro lost the fight against central control. But, like Sarmiento, da Cunha found much to admire in the frontiersman. Nevertheless, both concluded, in da Cunha's words, that "we are condemned to civilization. Either we shall progress or we shall perish." Admirable traits of a "noble savage" are sometimes attributed to "barbaric" frontiersmen. But ultimately the frontier savage, whether Indian or mestizo, must yield to the press of civilization (da Cunha 1944: 54).

In Brazilian mythology, the sertão or frontier is a place of racial and social democracy. João Capistrano de Abreu (1853–1927) was one of the first Brazilians to take up the frontier theme. His nationalism and "new worldism" invite comparison with Turner. Inspired by the writings of João Capistrano de Abreu, Cassiano Ricardo, Freyre, da Cunha, and other Brazilians came to believe that the miscegenation characteristic of the nation gave rise to more democratic race relations. The mestizo bandeirantes, residents of colonial São Paulo who hunted Indians to enslave them, became the heroes of this myth. Ricardo depicted the slavers as explorers who successfully bridged the cultural and racial gap between the Portuguese and indigenous cultures. The mythical ban-

---

[13]M. Lombardi 1975: 453–54. For both contemporary and modern views of the slave hunters, see Morse 1965.

deirante becomes the moral equivalent of Turner's hardy frontiersman, an archetype of Brazilian national identity and a force in cementing Brazilian national unity. The bandeirantes explored and expanded the national territory (at the expense of Spanish America) and stimulated the economic development and settlement of the frontier. The reality of the rapacious, brutal, plundering bandeirante raids was quite different from this mythology (Clementi 1981: 40–41; M. Lombardi 1975: 444, 449–51).

COMPARING PLAINS FRONTIERS

Turnerian frontier mythology in the United States emphasizes the frontier as a place of opportunity, a social safety valve for oppressed urban workers. But on the cattle frontier, cowboys for the most part had only the opportunity to work long hours for low pay. Few enjoyed upward mobility into the ranks of landholders. Laws in several Latin American nations imposed sharp restrictions on the rural population. Insofar as military and legal powers permitted, Latin American governments attempted to curtail and control their unruly rural populations. The burden of restrictions fell with special force on horsemen, who might form an impromptu cavalry for a threatening caudillo or political strongman (Morrisey 1951: 3–6, 41–42).

Turner's critics have especially questioned whether the frontier experience stimulated American democracy. Others have expressed doubt that the frontier offered a "safety valve" of enhanced opportunity for the common man. Frontiers of Latin America offered neither greater democracy nor more opportunity than more settled regions (Hofstadter and Lipset 1968: 15–42, 120–51, 172–200).

Neither did frontiers promote democracy. To be sure, a small rancher and his one or two hired hands might develop a familial, egalitarian relationship. But in general the livestock industry replicated and sometimes magnified class distinctions from society at large. Race, wealth, and culture determined one's standing. Whites looked down on non-whites, as in society at large. And whites controlled frontier resources, just as they controlled opportunity and assets elsewhere in society (Zavala 1957: 45, 56).

The advent of the farmer's frontier is generally associated with the decline of the ranching frontier. But the relationship between farming and ranching frontiers varies widely across the Americas. In general, the wealthy landed elites of Latin America preserved special prerogatives for cattle ranching. Under Spanish law and custom, it fell to agriculturalists, often Indian peasants, to protect crops from marauding livestock. This bias, coupled with labor shortages, retarded agricultural development in some plains areas of Latin America for centuries. Most often, Indian agriculture suffered as Spanish livestock raising expanded.

Economic significance is often related to historical visibility. Regions, frontier or other, that lacked economic importance rarely loom large in a nation's historiography. But this argument only partially explains the relative significance attached to cattle frontiers of the Americas. Ranching played a secondary role in the economic development of Brazil, Venezuela, and Chile. Agricultural or mineral development overshadows the livestock economy. And in those three nations, the cowboy figure remains of regional, not national, significance. In contrast, the cattle industry played the central economic role in Argentina and Uruguay until the late nineteenth century. The gaucho is a prominent topic for national historians in both countries.

But the economic argument breaks down for the United States. The ranching industry in the United States was ephemeral (circa 1865 to 1885) and was far overshadowed by the rise of industry during the same period. Yet the cowboy and the frontier loom large in the nation's written history. Clearly, forces beyond economic development are at work in shaping the significance of frontier imagery in a nation's history.

Taking inspiration from Turner, Walter Prescott Webb and David Potter focused on frontier abundance as a key historical force. According to Webb, the silver, gold, and new lands of the Americas fueled a four-century economic boom for Europe. New World natural riches created Old World wealth. In Potter's variant of the frontier riches thesis, resources and open lands in the American West helped shape the national character. The frontier remained an important historical force until industrialization and urbanization opened other avenues to abundance (Webb 1951: 8–28; Potter 1973: 124, 155–65).

By drawing from Turner, Webb, and Potter, we might argue that differential abundance accounts for some differences between Spanish and Anglo frontiers. The Spanish found numerous readily accessible sources of wealth in Latin America. As Webb emphasized, precious metals in Mexico and Peru fueled fortunes for some. More importantly, the Spanish harnessed massive numbers of Indians to labor for them in a wide range of enterprises. "Red gold," in the form of Amerindian labor, began the economic boom of Latin America. Black slaves, imported from Africa, quickly augmented the labor pool.

The Spanish "seeded" several plains regions with livestock, often inadvertently. Within a few decades after initial Spanish exploration, herds of wild cattle and horses flourished in plains regions from the Río de la Plata to the Spanish borderlands. In terms of gold, silver, labor, and livestock, the Spanish enjoyed tremendous riches in their frontier regions.

The Anglo-American frontiers of the United States and Canada lacked easily extracted sources of wealth. British North America did not include large concentrations of Amerindians suitable for impressed labor. The Aztec and Inca empires in Spanish America had already organized and concentrated the work force. The Spanish simply took over governance from indigenous rulers. Nothing comparable to these vast Amerindian empires of Latin America existed in the British colonies. In British North America, this slower, more difficult path to riches gave rise to a society of settlers, not conquistadors.

SEEING BOTH SIDES OF THE FRONTIER

As we have seen, frontier imagery has been rife with mythology and stereotypes. In addition, our vision of the frontier has been dominated by one side, that of conquering white society. Ethnohistorians have rightly criticized Turner for an insensitivity to indigenous populations in frontier regions. Researchers today have extended their vision to both sides of the frontier by including indigenous societies.

Indian-white race relations and the Indian policies of various nations have also come under examination. John Hemming (1978, 1987) has criticized Brazilian governmental policy toward Amazonian Indians. Equally critical of Argentina's "final solution" against the Indians of the pampa are Julio Aníbal Portas (1967) and Kristine L. Jones (1984). Ricardo Ferrando Keun (1986) provides an important study of Indian pacification on Chile's southern frontier. He argues that long Indian conflict had a strong formative impact on the Chilean frontier population.[14]

If we extend this corrective ethnographic vision, frontiers might well be viewed as membranes separating indigenous and European cultures. Influences pass in both directions, but the dominant pressure on the membrane is from the European side. White, European values meet and mix with indigenous cultures on plains frontiers. The two societies compete for and fight over the natural resources of the frontier. Frontiersmen often blend the language, equipment, and values of both European and Amerindian cultures (Forbes 1962: 63–73, 1968; Weber 1986: 81; Baretta and Markoff 1978: 593–95).

Spanish cultural values penetrated to frontier regions in Latin America. The medieval Spanish Catholic culture carried a stigma against manual labor. White elites avoided manual labor, so much work was left entirely to mestizos, blacks, and Indians. As in the antebellum American South, slaves tended cattle in most ranching areas of Latin America. Spanish colonies languished where labor was in short supply. Sharp lines of class, culture, and race stratified Spanish colonial society. The Spanish carried over these prejudices to frontier society where virtually no social leveling took place (Weber 1986: 70, 73; Bannon 1970: 5; Bolton 1921: 233–34).

Marvin Mikesell (1960) has shown that British settlers in North America created frontiers of exclusion that sharply divided whites and

---

[14]Scholarship on the Indian frontier lags behind that in the United States and Canada. See, for example, Pearce 1965; Drinnon 1980; Fagan 1984; Jennings 1975; Dickason 1984.

Amerindians. Despite their racial biases, the Spanish and Portuguese mixed with indigenous societies to create a new mestizo race. In Latin America, much more so than in Anglo America, Amerindian influence complemented and modified Hispanic tradition. The gaucho, for example, got his most formidable weapon, the bolas, and his favorite beverage, mate, from indigenous cultures (Slatta 1983: 7–8, 78–80, 87). For example, the vocabulary of the gaucho and the llanero, the cowboy of the tropical plains of Venezuela and Colombia, is heavily peppered with indigenous terms (Coluccio 1964; de Armas Chitty 1966). There is virtually no indigenous element detectable in Anglo-American cowboy life. The Anglo-American frontier of exclusion and the reservation system isolated Amerindians from Anglo settlement.

Despite a large body of criticism, the frontier concept, embellished by many Turnerian images, retains much of its compelling power. Clearly the idea will not die, nor should it. But further refinement is necessary. William Norton, a Canadian geographer, has laid out a number of suggested options, including viewing the frontier as "a zone of land competition, ecological imperialism, recent settlement, contact, transfer, acculturation, or a cultural region" (1983: 119). Further comparative questioning, such as that done over thirty years ago by Dietrich Gerhard (1959), is also needed. Comparative works in agricultural history, like those of Donald Denoon (1983) and John Fogarty (1985), offer useful research models.

A wide range of frontier attributes, real and imagined, has developed in Latin America. This historical imagery is still relevant, because the frontier remains a potent political symbol. We speak of the remaining frontiers of undersea and space exploration. Brazil's march inland to Brasilia and the Amazon and Argentina's proposed Patagonian march to the south remind us that frontiers still symbolize hope for a better future. Our look at plains frontiers of Latin America shows us that the compelling concept retains its power to mobilize and mythologize.

REFERENCES

Alfonso, Luis J. 1872. *Breve análisis del pasado de Venezuela*. Caracas: Imprenta Nacional.

Bannon, John Francis. 1970. *The Spanish Borderlands Frontier, 1513–1821*. New York: Holt, Rinehart, and Winston.

Baretta, Silvo Duncan, and John Markoff. 1978. "Civilization and Barbarism: Cattle Frontiers in Latin America," *Studies in Comparative Society and History* 20 (October): 587–620.

Bauer, Arnold. 1971. "Chilean Rural Labor in the Nineteenth Century," *American Historical Review* 76:4 (October).

Belaunde, Victor Andres. 1923. "The Frontier in Hispanic America," *Rice Institute Pamphlet* 10:4 (October): 202–13.

Billington, Ray Allen. 1966. *America's Frontier Heritage*. New York: Holt, Rinehart, and Winston.

Bolton, Herbert Eugene. 1921. *The Spanish Borderlands: A Chronicle of Old Florida and the Southwest*. New Haven: Yale University Press.

———. 1933. "The Epic of Greater America," *American Historical Review* 38:3 (April): 448–74.

Bowman, Isaiah. 1931. In *The Pioneer Fringe*, edited by G.M. Wrigley. New York: American Geographical Society.

Brackenridge, Henry Marie. 1819. *Voyage to South America*. 2 vols. Baltimore: Cushing and Jewett.

Brand, Donald D. 1961. "The Early History of the Range Cattle Industry in Northern Mexico," *Agricultural History* 35:3 (July).

Buenos Aires Province. 1822. *Registro oficial*. Buenos Aires.

———. 1864. Comisión de Hacendados del Estado de Buenos Aires, *Antecedentes y fundamentos del proyecto de código rural*. Buenos Aires.

Castellanos, Alfredo. 1975. *La cisplatina, la independencia y la república caudillesca, 1820–1838*. Vol. 3 of Historia uruguaya. 2d ed. Montevideo: Banda Oriental.

Castillo, Hugo F. 1983. "Agrarian Structures in a Region of Recent Colonization: La Frontera, Chile, 1850–1920." Ph.D. diss., University of North Carolina at Chapel Hill.

Chasteen, John C. 1988. "Twilight of the Lances: The Saravia Brothers and Their World." Ph.D. diss., University of North Carolina, Chapel Hill.

Clementi, Hebe. 1981. "National Identity and the Frontier," *American Studies International* 19:3–4:36–44.

Codazzi, Agustin. 1940. *Resumen de la geografía de Venezuela*. Caracas: Ministerio de Educación Nacional.

Coluccio, Félix. 1964. *Diccionario folklórico argentino*. 2 vols. Buenos Aires: Luis Lasserre.

da Costa Franco, Sergio. 1963. "A campanha." In *Rio Grande do Sul: Terra e povo*, by Alda Cardoza Kremer et al. Porto Alegre: Editora Globo.

da Cunha, Euclides. 1944. *Rebellion in the Backlands*. Translated by Samuel Putnam. Chicago: University of Chicago Press. Originally published as *Os Sertoes*.

de Armas Chitty, José Antonio. 1966. *Vocabulario del hato*. Caracas: Universidad Central de Venezuela.

Denoon, Donald. 1983. *Settler Capitalism: The Dynamics of Dependent Development in the Southern Hemisphere*. New York: Oxford University Press.

Díaz, Benito. 1959. *Juzgados de paz de la campaña de la Provincia de Buenos Aires, 1821–1854*. La Plata: Universidad Nacional de La Plata.

Dickason, Olive Patricia. 1984. *The Myth of the Savage and the Beginnings of French Colonialism in the Americas*. Edmonton, Canada: University of Alberta Press.

Drinnon, Richard. 1980. *Facing West: The Metaphysics of Indian-Hating and Empire-Building*. Minneapolis: University of Minnesota Press.

Fagan, Brian M. 1984. *Clash of Cultures*. New York: W.H. Freeman.

Febvre, Lucien. 1973. "Frontiere: The Word and the Concept." In *A New Kind of History from the Writings of Lucien Febvre*, edited by Peter Burke and translated by K. Folca. London: Routledge and Kegan Paul.

Fogarty, John. 1985. "Staples, Super-Staples, and the Limits of Staple Theory: The Experience of Argentina, Australia and Canada Compared." In *Argentina, Australia and Canada: Studies in Comparative Development, 1870–1965*, edited by D.C.M. Platt and Guido DiTella. London: McMillan.

Forbes, Jack D. 1962. "Frontiers in American History," *Journal of the West* 1:1 (July): 63–73.

———. 1968. "Frontiers in American History and the Role of the Frontier Historian," *Ethnohistory* 15:2 (Spring): 203–35.

Frances, May. 1890. *Beyond the Argentine, or, Letters from Brazil*. London: H.W. Allen.

Gallegos, Rómulo. 1931. *Doña Bárbara*. Translated by Robert Malloy. New York: Peter Smith.

———. 1945. *Cantaclaro*. Caracas: Ministerio de Educación.

———. 1954. "Necesidad de valores culturales." In *Una posición de la vida*. Mexico: Humanismo.

Gerhard, Dietrich. 1959. "The Frontier in Comparative Perspective," *Comparative Studies in Society and History* 1 (March): 205–29.

Gerstacker, Frederick. 1968. *Viaje por Venezuela en el año 1868*. Translated by Ana María Gathmann. Caracas: Universidad Central de Venezuela.

Granada, Daniel. 1896. *Reseña histórico-descriptiva de antiguas y modernas supersticiones del Río de la Plata*. Montevideo: Barreiro y Ramos.

Griffin, Charles C. 1957. "Francisco Encina and Revisionism in Chilean History," *Hispanic American Historical Review* 37:1 (February): 1–28.

Hamilton, Charles G. 1960. "English-Speaking Travelers in Brazil, 1851–1887," *Hispanic American Historical Review* 40:4 (November): 533–47.

Hemming, John. 1978. *Red Gold: The Conquest of the Brazilian Indians*. Cambridge: Harvard University Press.

———. 1987. *Amazonian Frontier: The Defeat of the Brazilian Indians*. Cambridge: Harvard University Press.

Hennessy, Alistair. 1978. *The Frontier in Latin American History*. Albuquerque: University of New Mexico Press.

Hofstadter, Richard, and Seymour Martin Lipset, eds. 1968. *Turner and the Sociology of the Frontier*. New York: Basic Books.

Iturbe, Juan. 1942. "Nuestros llanos: Apuntes fisiográficos, biológicos y agro-pecuarios." Pamphlet. Caracas: La Nación.

Izard, Miguel. 1979. *El miedo a la revolución: La lucha por la libertad en Venezuela (1777–1830)*. Madrid: Editorial Tecnos.

Jennings, Francis. 1975. *The Invasion of America: Indians, Colonialism, and the Cant of Conquest*. Chapel Hill: University of North Carolina Press.

Jones, Kristine L. 1984. "Conflict and Adaptation in the Argentine Pampas, 1750–1880." Ph.D. diss., University of Chicago.

———. 1986. "Nineteenth Century British Travel Accounts of Argentina," *Ethnohistory* 33:2:195–211.

Katzman, Martin T. 1975. "The Brazilian Frontier in Comparative Perspective," *Comparative Studies in Society and History* 17:3 (July): 266–85.

Keun, Ricardo Ferrando. 1986. *Y así nació la frontera: Conquista, guerra, ocupación, pacificación, 1550–1900*. Santiago: Editorial Antártica.

Landaeta Rosales, Manuel. 1963. *Gran recopilación geográfica, estadística e histórica de Venezuela*. 2 vols. Caracas: Banco Central de Venezuela.

Lattimore, Owen. 1962. "The Frontier in History." In *Studies in Frontier History: Collected Papers, 1928–58*. New York: Oxford University Press.

LeGrand, Catherine. 1986. *Frontier Expansion and Peasant Protest in Colombia, 1850–1936*. Albuquerque: University of New Mexico Press.

Lombardi, John V. 1976. *People and Places in Colonial Venezuela*. Bloomington: University of Indiana Press.

Lombardi, Mary. 1975. "The Frontier in Brazilian History: An Historiographical Essay," *Pacific Historical Review* 44:4 (November): 437–57.

Loveman, Brian. 1979. *Chile: The Legacy of Hispanic Capitalism*. New York: Oxford University Press.

Machado, Manuel A., Jr. 1981. *The North Mexican Cattle Industry, 1910–1975: Ideology, Conflict, and Change*. College Station: Texas A&M University Press.

Marfany, Roberto H. 1940. *El indio en la colonización de Buenos Aires*. Buenos Aires: Comisión Nacional de Cultura.

Martínez Estrada, Ezequiel. 1971. *X-Ray of the Pampa*. Translated by Alain Switlicki. Austin: University of Texas Press.

Matthews, Robert P., Jr. 1974. "Rural Violence and Social Unrest in Venezuela, 1840–1858: Origins of the Federalist War." Ph.D. diss., New York University.

McBride, George M. 1971 [1923]. *The Land Systems of Mexico*. New York: Octagon Books.

Mikesell, Marvin W. 1960. "Comparative Studies in Frontier History," *Annals of the Association of American Geographers* 50:1 (March): 62–74.

Mood, Fulmer. 1948. "Notes on the History of the Word Frontier," *Agricultural History* 22:2 (April).

Morrisey, Richard J. 1951. "The Shaping of Two Frontiers," *Americas* 3:1 (January).

Morse, Richard M., ed. 1965. *The Bandeirantes: The Historical Role of the Brazilian Pathfinders*. New York: Knopf.

Mulhall, Michael G. 1873. *Rio Grande do Sul and Its German Colonies*. London: Longmans, Green.

Norton, William. 1983. "The Cultural Landscape of the Historical Frontier," *Journal of Cultural Geography* 3:2 (September).

Paxon, Frederic L. 1933. "A Generation of the Frontier Hypothesis: 1893–1932," *Pacific Historical Review* 2:1 (March): 34–51.

Pearce, Ray Harvey. 1965. *The Savages of America: A Study of the Indian and the Ideal of Civilization.* Baltimore: Johns Hopkins University Press.

Portas, Julio Aníbal. 1967. *Malón contra malón: La solución final del problema del indio de la Argentina.* Buenos Aires: La Flor.

Potter, David M. 1973. *People of Plenty: Economic Abundance and the American Character.* Chicago: University of Chicago Press.

Prado, Caio, Jr. 1971. *The Colonial Background of Modern Brazil.* Translated by Suzette Macedo. Berkeley: University of California Press.

Rausch, Jane M. 1984. *A Tropical Plains Frontier: The Llanos of Colombia, 1531–1831.* Albuquerque: University of New Mexico Press.

Rock, David. 1987. *Argentina, 1516–1987: From Spanish Colonization to Alfonsín.* 2d ed. Berkeley: University of California Press.

Rodríguez, Adolfo. 1979. "Los mitos del llano y el llanero en la obra de Rómulo Gallegos." Pamphlet. San Fernando: Cronista del Estado.

Rodríguez Molas, Ricardo. 1968. *Historia social del gaucho.* Buenos Aires: Maru.

Sachs, Karl. 1955. *De los llanos: Descripción de un viaje de ciencias naturales a Venezuela.* Translated by José Ezquierdo. Caracas: Edime.

Sarmiento, Domingo F. 1971. *Life in the Argentine Republic in the Days of the Tyrants; or, Civilization and Barbarism.* Translated by Mrs. Horace [Mary] Mann. New York: Hafner.

Scobie, James R. 1964. *Revolution on the Pampas: A Social History of Wheat.* Austin: University of Texas Press.

Slatta, Richard W. 1983. *Gauchos and the Vanishing Frontier.* Lincoln: University of Nebraska Press.

———, ed. 1987. *Bandidos: The Varieties of Latin American Banditry.* Westport: Greenwood.

———. 1989. "Civilization Battles Barbarism: Argentine Frontier Strategies, 1516–1880," *Inter-American Review of Bibliography* 39:2.

Slatta, Richard W., and Arturo Alvarez D'Armas. 1985. "El llanero y el hato venezolano: Aportes bibliográficos," *South Eastern Latin Americanist* 29:2–3 (September): 33–41.

Solberg, Carl E. 1969. "A Discriminatory Frontier Land Policy: Chile, 1870–1914," *Americas* 26:2 (October).

———. 1970. *Immigration and Nationalism: Argentina and Chile, 1890–1914.* Austin: University of Texas Press.

Tejera, Manuel. 1875. *Venezuela pintoresca e ilustrada.* Paris: Librería Española.

Turner, Frederick Jackson. 1894. *The Significance of the Frontier in American History.* Madison: State Historical Society of Wisconsin.

Vallenilla Lanz, Laureano. 1930. *Disgregación e integración.* Caracas: Universal.

Vellinho, Moises. 1968. *Brazil South: Its Conquest and Settlement*. New York: Knopf.
Viana, Oliveira. 1972. *O campeador riograndense*. Vol. 2 of Populacoes meridionais do Brasil. Rio de Janeiro: Paz e Terra.
Vila, Marco Aurelio. 1975. *Las sequías en Venezuela*. Caracas: Fondo Editorial Común.
Vila, Pablo. 1969. *Geografía de Venezuela*. 2d facs. ed. Caracas: Ministerio de Educación.
Walther, Juan Carlos. 1964. *La conquista del desierto*. 2d ed. Buenos Aires: Círculo Militar.
Webb, Walter Prescott. 1951. *The Great Frontier*. Austin: University of Texas Press.
——. 1957. "The Western World Frontier." In *The Frontier in Perspective*, edited by Walker D. Wyman and Clifton B. Kroeber. Madison: University of Wisconsin Press.
Weber, David J. 1986. "Turner, the Boltonians, and the Borderlands," *American Historical Review* 91:1 (February).
Wilde, José Antonio. 1966. *Buenos Aires desde setenta años atrás (1810–1880)*. Buenos Aires: EUDEBA.
Xavier, Paulo. 1963. "A estancia." In *Rio Grande do Sul: Terra e povo*, by Alda Cardoza Kremer et al. Porto Alegre: Editora Globo.
Zavala, Silvio. 1957. "The Frontiers of Hispanic America." In *The Frontier in Perspective*, edited by Walker D. Wyman and Clifton B. Kroeber. Madison: University of Wisconsin Press.

THE UNITED STATES-MEXICO BORDER

3

Urbanization and Development of the United States-Mexico Border

Rebecca Morales and Jesús Tamayo-Sánchez

In recent decades, as the world economy has become increasingly integrated, borders and their activities have changed in response. This is particularly apparent along the U.S.-Mexican border, the most significant international border between an industrializing and a developed country. Border urban areas are especially sensitive barometers of change because it is here that prevailing methods of production and patterns of consumption take spatial expression. In retrospect, the legacy of urbanization along the U.S.-Mexican border reflects the juncture of two distinct economic systems. Consequently, the structure of urban activities uniquely captures the concept of interdependence evident today. Since border urban regions give form to international trends, the purpose of this chapter is to trace the evolution of urbanization along the U.S.-Mexican border as a product of broader forces in the two economies.

Throughout the years, Mexico and the United States have seen major changes in their economic systems, which greatly influenced growth along the border. For the most part, these occurred during three periods: (1) the nineteenth-century shift from mercantilism to capitalism in the regional economy; (2) the 1900s–1960s' maturation of industrial production; and (3) the 1960s–1980s' world trend toward economic interdependence. Using these three periods as a framework, this essay will examine the process of urbanization from the colonial period to the present. At times, the United States has been the primary protagonist; at other times, it has been Mexico. Consequently, the discussion that follows does not attempt to give balance to a process of unbalanced growth.

Period I: Border Urbanization in the Nineteenth Century

The contemporary border evolved through a series of demarcations. The first was the boundary created by the Adams-Onis Treaty of 1819. It separated the United States from Nueva España, the colonial territory of Spain later to become Mexico. In 1821, the province of Nueva España attained independence as Mexico, and until 1847 the U.S.-Mexican border remained officially unchanged. This delineation ended with the secession of Texas and the Mexican-American War of 1847. The border, as accorded in the Treaty of Guadalupe Hildago, 1847, was again modified five years later through the Gadsden Purchase (1853–1854). By 1854, not only had the border been significantly altered from the first designation, but with these agreements Mexico ceded approximately one-half of its land base to the United States. While on the surface the land acquisition appeared to present an opportunity for expansion by the United States, several conditions had to be met before the West could be considered part of the national economy. These consisted of: (1) U.S. colonization of western lands (1819–1848); (2) introduction of capitalism into the regional economies (1848–1865); and (3) integration of the West with the eastern part of the United States (1865–1910). A glimpse into the past shows how this was accomplished.

The Southwest Shifts Hands, 1819–1848

The colonization of northern Mexico under Spanish rule began with quests for minerals and expeditions by adventurers and missionaries. Early pathfinders opened the region for military outposts and religious settlements. Based on the latifundia form of Spanish land tenure, this area, known as the Interior Provinces of New Spain, grew as a peripheral frontier to be exploited for its resources.

The Interior Provinces of New Spain, as designated in 1772, consisted of Texas, New Mexico, California, Sonora, Sinaloa, Nueva Vizcaya, Coahuila, Chihuahua, Nuevo León, and Nuevo Santander. Life was difficult for settlers in the region. On reflection of the period, one historian wrote that local residents were controlled by "the heavy hand of bureaucracy, [an] unrealistic tax structure, and the rigid supervision of every phase of life, coupled with the ever-present Indian menace" (Faulk 1968: 82).

Consequently, when the French Revolution and skirmishes in the New World diverted Spain's attention, subjects of New Spain began to rally for independence. Their efforts culminated in the Mexican War for Independence (1810–1821), and ultimately recognition of Mexico as a sovereign nation. Along with independence, Mexico inherited a northern border demarcated by the Adams-Onis Treaty (also known as the Florida Treaty or the Treaty of 1819) which separated the Louisiana

Territory from the Interior Provinces of New Spain. This was a short-lived boundary, however, as the new nation soon became saddled with territorial disputes created by settlers from the United States.

From trailblazers such as William Becknell, the founder of the Santa Fe Trail (1821), to explorers looking for pelts, to immigrants who ventured across the country in search of land, the mainstay population of the region showed little allegiance to Mexico. They chose the secession of Texas in 1836 over ceding their political and economic decision-making power to Mexico. To prevent recapture by Mexico, the newly created Lone Star Republic of Texas surrendered its independence to the United States in 1845. Tensions between the United States and Mexico mounted. Overtures toward annexation of California, unsettled land claims, and U.S. military offenses ultimately triggered the Mexican-American War of 1847. With termination of the war and the signing of the Treaty of Guadalupe Hidalgo in 1848, the border was once again redrawn and extended from the mouth of the Bravo/Grande River to San Diego.

THE REGIONAL ECONOMY TAKES DEFINITION, 1848–1865

With annexation of the West essentially complete, internal development of the United States accelerated. Attracted by the Gold Rush of 1848, prospectors flooded into the region and found it rich in other minerals as well. Though the potential for prosperity seemed limitless, growth was constrained by the lack of easy access. To open the region, Mexico was coerced into selling a final parcel of land, known as the Gadsen Purchase of 1853. This property made possible construction of a transnational railroad within the United States (1865). Now, with the final transportation link in place, integration of the region into the national economy was technically feasible.

Yet the reality of this only occurred when the United States developed a coherent regional economy. In many parts of the Southwest, Native Americans controlled large parcels of land or key continental routes, a barrier that was ultimately overcome through near total extinction. Additional conflicts between the industrial economy of the North and that of the plantation South culminated in the Civil War of 1865. By the end of the war, the Indian or indigenous and plantation economic systems were essentially abolished, and industrial expansion proceeded westward.

RISE OF THE INDUSTRIAL UNITED STATES AND RESTORATION OF THE MEXICAN REPUBLIC

At the end of the nineteenth century, the United States' industrial capacity was growing rapidly. Market expansion at home and abroad was further aided by construction of the Panama Canal (1904) and inventions such as the telegraph and electric light. In the search for markets and sites for investment, Mexico provided a natural complement to burgeoning entrepreneurial interests in the United States.

Due largely to foreign investment, economic growth in Mexico reached an all-time high between 1876 and 1911. Known as the "Por-

TABLE 3.1
CHRONOLOGY OF BORDER CITIES

Founded as forts, missions, and civil centers under Spanish rule	
Paso del Norte (Ciudad Juárez), Chihuahua	1659
Sonoyta, Sonora	late 17th century
Ojinaga, Chihuahua	1712
Camargo, Tamaulipas	1749
Reynosa, Tamaulipas	1749
Laredo, Texas/Nuevo Laredo, Tamaulipas	1749
Revilla (Ciudad Guerrero), Tamaulipas	1750
Mier, Tamaulipas	1751
San Diego, California	1769
Founded as civil centers and forts under Mexican rule	
Matamoros, Tamaulipas	1821
Tijuana, Baja California	1840
Brownsville, Texas	1846
Founded after creation of the international boundary	
A. As forts and supply stations	
El Paso, Texas	
early settlements	1849
official	1873
Nuevo Laredo, Tamaulipas	1849
Presidio, Texas	1849–1851
Eagle Pass, Texas/Piedras Negras, Coahuila	1849–1851
B. Post-Civil War transportation and commercial era	
Nogales, Arizona/Nogales, Sonora	1888
Del Rio, Texas/Ciudad Acuna, Coahuila	1890s
Columbus, New Mexico/Palomas, Chihuahua	1890s
Naco, Arizona/Naco, Sonora	1900s
Douglas, Arizona/Agua Prieta, Sonora	1900–1901
Tecate, Baja California	1900–1921
Calexico, California/Mexicali, Baja California	1900–1901
Yuma, Arizona/San Luis Río Colorado, Baja California	1900–1901
San Ysidro, California	1920s
Lukeville, Arizona	1920s

Source: Adapted from Gildersleeve 1987: 75.

firiato" in reference to the thirty-year reign of President Porfirio Díaz, it was a period of political centralization coupled with extensive economic development. Railroad lines built by U.S. firms connected Mexico City to Ciudad Juárez and Nuevo Laredo (1891), resulting not only in growth of the domestic market, but also in stronger ties between Mexico and the United States. As noted by historian James Cockcroft:

> [T]he new lines, built by Indian wage labor and owned by foreign capital, linked the rich mining areas of northern and central Mexico to key gulf ports, Texas border towns, and industrial centers like Chicago and Pittsburgh, facilitating the export of raw materials and labor power. Mexican migrant laborers began to move north (1983: 88–89).

Drawn by potential urban employment, thousands of peasants migrated from Mexican fields to factories in both Mexico and the United States. Mexicans residing in the United States grew by a factor of three between 1880 and 1910 (Cockcroft 1983: 91). While Mexican labor moved to the United States, U.S. capital was moving south. In 1897, U.S. investments in Mexico, mainly in railroads, mining, and oil extraction, equalled more than $200 million, well in excess of U.S. investments elsewhere in the world. Throughout the Porfiriato, industrial production grew threefold, agriculture doubled, and mining realized a tenfold increase. But the rapid growth fueled social unrest. Beginning with a 1906 strike at an American-owned mine in Cananea, Sonora, discontent and uprisings climaxed in the prolonged Mexican Revolution of 1910–1921.

With the Revolution, the preindustrial period of urbanization along the border came to a close. The majority of border cities had by now come into existence, and functioned as conduits for trade between the United States and Mexico. Twin cities emerged and prospered from international commercial exchange and production. The formation of border urban areas is summarized in table 3.1.

PERIOD II: URBANIZATION OF THE BORDER, 1900–1960S

From the turn of the century to the mid-1960s, the U.S. economy moved rapidly toward industrialization. For the most part, U.S. border cities grew on the basis of trade and services. Mexican border cities along the western edge serviced an urban population, while those in the eastern half had a more rural orientation. Several twin cities developed which shared strong symbiotic relationships. The following discussion follows the development of several urban areas by focusing on eight benchmark events between the 1900s and 1960s.

HYDRAULIC INFRASTRUCTURE AND THE GROWTH OF AGRICULTURE, 1900–1950S

With construction of the Imperial Canal in 1901, passage of the Newlands Reclamation Act in 1902 which allocated federal funds for the construction of large-scale irrigation and reclamation projects, and construction of the Roosevelt Dam (1905–1911) near Phoenix, Arizona, fallow western lands became useable for intensive agricultural production. Massive water projects combining reclamation and flood control brought millions of acres of land in the Southwest into cultivation. The most ambitious infrastructure developments consisted of construction of Boulder Dam (1931) and the All-American Canal (1940), which introduced water into the Imperial and Coachella valleys of Southern California, transforming them into major producers of citrus and vegetables. The All-American Canal replaced the old Imperial Canal, part of which had been built in Mexican territory. The Hoover (1935) and other dams regulating Colorado River tributaries also provided water to support the explosive urban growth of Los Angeles and other Southern California cities.

As southwestern U.S. agricultural lands opened up, the Mexican border communities of Mexicali, Reynosa, Matamoros, and Ciudad Juárez became catchment and deployment centers for seasonal farm labor. Towns along the Rio Grande Valley in Texas experienced spurts of growth following post-World War I private irrigation efforts, and again after passage of the Rio Grande Compact (1938), which allocated Rio Grande water for irrigation. Mexican government irrigation plans dating from the 1930s supported the irrigation districts of Mexicali and the Bajo Río San Juan and Palestina irrigation districts. Jointly, these improvements fostered growth in the region.

Mexicali demonstrates how strong ties with agriculture shaped the development of border cities. Originally Mexicali was a "planned city" designed by the Colorado River Land Company (1903–04). The plan called for a grid pattern of streets coupled with a series of canals channeling Colorado River water through the center of town. Orderly streets directed toward the border mirrored the northern orientation of the population. Residential land use resembled the U.S. style of "house-on-lot" layout rather than the Latin style of building houses flush with the street. For years, the local economy depended on commuters to the United States who retained permanent residence in Mexico, a pattern that was finally disrupted in the mid-1960s, when mechanization and the fall of cotton prices displaced numerous farm laborers. As unemployment began to rise, Mexicali experienced a surge of casual housing, or squatter settlements. Since then, the economic base steadily shifted toward industrial employment. Today Mexicali's diversified economy relies not only on agriculture but also on industrial development and, to a lesser extent, tourist trade.

Mexican Revolution, 1910–1921

Mexican migration to the United States of workers attracted by employment in U.S. railroads, mines, and ranches became noticeable during the Porfiriato, and grew even stronger with the outbreak of the Mexican Revolution in 1910. At the beginning of the Revolution, more than twenty thousand miles of railroad track had been laid, which provided a major means of transport. Between 1900 and 1930, an estimated 1.5 million residents fled their country, resulting in a loss of nearly 10 percent of Mexico's population (Cross and Sandos 1981: 10).

Often those who emigrated were recruited to work on the construction and maintenance of railroads in major rail cities, such as Chicago and Kansas City. Within a few decades, Mexicans had become the backbone of the labor force in many urban sectors; from 17.1 percent of the labor force of nine western railroads in 1909, they rose to 59.9 percent by 1929. At the beginning of the century, as the United States rapidly industrialized, Mexicans were easily absorbed into all types of employment, including "steel mills, mines, meatpacking plants, brickyards, canneries, . . . and with the new century came the need for workers to pave city streets, construct new buildings, and erect dams and bridges" (Hoffman 1976: 7). Mexican farm labor worked the fields of the Imperial and San Joaquin valleys in California, the Salt River Valley of Arizona, and the Lower Rio Grande Valley of Texas. Despite passage of the Immigration Act of 1917, which established a literacy test and tax on immigrants, most Mexicans were exempted, largely because of labor shortages that developed after the onset of World War I. Due to the high demand for labor, border cities were pass-throughs for numerous destinations across the United States, ranging from Omaha to Detroit, New Orleans, and, of course, cities in the Southwest.

The Prohibition Era, 1915–1933

While one kind of bond was being forged between U.S. industrial cities and Mexico, another was developing between Southern California and northern Mexico around the provision of personal services. The years prior to the Great Depression were marked by rapid growth in Southern California. Built around an excellent natural harbor, San Diego was an ideal site for the location of a major naval base. Both naval employment and the aircraft industry expanded during World War I. Complementing the burgeoning population of San Diego was the explosive growth of Los Angeles. The old Pueblo de Nuestra Señora de Los Angeles was transformed by the entertainment industry into a city known for glitter, the tinsel of Hollywood, and good times. In keeping with the reform movement sweeping the country, however, some of the bawdier forms of entertainment came under public scrutiny, and California outlawed horse racing (1915), prostitution (1917), and dance halls (1917). Within a matter of years, the Eighteenth Amendment to the U.S. Constitution was passed (1920), which prohibited production and sale of alcoholic beverages. As these activities closed down in Southern California, the Mexican border towns of Tijuana, Nogales, and Ciudad Juárez picked up the slack in vice trade. In response to the high demand for liquor, wineries, breweries, and distilleries were established (e.g., Cervecería Mexicali, Mexicali 1923; Fábrica de Whiskey Bourbón, Tecate 1917), and the service economy boomed (Piñera Ramírez 1983).

One of the most colorful histories of this period is found in the archives of Tijuana. When its northern neighbor organized the San Diego-Panama Exposition (1915–1916), Tijuana took advantage of the opportunity to expand tourism by erecting a "Feria Típica Mexicana" (1916). The fair offered all the diversions unavailable in San Diego: boxing, cockfighting, gambling, and bullfighting, plus a casino and night club. Horse racing, which opened in 1916, became a popular tourist attraction. Much of the financing for these activities came from U.S. gangsters and racketeers. The Tijuana racetrack illustrates how complex these arrangements could be: "the property at the time of the track's construction was owned in part by John D. Spreckels, the sugar and rail financier. Former San Francisco boxing promoter James Wood Cofforth [Sunny Jim] handled the racing; former Bakersfield cabaret owner Carl Withington handled the gambling, and Ed Baker controlled the importing of spirits into Tijuana and Mexicali, while Withington ran the Mexicali Brewery" (Price 1973: 51).

For a while the moralistic fervor of the United States dampened Tijuana's economy. In 1917, persons in military uniform were prohibited from crossing the border and passports were required from citizens attempting to return. Yet things picked up again after passage of the Eighteenth Amendment. Throughout the Roaring Twenties movie stars like Charlie Chaplin, Fatty Arbuckle, Tom Mix, and Buster Keaton could be seen there. The high-rolling period continued until repeal of Prohibition (1927) followed by the Depression (1929), and then the bubble burst. Foreign investors closed shop, the clients stopped coming, and it was clear this city had followed a poor model of development.

IMMIGRATION REGULATIONS/THE GREAT DEPRESSION/REPATRIATION, 1924–1939

When the U.S. economy was expanding or when war mobilization created a shortage of labor power, Mexican workers found a ready market. This was a different matter altogether when labor markets were slack, as occurred after termination of World War I and again during the Depression. To address the unemployment problem in the United States, an unlikely coalition of "small farmers, progressives, labor unions, eugenicists and racists" rallied behind passage of the National Quota Act of 1921, which placed a limit on immigrants from Europe and

Asia (Hoffman 1976: 26). The National Quota Act expansion of 1924 established visa policies that further constrained Mexican entry, as did creation of the Border Patrol in 1925. By 1930, virtually no visas were granted to Mexicans who were common laborers unless they had previously resided in the United States (Hoffman 1976: 32).

When the stock market crashed in 1929, efforts were stepped up not only to deny immigrants entry into the United States, but to repatriate Mexicans already there. The arguments for repatriation came from two sides. The federal government threatened deportation of immigrants holding jobs who were seen as depriving citizens of employment, while local public and private groups sought to remove unemployed immigrants who were already—or had the potential of becoming—public charges. In response to growing national pressure, a federal program began in 1931, followed by several local repatriation efforts.

By far the most intensive local repatriation program took place in Los Angeles, where Mexican families were rounded up and sent by train to El Paso. From there they crossed the border to Ciudad Juárez and took a train to the interior at the expense of the Mexican government, ostensibly to prevent congestion at the border. From March 23, 1931, to April 15, 1934, 13,332 Mexicans were repatriated from Los Angeles, of which only 3,317 were welfare cases (Hoffman 1976). From the start in 1929 to 1937, when most programs were terminated, 458,039 Mexicans were repatriated from across the United States.

During repatriation, cities immediately along the border developed a transient character. Since "laborsheds" reached far into the United States, it was further becoming apparent that the concept of border was not only porous, it was also relative and unconstrained by proximity.

LÁZARO CÁRDENAS ERA, 1934–1940

Similar to the New Deal recovery effort of the United States, Mexico entered a period of economic reconstruction following the Great Depression. Under the leadership of President Lázaro Cárdenas, policies for reviving the economy included stabilizing employment, stimulating demand by raising the minimum wage, instituting agrarian reform through land redistribution, and investing in rural infrastructure. Cárdenas vigorously enforced existing laws governing black-market activities by closing casinos and brothels, and shutting down remaining vestiges of the "personal services" trade. After repeal of Prohibition in the United States and the onslaught of the Depression, border crossings dropped from 27 million in 1928 to 21 million by 1934 (Martínez 1975: 83). What little spending could be attributed to Americans was directed more at staple goods than tourist items, and that was largely a function of the lower prices which resulted from devaluation of the peso in 1931. However unintended, the joint attack on the vice trade, coupled with devaluation, led to even higher unemployment and a soaring cost of living along the Mexican border.

With Tijuana's economy on the brink of collapse, Cárdenas drew on a policy General Abelardo Rodríguez's government had tried earlier. The former president had designated Tijuana a *perímetro libre* (free perimeter) and Ensenada a *puerto libre* (free port) through executive decree. This permitted duty-free entry of foreign commodities into the two locations. During his term, Cárdenas applied a "free zone" designation to Baja California Norte, which was expanded two years later to include the entire Baja California peninsula and the northwest of Sonora. Mexican border towns not included in the free zones were allowed free importation of consumer goods under 1935 custom law provisions. As a consequence of these designations, Tijuana's economy picked up, its population nearly doubled, and the commercial work force grew by a factor of three between 1930 and 1940 (see table 3.2).

TABLE 3.2
GROWTH OF THE LABOR FORCE BY SECTOR IN FIVE
MEXICAN BORDER MUNICIPALITIES, 1930–1940

	Agriculture			Commerce			Manufacturing		
	1930	1940	% Change	1930	1940	% Change	1930	1940	% Change
Matamoros	5,947	12,961	118	563	1,634	190	353	907	157
N. Laredo	2,011	1,934	−4	934	2,303	147	819	1,453	77
C. Juárez	4,559	3,723	−18	1,816	4,602	153	1,827	3,077	68
Mexicali	9,213	9,568	4	856	1,773	107	671	1,160	73
Tijuana	1,145	1,820	59	594	2,350	296	657	988	50

Source: Martínez 1975: 168.

Other border cities also grew. Ciudad Juárez, the main point of entry for repatriates, became the largest city on the Mexican side of the border, with 73,685 residents, followed by Mexicali (45,883) and Tijuana (43,464). Viewed in retrospect, national policies such as peso devaluations and the designation of free zones demonstrated that the border economy was highly responsive to external decisions, in addition to being remarkably resilient.

WORLD WAR II, 1939–1945

With the New Deal programs of President Franklin D. Roosevelt and the stimulus created by World War II, the U.S. economy was again on the rise. Throughout the war, Los Angeles and San Diego saw their populations mushroom. San Diego's manufacturing base nearly doubled, due largely to employment in the aircraft industry. With money in their pockets and nowhere to spend it, Southern Californians turned to Mexico for many hard-to-obtain purchases. Suddenly Tijuana was filled with "Army, Navy and aircraft workers" trying to buy "alarm clocks, meat, gasoline, butter, cream, shoes, woolens, hardware, sporting goods, silk stockings, chewing gum, and . . . hairpins." To meet the demand, Tijuana merchants accepted U.S. Office of Price Administration ration coupons for the purchase of shoes and meat (Price 1973: 59–60).

Military bases provided another impulse to the border economy. When Fort Bliss (near El Paso, Texas) grew from 3,999 soldiers in 1938 to nearly 25,000 by 1941, Ciudad Juárez's tourist trade boomed (Martínez 1975: 96). The city put its revenues to work building infrastructure, schools, and homes. It also began a series of social reforms. "Commercial, industrial, educational, cultural, and entertainment facilities . . . proliferated. New stores, shops, markets, factories, schools, libraries, theaters, auditoriums, parks, not to mention bars, cabarets, and brothels, transformed Juárez into a modern metropolis by the 1950's" (Martínez 1975: 97). During the war years, commerce and tourism thrived along the border. Over three-fourths of Mexico's entire tourist income during this period was derived from the border region.

Throughout the United States, the demand for wartime workers was drawing people out of agriculture into higher-paying urban industrial jobs, and out of the civilian work force for military service. In a repeat of history, the severe labor shortage created by the war mobilization once again made Mexican labor appealing, and once again recruitment took place. The sad irony was that this was less than one decade after the expulsion of Mexican workers from the United States under the aegis of federal and local repatriation programs.

The Bracero Program, 1942–1964

To relieve the agricultural labor shortage, the United States established the Emergency Farm Labor Program, or Bracero Program. The terms of the program were contained in a 1942 Bilateral Agreement between the United States and Mexico. Augmenting this was Public Law 78, passed in 1951 to regulate the recruitment, placement, and treatment of Mexican workers (Cross and Sandos 1981: 36). When the war ended and the economy continued to expand, persistent labor shortages in less remunerative agricultural jobs created a rationale for extending the farm labor program. From the time it was initiated in 1942 with the employment of 50,000 Mexican workers, to its dissolution in 1964, over 4.6 million contracts were issued. This represented a significant labor subsidy to U.S. agriculture.

The history of the Bracero Program is spotty at best, with all participants in some way tainted by their involvement. It has been argued that the program was a safety valve for rural Mexican farmers displaced by the large-scale farming which emerged from the Green Revolution of President Miguel Alemán. Mexico had realized an unprecedented average 9.4 percent increase in agricultural output per year during this administration, but the policies marginalized smaller farmers and triggered a massive out-migration from the countryside to urban areas (Cross and Sandos 1981: 18). Though they were destitute, displaced farmers were not given preference in the Bracero Program (see table 3.3). Moreover, obtaining a bracero contract often required paying bribes at several stages of the process, an impediment few could afford. Consequently, many crossed over into the United States without documents. As the Bracero Program progressed, what was originally a safety valve became a crutch that institutionalized both "legal" and "illegal" migration to the United States.

TABLE 3.3
NUMBER OF BRACEROS BY ORIGIN FOR SELECTED YEARS

State	1942–44	1953–54	1960–64
Durango	1,438	61,004	62,048
Guanajuato	19,848	58,761	132,263
Jalisco	8,202	54,458	110,054
Michoacán	34,069	48,371	143,527
San Luis Potosí	7,718	23,560	58,456
Zacatecas	7,619	56,962	91,831
Other	58,511	191,319	564,875
Total Mexico	137,405	494,435	1,163,054

Source: Based on Cross and Sandos 1981: 44.

U.S. growers contributed to the illegal migration by abusing contracted laborers and hiring workers without papers. Since workers could skip the bribe-ridden path and still find employment, illegal crossings increased. With urban economies growing and offering better-paying service or manufacturing jobs, many were drawn there as well.

In retrospect, the legacy of the program was an accelerating stream of documented and undocumented temporary workers into the United States. As a result, border cities became way stations from which migrants staged their next crossing. Entire neighborhoods comprised of largely temporary residents cropped up in Tijuana and Ciudad Juárez, lending permanence to transience. By 1951, Tijuana was reputed to be the fastest-growing city in Mexico. Counterpart neighborhoods developed in the United States as well—communities where conventions governing the rest of urban life, such as the right to vote, did not apply.

OPERATION WETBACK, 1953–1956

The spread of undocumented workers came to a temporary halt when the United States entered a recessionary period (1953–55) after the Korean War. With unemployment on the rise, Mexicans were rounded up and deported under the auspices of "Operation Wetback." Headed by Lieutenant General Joseph M. Swing, a man who had at one time accompanied General Pershing into Mexico in pursuit of Pancho Villa, Operation Wetback became a "militaristic" campaign (Acuna 1981). Under Swing's direction, the Immigration and Naturalization Service (INS) conducted special drives in California, Texas, and elsewhere across the nation. During 1953, "the INS deported 875,000 Mexicans; 20,174 Mexicans were airlifted into the interior from Spokane, Chicago, Kansas City, St. Louis, and other cities" (Acuna 1981: 157). By some accounts, 1,075,168 Mexicans were deported in 1954 and 242,608 in 1955, though actual figures are the object of dispute (Kiser and Kiser 1979: 101; Acuna 1981). Subsequently many workers traded their illegal status for legal entry through the Bracero Program (Kiser and Kiser 1979). Since deportees were left at the border and not all of them returned home, the population of border cities increased rapidly. Unlike the repatriation of the 1930s, Mexico did not supply transportation to the interior this time.

By the time the Bracero Program was finally terminated in 1964, thousands of workers had returned to Mexico. Border cities grew at record levels. These "boomtowns" fast surpassed U.S. counterparts in size and urban service needs. Infrastructure rarely kept pace with demand. Inflation soared, causing the cost of living to rise. To keep up with costs, residents relied on rural methods of subsistence as strategies for survival. Though Mexican communities often maintained daily ties with their "twin cities" directly opposite across the border (e.g., sharing recreational or fire prevention facilities), the main sphere of economic influence came not from neighboring cities but from major urban centers of the United States, with their large product and labor markets. By now it was apparent that the economies of the two nations were both intertwined and increasingly international in scope.

PERIOD III: THE RESTRUCTURED ECONOMY, 1960s–1980s

By the time the Bracero Program ended (mid-1960s), the global economy had entered a period of economic restructuring that ultimately reshaped ties between Mexico and the United States. The restructuring was traced to a number of factors, including: (1) international monetary, financial, and price instability; (2) a rise of competitive trading blocs; and (3) the oil shocks of 1973 and 1979. Within the United States, these culminated in a drop in productivity and a series of deep recessions during which it was apparent that U.S. firms were in a vulnerable position worldwide. Within Mexico, this was felt as a mounting trade deficit that required drastic ameliorative measures aimed at increasing exports. Both reactions resulted in heightened U.S. investments along Mexico's northern border.

At the beginning of the second half of the 1970s, foreign competition was making its imprint in the United States. Corporate profits fell from a 15 percent average annual return in the mid-1960s to 9.7 percent in 1978. To lower costs and increase returns, firms began reorganizing their methods of production. In many cases, this led to the closing of industrial plants and capital flight. The shifting of production to other countries was facilitated by the international conglomerate nature of large U.S. corporations, a quality which characterized most basic manufacturing. By 1982, one out of every three manufacturing jobs that existed in 1978 had disappeared.

The United States appeared to be losing its saliency in the manufacture of mass-produced goods. Developing nations such as Mexico, using low-cost labor, were becoming competitive in the manufacture of many consumer durable goods. The notion of a global assembly line—with parts sourced from around the world, assembled in export-processing zones, perhaps in Mexico, and then shipped to industrialized nations such as the United States—was becoming manifest.

While this was one trend, yet another came later. Though many mass-produced goods were increasingly made abroad, items characterized by extensive product differentiation and dependent upon flexible manufacturing systems remained in the United States. Firms adopting methods of flexible manufacturing continued to import from developing countries, but they were generally low-value-added products for final assembly in the United States, rather than final goods.

Ultimately both forms of industrialization—i.e., one based on the global assembly line and the other based on flexible manufacturing—coexisted along the border. Mexican cities began to sprout a broad range of industrial activities, from the most labor intensive to the most complex and capital intensive. The shift in the economy of the region took place over two discernable periods: 1961 to 1976, when the Mexican government attempted to influence border development through concerted national economic policies; and 1976 to the present, when a series of peso devaluations heightened economic uncertainty along the border while simultaneously adding to the process of economic integration.

PRONAF/BIP/ARTÍCULOS GANCHOS, 1961–1976

The northern border has always posed a special dilemma for Mexico. Because it is removed from the center of Mexican economic activity, attempts to stimulate the border economy have often resulted in increased investment or trade relations with the United States. This, in turn, only further weakens regional links with the national economy. This is the situation that Mexico now faces.

During the early 1960s, economic conditions along the border began to deteriorate under the weight of exploding population growth, high unemployment, and an overburdened infrastructure. To revive the economy, the Mexican government proposed a program aimed at infrastructure development. The Programa Nacional Fronterizo (PRONAF), begun in 1961, provided funds for constructing buildings, paving roads, and extending utilities to industrial parks. In addition, there were incentives aimed at spurring sales of Mexican goods. Jointly, the capital improvements and incentives were expected to stimulate investment in industry, services, and trade, which would result in the local manufacture of imported goods, or import substitution. Although the program enjoyed limited success, a more explicit employment program was needed to absorb the anticipated flood of workers released at the termination of the Bracero Program in 1964.

The policy adopted for alleviating the high unemployment had been tried previously in only a few places in the world. This was the Border Industrialization Program (BIP), which authorized establishment of *maquiladoras*, or in-bond assembly plants, in specially marked zones. Dual incentives enticed U.S. firms to move part of their production to Mexico: low-cost Mexican labor coupled with U.S. Tariff Codes 806.3 and 807, which taxed only the value added (i.e., labor) of goods transformed during intermediate stages of production. Enactment of this policy coincided with the beginning of capital flight from the United States. Initially, garment and electronics firms were quick to move to the maquiladoras, but within two decades a broad range of industries had followed their lead.

As the program matured, it became apparent that women were benefiting from jobs in the maquiladoras, not the men who were the former braceros. The maquiladoras were changing both labor markets and the economic profile of border cities. When the program opened in 1967, 72 U.S. plants were in operation. By 1985, there were 735 plants employing over 200,000 workers and generating over one billion dollars annually in foreign exchange (USITC 1986: xv, 39). Most plants were clustered in Ciudad Juárez (23 percent), followed by Tijuana (22 percent), Mexicali (10 percent), Nogales (7 percent), and Matamoros (7 percent) (USITC 1986: 25) (see table 3.4). Eastern cities, such as Matamoros and Ciudad Juárez, were closely linked with industrial centers of the Midwest, and tended to specialize in garment manufacture, electronics, and/or auto parts. Western cities, such as Mexicali and Tijuana, had primary ties to California and displayed more diversified product mixes.

As northern border workers began earning a significant income, U.S. items became attractive commodities. An estimated 60–75 percent of wages earned in Mexico during the 1970s were spent in the United States (Grunwald and Flamm 1985: 142). Ostensibly to prevent further

TABLE 3.4
PROFILE OF MEXICO'S IN-BOND INDUSTRY, 1983

City	No. of Operating Plants	No. of Employees
Ciudad Juárez	140	58,652
Tijuana	133	19,045
Mexicali	56	8,093
Nogales	43	14,008
Matamoros	40	16,823
Agua Prieta	24	4,655
Cd. Chihuahua and Ojinaga	23	6,813
Tecate	22	1,321
Ciudad Reynosa and Río Bravo	19	12,145
Ciudad Acuna	18	4,257
Piedras Negras	17	2,733
Guadalajara	14	4,976
Other	57	9,469
	606	162,990

Source: Hodak 1984: 68.

foreign trade leakages, the Mexican government introduced the Artículos Ganchos Program in 1971. Under this program, only a limited number of items could be brought into Mexico duty free by Mexican residents. As compensation, Mexican border stores could offer foreign (mainly U.S.) goods at prices commensurate with those charged in U.S. stores. This was intended to be a "hook" (*gancho*) for recapturing the Mexican consumer market.

By some measures, such as absolute numbers of jobs created or increase in foreign exchange generated, the programs initiated during the 1960s–1970s realized their intended effect. Using other measures, such as the rising number of undocumented workers crossing the border or the increased dependence of Mexican cities on foreign investment, their success remains elusive. Because of the nature of the BIP, few linkages have been created that would secure industries in the region. The northern border has become an industrial enclave comprised of largely female labor and whose corporate headquarters are usually located in the United States. In this respect, the BIP typifies the concept of the "new international division of labor," since production processes are disarticulated from management, research, and fabrication, creating an industrial labor force that is both fractionalized and operating within a narrow skill range. While this represents one dimension of the contemporary urban structure along the border, subsequent events have broadened the picture.

DEVALUATION OF THE PESO, 1976 TO THE PRESENT

While the BIP represented a concerted effort to attract industry to Mexico, peso devaluations of the last decade have had a similar, if unintended, effect. Between 1954 and 1976, the peso exchanged at a rate of 12.5 to the dollar. Throughout these twenty-two years, the peso became increasingly overvalued, creating both inflationary conditions within Mexico and a de facto subsidy to Mexican purchasers of U.S. products. By 1976, Mexico was no longer able to sustain this policy, and the peso was sharply devalued twice in one year. Initially this created severe economic hardship on Mexican border residents accustomed to shopping on the U.S. side. U.S. border merchants went broke, and commerce-dependent cities applied for federal economic disaster aid. Despite its negative effects, the devaluation lowered the cost of production in Mexico, which, in turn, stimulated investment.

The 1976 devaluation had a short-lived impact. Mexican consumers resumed shopping in the United States because, with economic growth, they now had an increase in their personal disposable income. Furthermore, inflation continued to be higher in Mexico than in the United States, which added to the price of Mexican goods (USITC 1986: 15). But then the overvalued peso, which was maintained by oil revenues and foreign borrowing, collapsed with the drop in the world oil market in 1982. Ultimately unfavorable trade conditions led Mexico to devalue the peso again in 1982.

The drastic devaluations that followed had a pronounced effect on U.S. cities dependent on Mexican trade. Laredo and McAllen were especially hard hit (see table 3.5). In December 1984, they had the highest and second highest unemployment rates in the United States (USITC 1986: 20).

Another effect of the devaluations was a rise in investment in northern Mexico by major U.S. manufacturers. One clear illustration is among automakers, who not only doubled maquiladora operations from

TABLE 3.5
NONAGRICULTURAL EMPLOYMENT IN SELECTED TEXAS SMSAS: 1982, 1983

SMSA	Number Unemployed			Unemployment Rate		
	1982	1983	% Decline	1982	1983	% Increase
Brownsville	65,700	58,250	11.3	11.4	17.7	55.3
McAllen	83,150	79,300	4.6	14.0	20.5	46.4
Laredo	37,500	30,450	18.8	11.0	27.3	148.2
El Paso	170,400	162,900	4.4	9.2	13.3	44.6

Source: USITC 1986: 18.

1985 to 1986 but shifted much of their engine production and auto assembly there as well (Morales and Hinojosa 1986). The meteoric increase in the amount of car-related shipments to the United States, which is expected to continue at least through the 1990s, topped $2 billion in 1985. This was more than four times the $460 million registered in 1981. Approximately 75 percent of the growth was in engines and ignition wiring sets. The value of the peso has been a critical factor contributing to this growth. In 1981, the exchange rate was 50 to 1; by 1987 it was at nearly 1,000 to 1, and it grew to over 2,200 to 1 by 1988.

The output and location of these post-devaluation plants vary considerably from the patterns associated with maquiladoras. For example, Ford's Hermosillo plant makes engines using state-of-the-art technology. None of the new engine or auto assembly plants use maquiladora designations, nor are they confined to cities immediately adjacent to the border. Rather, they tend to locate in places like Hermosillo or Saltillo that offer the advantage of proximity without the history of labor unions now identified with some border cities.

As northern Mexico continues to industrialize, it is becoming increasingly integrated with the U.S. economy. Just as the notion of border reached deep into the United States when Mexican labor mobility was a major determinant in the structure of U.S. urban economies, now the concept of border is being pushed back into Mexico as a result of the mobility of U.S. capital. However elusive the term "global economy" might appear, between Mexico and the United States this is taking a concrete form, as illustrated by recent developments in northern Mexico.

PROSPECTS FOR URBANIZATION ALONG THE U.S.-MEXICO BORDER

Upon reflection, the three major periods shaping urban growth along the U.S.-Mexican border—preindustrial, industrial, and global—have been characterized by progressive integration of the two economies. Despite increasing interdependence, a transient quality to the nature of development persists. While in prior years, border cities, with few exceptions, were dependent on income generated by migrant workers or tourists taking advantage of locally generated crafts and services, at present a more significant portion of revenues comes from an economic base comprised of dislocated industries. As the fortunes of Mexican cities rise or fall in response to external impetus, a multiplicative effect will continue to be felt in the United States. In this respect, the growing interdependence carries substantial risks.

In addition, it is evident that no one form of industrialization is taking precedence, but rather there is an extraordinary mix. The ties that have developed between the two countries are neither uniformly pernicious nor benign. As described by Alain Lipietz (1986), the current international economic landscape is defined not by national distinctions but by production and consumption relationships that transcend boundaries.

Finally, the most recent growth has been characterized by a shift in the geographic location of industrial and urban development. Within Mexico, much of the newest industrial capacity is going into northern Mexico. Further, most of the new development is occurring within a broad region rimming the border. As a result, the notion of border is not a linear but an economic space, within which diverse activities take place.

REFERENCES

Acuna, Rodolfo. 1981. *Occupied America: A History of Chicanos*. New York: Harper and Row.

Cockcroft, James D. 1983. *Mexico: Class Formation, Capital Accumulation, and the State*. New York: Monthly Review Press.

Cross, Harry E., and James A. Sandos. 1981. *Across the Border: Rural Development in Mexico and Recent Migration to the United States*. Berkeley: Institute of Governmental Studies, University of California, Berkeley.

Faulk, Odie B. 1968. *Land of Many Frontiers: A History of the American Southwest*. New York: Oxford University Press.

Gildersleeve, Charles R. 1987. "The International Border City: Urban Spatial Organization in a Context of Two Cultures along the United States-Mexico Boundary." Ph.D. diss., University of Nebraska at Lincoln.

Grunwald, Joseph, and Kenneth Flamm. 1985. *The Global Factory: Foreign Assembly in International Trade*. Washington D.C.: Brookings Institution.

Hodak, Dennis P. 1984. "Mexico's In-Bond Industry: Crucial Job Source and Dollar-Earner," *Business Mexico*, February, pp. 62–69.

Hoffman, Abraham. 1976. *Unwanted Mexican Americans in the Great Depression: Repatriation Pressures, 1929–1939*. Tucson: University of Arizona Press.

Kiser, George C., and Martha Woody Kiser, eds. 1979. *Mexican Workers in the United States: Historical and Political Perspectives*. Albuquerque: University of New Mexico Press.

Lipietz, Alain. 1986. "New Tendencies in the International Division of Labor: Regimes of Accumulation and Modes of Regulation." In *Production, Work and Territory*, edited by Allen J. Scott and Michael Storper. Boston: Allen and Unwin.

Martínez, Oscar. 1975. *Border Boomtown: Ciudad Juarez since 1848*. Austin: University of Texas Press.

Morales, Rebecca, and Raul Hinojosa. 1986. "International Restructuring and Labor Market Interdependence: The Automobile Industry in

Mexico and the United States." Paper presented at the Conference on Labor Market Interdependence between the United States and Mexico, El Colegio de México, Mexico City, September 25–27.

Piñera Ramírez, David, ed. 1983. *Panorama Histórico de Baja California*. Mexicali: Universidad Autónoma de Baja California.

Price, John A. 1973. *Tijuana: Urbanization in a Border Culture*. Notre Dame: University of Notre Dame Press.

USITC (United States International Trade Commission). 1986. "The Impact of Increased United States-Mexico Trade on Southwest Border Development." Report to the Senate Committee on Finance on Investigation No.332-223, Under Section 332 of the Tariff Act of 1930. USITC Publication 1915. Washington, D.C.: U.S. Government Printing Office.

4

The Maquila Industry and the Creation of a Transnational Capitalist Class in the United States-Mexico Border Region

Leslie Sklair

In Mexico, as in many other Third World countries in recent years, the belief in export-led industrialization (ELI) is beginning to displace other available development strategies, such as import substitution, varying degrees of autarky, or the traditional reliance on primary-product export. My purpose here is to explain how the *maquila* (in-bond) industry along the Mexico-U.S. border, by spearheading ELI, has helped create a transnational capitalist class which is gradually changing the ways in which Mexico, and to some extent the United States, relate to a global capitalism in the process of reformation.

Mexico has for at least a century been a prime location for foreign investment, mainly but by no means exclusively from the United States. While in the 1980s only about 2.5 percent of Mexican industrial firms were foreign owned, they produced more than 30 percent of Mexican industrial exports (*La Jornada*, June 8, 1985). Up until the 1970s, most of this foreign investment was in the "traditional" TNC sectors like automobiles, petroleum exploitation, pharmaceuticals, textiles, and so on, which combined import substitution with exporting. But from the 1970s, and increasingly in the 1980s, this picture began to change and the balance began to swing to the more specifically export-processing assembly industries, like electronics, machinery, auto parts, apparel, furniture, sports goods, and toys. This tended to be concentrated along Mexico's northern border under the rules of the maquila industry.

Foreign investment has to go somewhere and do something, and all over the world from the 1960s onward some of it went into specially constructed zones. The study of what can broadly be called "economic zones" and particularly "export processing zones" (EPZs) is important for at least two reasons. First, they have often been the physical expressions of industrial development policies in Third World countries. Second, they have invariably been set up to attract foreign investment. Thus, they do tend to concentrate the effects of the external environment of the global capitalist system in a particularly intense manner. In Mexico this has happened largely along the border.

THE BORDER ENVIRONMENT

In the mid-1960s the Mexican government introduced a Border Industrialization Program, a major plank of which was to permit Mexican and foreign-owned factories to operate along the border duty free (thus it is often termed the "in-bond" industry) on conditions that they exported all their products. These factories, mainly U.S.-owned, were also able to take advantage of tariff regulations covering the reimport of assembled unfinished goods using U.S.-manufactured components. These were the beginnings of the maquila program. Mexico now has 1,500 maquilas, employing almost half a million workers, and export earnings from the maquilas are in the region of U.S. $2 billion per year.[1]

This is a genuine success story and it is not an exaggeration to describe the maquila industry as "booking" along the border. One need only observe the dozens of maquila consulting and facilitating firms that have sprung up in Mexico and the United States over the last decade to confirm this impression.[2]

In *Where North Meets South*, Herzog (1990: 60) nicely understates the central dilemma of the border: "The boundary that separates the two nations today is hardly a logical one in terms of ecology, culture, and history." This illogicality encourages us to look at the 2,000-mile international border vertically as well as horizontally. Horizontally, it divides the richest country in the world from a country that is by no means the poorest but by common consent has been in a state of profound economic and deepening sociopolitical crisis since at least 1982.

However, if we look at the northern border states of Mexico and the southwest border states of the United States vertically—Baja California and California, Chihuahua and west Texas, Tamaulipas and south Texas, for example—some of the richest communities in Mexico face some of the poorest communities in the United States. Even the exception of San Diego, a very rich community, is misleading, as the actual border with

---

[1] For general accounts of the origins and growth of the maquilas, see Carrillo and Hernández 1985 and Sklair 1989, from which some of the material in this paper is taken and where full documentation can be found.

[2] The maquilas are not, strictly speaking, in EPZs, as they could be located anywhere within twenty kilometers of the border and, since 1972, in the interior of Mexico. The effects, however, are similar to the traditional EPZ.

Mexico is not San Diego proper, but San Ysidro, a poor, mainly Hispanic settlement.

For Mexico City and Washington, D.C., there is one border, the line that marks the extent of national sovereignty. For the border communities, the border exists for some practical purposes, but the borderlands within which they live out their daily lives facilitate and constrain what they do and how they do it. For nation-states, borderland communities are secondary to national borders, in fact and in symbol, while for borderland communities, the borders may be secondary to their borderlands, the economy, politics, and culture, the total social formation of that part of their borderland that happens to lie on both sides of the national frontier (Ross 1978).

My particular purpose here is to show how the creation of the maquila program and its history to the present were a result of the conjuncture of economic, political, and cultural-ideological forces acting horizontally along the border, but vertically through these borderlands. In brief, the argument is that the transnational corporations operating through the maquila industry have created a transnational capitalist class in the border region, and this has gradually begun to make a significant difference to the ways in which Mexico and the global capitalist system relate to each other.

Binational economic, political, and cultural-ideological contacts predate the maquila industry along the border but were given added dynamism by the establishment of the maquila regulations in the mid-1960s. Without underestimating the importance of PRONAF, the Mexican Northern Border Development Program energetically led by Antonio Bermúdez in the 1960s (Sklair 1989: 24–42), it cannot be denied that it was, to some extent, predicated on a hostility toward the United States and in particular toward the incursions of U.S. capitalists into Mexico.

There were, however, several genuinely binational initiatives, particularly connected with the socioeconomic development of the region. For example, the U.S.-Mexico Commission for Border Development and Friendship was established in 1967 as a result of a meeting in the previous year between the two presidents in Mexico City. It was unable to achieve anything very concrete apart from binational planning commissions in Matamoros/Brownsville and in Juárez/El Paso to work on transportation and environmental problems. The combined effects of "Operation Intercept," an attempt to stop transborder drug trafficking which was bitterly resented in Mexico, and the discontinuation of the Commission in 1970 effectively put an end to these binational commissions. Also in the 1960s, a Border Cities Association was formed by the chambers of commerce on both sides with the purpose of lobbying the respective governments and improving business along the border. Although this particular organization faded out by the end of the decade, informal, and in some cases formal, connections between the Mexican and U.S. business communities along the border were created during this period, many surviving to the present. Some of these grew into influential economic and political organizations, many concerned with the maquila industry.[3]

Environmental questions frequently created problems along the border. The allocation of the waters of the Rio Grande/Río Bravo del Norte, the river that marks the international boundary from El Paso/Ciudad Juárez to the Gulf of Mexico, is at the root of many of these problems. An International Boundary and Water Commission was established in 1889 to oversee boundary disputes, but its work in recent years has focused on water and, increasingly, on pollution. Public health has also loomed large in the concerns of border officials. As early as 1903 the authorities in El Paso required all cars crossing the border from Juárez to be fumigated. In the 1940s, a Border Health Association was set up to monitor public health issues between the United States and Mexico. This developed into the Pan American Health Organization, based in El Paso/Juárez and it is beset with problems of lack of resources and credibility in the respective seats of national government (Bath 1982).

There have also been attempts to create regional organizations along the border. The most important of these has been the Southwest Border Regional Commission (SBRC), one of the eight "Title V" economic development regions established to provide a vehicle for socioeconomic development in backward areas of the United States (Tocups 1980: 638). Each of the border states had its own commission, and they worked with the SBRC in identifying projects and in researching development plans. When the Title V Commission was terminated in 1981, the SBRC was replaced by the Governors' Southwest Border Regional Commission, which formalized the cross border contacts that the SBRC had been making with a conference in Ciudad Juárez in June 1980. This was the first time that cross-border diplomacy had been conducted by local rather than central government officials and the meeting was called "historic" in the *New York Times* (Tocups 1980: 640). This commission was supported by the Organization of U.S. Border Cities (a resuscitated version from the 1960s), federally funded from the Commerce Department. From the 1970s onward, therefore, there were several organizations on the U.S. side of the border devoted to socioeconomic development.

As PRONAF was being wound down in the early 1970s, several other national and regional organizations in Mexico were established to collect data and to stimulate socioeconomic development along the border.

---

[3] As Jamail (1981: 84) points out: "in almost every [U.S. border] community there is a group concerned with the maquiladora industry." See also Tocups 1980.

Most influential was the Intersecretarial Commission for the Development of the Northern Frontier and Free Zones, set up in 1971 by President Echeverría. Its purpose was to "bring the border region economically closer to the rest of the country, alleviate the unemployment situation, and encourage the Mexican consumer to shop at home," all unfulfilled aims of PRONAF (Ross 1978: 157).

The Mexican government introduced a program in March 1974 aimed at stimulating small and medium-sized industry along the border to produce goods for domestic consumption. The idea was to permit domestic firms to share in the fiscal benefits that the maquilas already enjoyed, mainly duty-free import of machinery, materials, and components. None of these measures was very effective in stimulating the growth of a manufacturing bourgeoisie north or south of the border.

In the 1970s economic promotion committees were set up to popularize official policy in the border cities, and these committees, by combining representatives of the federal and state governments and private entrepreneurs, seemed at last to be bringing to fruition the vision of PRONAF as expressed by Antonio Bermúdez: "the perfect coordination between government and private enterprise" (Sklair 1989).

In 1977, when Echeverría had been succeeded by López Portillo, a new organization, the Comisión Coordinadora del Programa Nacional de Desarrollo de las Franjas Fronterizas y Zonas Libres del País (CODEF), was established, to indicate that the incoming administration had its own policies for the development of the *frontera norte*. CODEF operated as a coordinating agency for all the interdepartmental policies that might affect the border (and the free trade zones not on the border) and was intended to reflect the interests of the border in national development planning. CODEF also set up economic promotion committees in the main border cities to coordinate planning at the local level. The next president, Miguel de la Madrid, replaced CODEF with a revamped Intersecretarial Commission in August 1983, specifically to implement the border policy outlined in the 1983–1988 National Development Plan. The commission was placed firmly under the control of the Industry Ministry (SECOFI) and, along with a new set of regulations for the maquila industry promulgated at the same time, represented yet another attempt to develop the *frontera norte* and to integrate it into the national economy and society and to control U.S. penetration.

The merchants who had been selling to Mexican consumers in U.S. cities all along the border (much to the chagrin of Mexicans like Bermúdez at PRONAF) saw their trade progressively wiped out as the pesos that their customers offered in exchange for goods were worth fewer and fewer dollars, due to dramatic devaluations beginning in 1976 and accelerating in 1982. The peso was devalued three times in 1982. It began the year at less than 27 to the dollar and ended the year at around 100.

Strict exchange controls were imposed by the government to stop the massive outflow of funds from Mexico into U.S. banks, a trend that had been gathering pace over the preceding years.

The combined effects of the exchange controls and the fall in the value of the peso were disastrous for many residents in the U.S. border cities and beyond. From San Diego in the west to Brownsville in the east, retail sales plunged, businesses failed, and unemployment rose. The situation was so serious that the Small Business Administration created a program of special loans for businesses that had been adversely affected. Border towns in Texas were worst hit. Unemployment in Texas as a whole increased from 5.9 percent in 1982 to 8.5 percent in 1983, but in Laredo, where the retail trade almost collapsed, it increased from 11.0 to 27.3 percent; in Brownsville it increased from 11.4 to 17.7 percent; and in McAllen the increase was from 14.0 to 20.5 percent (Prock 1983: 81). The lowest increase in unemployment along the Texas-Mexico border was in El Paso (from 9.2 percent in 1982 to 13.3 percent in 1983). Those who saw a connection between Juárez's booming maquila industry and El Paso's employment base during this difficult period suggested that U.S. border communities could best protect themselves from "exchange-rate shocks" by expanding their own manufacturing industries and encouraging the maquila industry across the border.

This is, of course, what the public and private maquila facilitators of the border cities, the embryonic transnational capitalist class, had been so assiduously trying to do since the late 1960s, when the Border Industrialization Program was getting off the ground. In the next section I shall look more closely at this concept of the transnational capitalist class and then go on to examine how it went about the task of redefining Mexico's quest for development and the creation of a capitalist industrial economy and society in the cities along the border.

THE CONCEPT OF THE TRANSNATIONAL CAPITALIST CLASS

The idea that regimes and their dominant classes in the Third World have institutionalized specific mechanisms for dealing with the global capitalist system, and vice versa, has been conceptualized in many ways. Major changes in the economic, political, and cultural-ideological structures of the global system in the last few decades force us to reconsider the traditional ways in which First World-Third World (and increasingly First World-Second World) class relations have been conceptualized. In doing this, it is necessary to begin to think about the global system itself, about the extent to which it can usefully be characterized as a *global capitalist system*, and the creation of what I shall term *transnational capitalist classes* (TCCs) within it.[4]

---

[4] This section borrows from Sklair 1990, where the concept of the transnational capitalist class is located within a theory of the global system.

Traditionally, domestically dominant classes in the Third World have related to First World transnational bourgeoisies either as "compradors" (serving the interests of their foreign masters) or as "indigenous proto-capitalists" (serving the interests of some supposed national autonomous development). The Eurocentric class categories of bourgeoisie and proletariat have always caused problems in the analysis of social structures in the Third World, and so it is hardly surprising that concepts like "comprador bourgeoisie" and "indigenous bourgeoisie" tended to blur as many issues as they clarified.

In an attempt to push this particular debate forward, several writers, usually quite unconnected, have begun to develop the idea of a "triple" alliance between the host state, foreign investors, and the outward-oriented elements in the indigenous bourgeoisie. Examples of this include the studies by Evans (1979) on Brazil, Gillespie (1984) on Egypt, and Ihonvbere and Shaw (1988) on Nigeria. This seems to me to be a promising move. However, where we cannot identify triple alliances, a society may still be dominated by a genuinely transnational capitalist class whether or not all three parties are represented. This class, the TCC, sees its interests bound up not with transnational corporations or foreign capital as such, but with the global capitalist system. It sees its mission as organizing the conditions under which the interests of the system can be furthered within the national context.

While what used to be called the comprador class may admit that its interests and those of the foreigners it serves are antagonistic to those of co-nationals, the transnational capitalist class conceives of its interests, and the interests of the global capitalist system that it serves, as more or less identical with those of the national development of its home country. Claude Ake (1985: 175) puts this very well when he argues that the processes of indigenization of foreign enterprises in Nigeria: "reinforced the division of labor between the Nigerian bourgeoisie (as specialists in maintaining the political conditions of accumulation) and foreign capital (as specialists in production)." As we shall see, this is not a bad description of the division of labor between the Mexican and the U.S. members of the maquila TCC.

Transnational capitalist classes do not identify with any foreign country in particular, or even necessarily with the First World, or the white world, or the Western world. They identify with the global capitalist system, reconceptualize their several national interests in terms of the global system, and take on the political project of reconceptualizing the national interests of their co-nationals in terms of the global capitalist system.

Although the comprador class in one form or another has existed for centuries, the transnational capitalist class is a relatively new phenomenon. The basic difference between the two is that whereas compradors are entirely beholden to the TNCs and foreign interests, the TCC can develop into a class that can, under certain circumstances, begin to dictate its own terms to the TNCs and foreign interests. The logical extension of this argument is that some form of interdependence might be possible, where Third World countries could carve out niches for themselves in the crevices that the hegemon TNCs leave unattended. It is a short step from the interdependence thesis to a full-blown "production sharing" conception of the global system, the positive capitalistic version of international division of labor theory that provides the central ideology of the maquila industry in Mexico, what I have called the strategy of "export-led industrialization fuelled by foreign investment and technology" or ELIFFIT (in Sklair 1989: 1–23).

The TCC in the Third World will undoubtedly be connected with transnational corporations, though its members will not necessarily work for them or be dependent on them. They may work through their own TNCs, which may be in a position to challenge other TNCs anywhere in the world or as independent professionals. Insofar as these people share the interests of and are engaged in the practices of the global capitalist system, they are members of the transnational capitalist class. So the transnational capitalist class includes fractions of both the old indigenous bourgeoisie and the comprador bourgeoisie.

THE MEXICO-U.S. BORDER AND THE MAQUILA INDUSTRY

Maquila workers, like all Mexican workers, suffered a decline in real standards of living in the 1980s, while the profits of the TNCs increased substantially. Every plunge in the dollar value of the peso heralded a new surge in maquila startups. The decline of the peso hit the maquila worker on the border particularly hard because Mexican border communities have always looked to the United States for many of their household purchases. Mexican alternative products are often unavailable, too expensive, of inferior quality, or even disguised imports from the United States. The U.S. working class along the border has also suffered during the 1980s.

However, both Mexican and U.S. transnational capitalists and professionals along the border have done very well out of the maquilas. Industrial park development, and legal and commercial services for the maquila industry, have created a new class of wealthy Mexican maquila facilitators (and, of course, U.S. maquila facilitators too). This phenomenon has been noted with increasing frequency in the last decade and it merely confirms what rational expectation would lead us to predict. Baird and McCaughan (1975: 9) succinctly describe the membership of the "political cliques" that ran the Border Industrialization Program in its first decade: "a local government official, lawyer, accountant, banker, customs broker, labor contractor and in most cases the owner of factory land and buildings. U.S. businessmen from industrial development committees and chambers of commerce from nearby U.S. cities also usually form part of this clique."

What the maquila industry had to do if it was to succeed on a more permanent basis was to create a class that could build a capitalist industrial culture to serve its needs along the border. Howard Boysen, a major maquila facilitator in San Diego/Tijuana, put this neatly when he said that the maquilas produce "middle-class men who are learning skills of programming and management, buying houses, educating their children and limiting the size of their families" (*National Journal*, July 7, 1979). That this was not just a view from north of the border is confirmed by González Baz, of the prominent Juárez/El Paso maquila industry law firm: "Maquiladoras have made the difference for the border. . . . For the first time in history there is a solid, strong middle class here" (*Oakland Tribune*, September 29, 1982). And Whiteford, in his study of the Mexicali Valley, argues that the maquila industry created an "emerging regional bourgeoisie . . . able to acquire considerable wealth and power as the program [BIP] expanded" (1986: 34).

This "border ruling class," what I prefer to call the maquila transnational capitalist class, differs considerably from the traditional landed oligarchies. The maquila ruling class is a new bourgeoisie in a recognizably Western capitalist sense, and it is more than a comprador class dependent on the presence of foreign capital for its own existence and survival. This does not necessarily make it any less patriotic or even chauvinist in its practice or ideology, for in Mexico there are many economic nationalists who have no scruples about stealing public funds, and there are many compradors who genuinely try to put foreign investment to use in the development of their country.

Salas-Porras, in her studies of the effects of the maquila industry on Mexico's regional bourgeoisie, argues that this new class has at least two distinctive characteristics that can be directly related to the growth of the maquilas. The base of this class is in services for the maquilas rather than productive investment in the plants themselves; and its members exploit the peculiar "private-public sector" symbiosis that exists in Mexico (and elsewhere) in their own interests against the public interest (1987). She draws attention to the favorable terms on which state-owned facilities are made available to private maquila facilitators for the benefit of the maquilas, a paradigm case of the way in which a transnational capitalist class can seem to serve the "national" interest while serving the interests of global capital. It is for this reason that Tamayo, for example, has argued that the "nationalization of the 'political class' at the border" (presumably the *de-U.S.-ification* of it) is necessary if national integration is to be achieved (in Gibson and Corona Rentería 1985: 91).

Every ruling class requires subordinate classes to rule. The maquila industry has effectively replaced or supplemented the underclasses that were created by mines, land, and cattle along the border, some of which were themselves created by U.S. business interests, with an industrial proletariat. Whiteford puts this in uncompromising terms: "the assembly-plant workers are thus the urban counterpart to [Mexicali's] landless rural laborers: both groups are non-unionized, poorly paid, and deprived of the social benefits of economic development in the Mexicali region" (1986: 34). The next section will look in more detail at how this new transnational class imposed its project on three main centers of the maquila industry along the border.

The Transnational Capitalist Class in South Texas/Tamaulipas

The concrete push to create a maquila industry in Matamoros and Reynosa came from the Texas side of the border. The United States has for decades had a network of local chambers of commerce stretching down to even quite small towns. While these have traditionally represented the interests of retailers and the commercial sectors (and the professionals who service them), when the opportunity for industrial development presented itself, an organizational framework already existed in many places.[5] In Brownsville and McAllen the preexisting chambers of commerce both set up administrative structures to handle questions of industry shortly after the BIP was announced. In Brownsville, the chamber created an industrial development department, and in McAllen an industrial board was established. Both specifically recruited industrial development managers, who stayed in their jobs for many years. An expertise and network of local, cross-border, and, in some cases, global connections were built up, and a corps of industrial development specialists evolved. Their success can be gauged in the words of a local newspaper: "while other segments of the valley economy remain stagnant, the maquiladora industry is booming. Consequently, the economic development strategies of Brownsville and McAllen and smaller valley communities have centered around promotion of the maquiladoras" (*Brownsville Herald*, November 5, 1985).

Neither Brownsville nor Matamoros had any real manufacturing industrial base in the 1960s. Lindsey Rhodes, of the Brownsville Chamber of Commerce, reasoned that the local selling point for the average U.S. corporation would be "the Mexican border is your Japan at the back door," and that logistics relative to the Far East rather than the cheapness of labor would be the clinching factor. Rhodes sought U.S. companies that were either already producing offshore or might be persuaded to do so.

In Matamoros there were also some entrepreneurs who saw the potential of the maquila industry. One such was Sergio Martínez, an accountant who worked with the Brownsville Chamber and was in-

---

[5]By 1965 there were said to be about two hundred local industrial development corporations in Texas (Hale 1965: Part 1:3).

volved in the negotiations with some of the earliest maquilas in the city, for example, the Electronic Control Corporation, which began by assembling light dimmers, probably the first manufacturing maquila in Matamoros. For the Brownsville Chamber of Commerce, the point of the exercise was to create a twin-plant industry in Brownsville and Matamoros.

The first years of the maquila industry in Matamoros and Brownsville were rather bleak. By the end of 1968, only five manufacturing and two shrimp-processing maquilas were in operation in Matamoros. This modest beginning, however, was sufficient to stimulate interest in the potential of Matamoros/Brownsville as a maquila site. The breakthrough came with the establishment of the Zenith plant in 1969–1970. Zenith, now one of the largest single employers in the whole maquila industry, came to Matamoros to assemble television tuners. The company, as it were, put its stamp of approval on the valley as a maquila site. Where Zenith went, others followed, particularly in the electronic assembly business. In the early 1970s, a further seventeen maquilas were signed up and, of rather more significance, four of these were subsidiaries of Fortune 500 corporations. They were all involved in one way or another with the electronic components industry. More Fortune 500 corporations followed in the mid-1970s, like Parker-Hannifin, DuPont de Nemours, ITT, Quaker Oats (Fisher Price), and the Eaton Corporation. Between 1969 and 1988, eighteen Fortune 500 firms established maquilas in Matamoros. The presence of major TNC executives is a qualitative feature of the local transnational capitalist class.

Matamoros, like other maquila locations along the border, saw the advantages of industrial parks, and around 1970 moves in this direction started in the city. A group of Mexican entrepreneurs formed a company, Empresas Cylsa, in September 1970 to buy land. This was the origin of the Matamoros industrial park. Cylsa's 1,000-acre site was split up into a 400-acre industrial zone to the north of the irrigation canal that bisected the area, and the rest was set aside for housing, some for the workers who would hopefully be required in the maquilas. In its first few years, the park leased factories to Zenith, the Fisher Price toy division of Quaker Oats, and to a wire harness plant of ITT.

The success of the industrial park persuaded other public and private bodies to enter the field. In the mid-1970s, the Mexican government, in the shape of Nacional Financiera (the industrial development bank controlled by the state but containing some private capital), created the Ciudad Industrial de Matamoros (CIMA), which attracted some local Mexican companies, mostly small metal-working firms, and later began to bring in maquilas of U.S. corporations. Another private park opened in 1979, Fraccionadora Industrial del Norte, S.A. (FINSA), the creation of a local entrepreneur, Sergio Argüelles, and possibly the most important private facilitator in Matamoros/Brownsville. Argüelles accumulated 180 acres of undeveloped land in the industrial zone in the west of the city, about ten minutes away from the international crossing. Working through a shelter and subcontract company, Grupo Nova, Argüelles and his associate René González Rascón, pursued a targeted group of U.S. corporations. FINSA's first coup was to land the Inland Division of General Motors. The negotiations for this were said to have taken sixteen months, but it was clearly worth every minute because GM, like Zenith, is a major maquila corporation whose name on a promotional brochure is worth its weight in gold to private and public facilitators alike. By 1988, there were three General Motors plants in the FINSA park, employing more than five thousand people producing many types of automotive components.

Another feather in FINSA's cap was to attract the first Japanese maquila to Matamoros, Fabricación Metálica de Matamoros, a subsidiary of the Mitsubishi Corporation. Although a small metal industry plant employing fewer than one hundred workers, the symbolic breakthrough that it represented should not be underestimated. A planned expansion of a further seven hundred adjacent acres will turn the park into the largest maquila park on the border, and sister parks in Nuevo Laredo and Nuevo Progreso will make FINSA the largest private facilitator in the area. The transnational capitalist class was now clearly emerging.

There are three major differences between Reynosa/McAllen and Matamoros/Brownsville. The first, and most obvious, is that whereas one can walk across the international bridge that joins Matamoros and Brownsville from the downtown areas of both cities, McAllen is about ten miles from the Mexican border and is therefore a "twin city" to Reynosa only in the same sense that San Diego is to Tijuana. The actual "twin" is Hidalgo, a very poor, mainly Hispanic settlement like San Ysidro, San Diego's border town. Therefore, the Mexican influence in downtown McAllen appears less marked than it is in downtown Brownsville, just as U.S. influence appears less marked in Reynosa than it is in Matamoros. There is less day-to-day commerce, in both the social and economic senses of the term, between Reynosa and McAllen than there is between Matamoros and Brownsville. The second difference is that Reynosa has a massive PEMEX plant, one of the largest industrial facilities in the valley and in northern Mexico as a whole. The influence of the company, the largest in Mexico and the source of most of the foreign currency that Mexico earns, is to be seen all over the city and across the border.[6] The third difference is that McAllen has one of the most successful foreign trade zones in the United States, and this zone plays a central part in facilitating the efficient operation of the maquila industry in the area.

The creation of the maquila industry in Reynosa/McAllen was largely a product of the efforts of public facilitators in McAllen and

---

[6] As long ago as 1967 Texas was celebrating the fact that PEMEX would be giving its workers the equivalent of $350,000 in Christmas bonuses, as over half of this was likely to be spent in the United States (*Journal of Commerce*, November 30, 1967, p. 2).

private facilitators in Reynosa, although both public and private facilitators in both cities (and some who straddled both camps) did take part. In Reynosa, two local entrepreneurs, Antonio Villareal and Arturo González, saw the prospects for a maquila industry at an early stage. They were active in setting up a joint industrial team of the Reynosa and McAllen chambers of commerce to promote the industry in the two cities. The McAllen Chamber of Commerce had an industrial board to handle maquila business, run by Frank Birkhead. He and Wade Terrell, the manager of the chamber, were the main figures on the McAllen side. Noting the steady buildup of maquila plants in the other locations along the border, they saw no good reason why Reynosa and McAllen should not have some share. However, it proved to be a difficult task to attract U.S. corporations.

The first real breakthrough came in 1969, when a U.S. apparel company not only decided to establish a maquila in Reynosa but also to set up a twin plant in McAllen. This maquila was built on land acquired from Antonio Villareal, a member of the binational team and an engineer by profession. Villareal had been buying up land through his company, Fraccionamiento Reynosa, and now began to plan an industrial park in Reynosa. He had been able to acquire land on the eastern edge of the city near the airport and in an area adjoining suburban *colonias* which would provide the labor force for the maquilas. Over the next few years, Villareal and his associates developed the Parque Industrial Reynosa, preparing industrial sites, building houses, and organizing bus services.

The binational team kept up its promotional work, with rather more of an official input from Reynosa as time went on, and each year one or two more companies came in. The number of maquilas crept up to nine in 1972. Then in 1973 McAllen got onto the front page of the *Wall Street Journal* in an article on the booming maquila industry, and the Industrial Board received more than fifty telephone calls in one day from prospective clients.

The breakthrough for Reynosa/McAllen, as in Matamoros/Brownsville, came in 1978 with the establishment of a Zenith television components maquila. The Zenith plant single-handedly transformed the situation by doubling the maquila labor force in one year, doubling the area of factory floor in use (the plant covered a massive 250,000 square feet), and giving the seal of approval to the Parque Industrial Reynosa for all in the maquila industry to see. Not only did Zenith transform the maquila industry in Reynosa, but it also transformed it in McAllen because it was the first important client to establish itself in the McAllen Foreign Trade Zone.

In 1980, rather belatedly, the Mexican authorities began to build their own industrial park in Reynosa. This was a joint venture of national agencies, the state government of Tamaulipas, and CANACINTRA in

Reynosa. The original plan was to take a 400-hectare area about nine kilometers south of Reynosa, where housing was already being developed, and design a full-service industrial park specifically for the maquila industry.

Confidence that the maquila industry in Reynosa/McAllen would share fully in the anticipated growth of the industry nationally in the late 1980s was high in local circles. The maquila association is a major propagator of this confidence. It started in 1981 and, as was the case in Matamoros, Zenith dominated at first, but as new large firms began slowly to come in (TRW, General Motors, and General Electric), these began to play a bigger role. The association has for some years been involved in infrastructural improvements in the maquila parks areas of the city, both on its own and in joint projects with the authorities.

Ciudad Juárez/El Paso

An industrial development board was established in Juárez in the mid-1960s, with an office in El Paso. Its membership included businesspeople, bankers, lawyers, educators, and local officials. The Juárez board made no bones about the specific attraction of the city in publicity material it distributed in El Paso in the late 1960s. The weekly wage based on the January 1968 minimum, for example, was just over $20 for a 48-hour week. Even in 1968, this spoke for itself.

The competition between Mexican border cities for maquilas has always been intense, and in the mid-to-late 1960s it was not Juárez that attracted the bulk of the first wave of large maquilas, but cities like Mexicali and Nuevo Laredo. However, after 1970 the maquila industry in Juárez took off, and although it lagged behind Tijuana in terms of the numbers of plants, from that time on Juárez was to have more maquila employees than any single city in Mexico. It also boasted the largest collection of Fortune 500 companies, an achievement that the public and private facilitators never tired of publicizing.

A feature of the Juárez maquila industry at this time was the apparent success of "twin plants" in El Paso. This is of great interest both in relation to the early growth of the industry and in relation to the structure of the transnational class that was being created. The very fact that the city of El Paso devoted a section of its 1971 community renewal program to the maquila industry is itself significant.

The leading force on the Mexican side of the border was the Bermúdez family, who had a construction company and saw the opportunity of building industrial parks for the maquilas along the border. The Antonio J. Bermúdez Park, named for the patriarch of the family who had brought PRONAF to Juárez, employed a U.S. citizen, William Mitchell, to sell the "maquila in the park" idea to U.S. corporations. Mitchell saw very clearly that success lay with those who could attract the big players in the game, and he aggressively went after some Fortune 500 companies. His first major success was RCA, which already had a joint venture in Mexico City but was convinced by Grupo Bermúdez to turn it into a maquila in the new park they were building in Juárez. (Actually the park was built around RCA, rather than vice versa.) The first priority, consistent with the policy of attracting and retaining Fortune 500 companies, was to build a park to international standards, with on-site facilities that would eliminate as much of the difficulty of operating in Mexico as possible.

The maquila activities of Grupo Bermúdez expanded considerably in the 1970s and 1980s. It has established other maquila parks in Juárez, an industrial park in El Paso, the Pan American Center for Industry, and a series of parks outside Juárez, mainly in the state of Chihuahua. In addition, Grupo Bermúdez is involved in maquila parks in Coahuila and the Yucatán and actively seeks fresh sites on a continuing basis.[7]

Also active in building industrial parks for the maquila industry from the 1970s on was a group of Mexican entrepreneurs who, like Bermúdez, expanded from purely domestic enterprise. The Grupo Omega, directed by Oscar Cantú Murguía, and the Grupo Juárez of Francisco Villareal both established industrial parks for the maquila industry, offering a variety of services. Several other individuals and groups in Juárez also began to lease out factory space (see Salas-Porras 1987: 55–56). These were joined by a substantial core of professional and commercial personnel who were able to service the growing maquila industry. The Juárez law firm González Vargas et al. were the first legal experts in the city to take an active interest in the maquilas, and they built up a thriving business in advising and representing U.S. and Mexican companies.[8] Other law firms followed suit. It would be incorrect, however, to suggest that the Mexican element from Juárez totally dominated the maquila industry in the early years, much less today.

Then as now, the public facilitators in El Paso, those attached to the Chamber of Commerce and the Industrial Development Corporation, and various other nonprofit but profit-oriented organizations, were quick to see the significance of the maquilas for the prosperity of El Paso and for the creation of economic opportunities for the new transnational class that was forming all along the border. Likewise, groups of private facilitators were active in the establishment and growth of the industry. These private facilitators were often men, and more presently some women, who usually began by working for the larger maquilas in Juárez and elsewhere. By dint of their vision for the industry as a whole, they became activists for the maquilas in the local and wider community.

---

[7]In 1988 Grupo Bermúdez handled around 40 percent of Juárez maquila employment and over 10 percent of the national total.

[8]Under the name of Bryan, González Vargas, González Baz, Delgado y Rogers, it was said to be the largest law firm in Mexico outside Mexico City.

Some circulated between executive roles in industrial parks and specific maquilas and independent consultancy and quasi-official state positions (though this was much more characteristic of the Mexican side) and back again.

The physical growth of the maquila industry in Juárez was matched by the growth in number and level of activity of the public and private facilitators on both sides of the border. In 1980 the state of Chihuahua set up its own industrial promotion agency, Promotora de la Industria Chihuahuense, which has been instrumental since then in establishing no less than six industrial parks for the maquila industry. The Airport Industrial Park in Ciudad Juárez is one of Promotora's most successful ventures. In these parks the state government offers a variety of industrial facilities and services. The state has also actively encouraged the growth of the maquila associations which, while not formally part of the state apparatus, clearly enjoy a special relationship with it. In Juárez, the Asociación de Maquiladoras (AMAC) is active both politically on behalf of the industry and in a research and information-gathering capacity. AMAC, which is legally a private nonprofit organization, is funded by the maquilas themselves, through the affiliation that all registered maquilas must maintain with CANACINTRA.

The major public facilitators at work in the Juárez maquila industry are usually either straightforward arms of local government or nonprofit bodies that are at least partly supported from public funds, and they express the official ideology of the ruling strata on both sides of the border that the maquila industry is essential for the well-being of both the border communities and the national interest. The borderlands socioeconomic systems both permit and encourage people in such "public" organizations to flit back and forth between the public and the private sectors, and in this they are in no way unique.

Tijuana/San Diego

The first "maquila type" plants were established in Tijuana years before the official program got under way (see Mungaray 1983: 26). From the mid-1960s, private facilitators in California, principally the Cal Pacifico company, began to develop the shelter plan concept, a variation on subcontracting. Many of those were to become influential members of the transnational maquila class—like Richard Campbell, who founded a successful maquila park in Nogales; Richard Bolin, a prominent international production-sharing consultant; and Enrique Esparza, whose firm eventually became the leading facilitator in Tijuana.

Although there were several small companies running maquilas in the early 1960s, in 1966, when the BIP was introduced, some larger and more notable corporations began to look seriously at Tijuana. The electronics industry was well represented in this early inflow. Litton

Industries, operating under the name Triad de México, opened two plants, and Fairchild, one of the pioneers of the global electronics industry, also opened a component assembly plant in Tijuana in 1966.

Tijuana did, in fact, have a small industrial park at this time, the Centro Industrial Barranquita, established in the mid-1960s by a Mexican developer. This was not an industrial park in the accepted sense of the term, certainly nothing like the parks being created in Nogales or in Ciudad Juárez. It was more like a zoning device to encourage factories to locate near each other, and few services were provided beyond the provision of industrial space. The lack of proper industrial parks meant that certain types of U.S. firms (particularly Fortune 500 corporations) were less likely to establish maquilas in Tijuana, and, conversely, others (clothing "sweatshops," for example) were more likely to do so. The importance of industrial parks for the maquila industry has been insufficiently appreciated; an exception is the work of Salas-Porras (1987). The concentration effects of these parks also give the transnational capitalist class a particular character that a more dispersed industry will not provide.[9]

For the "true believers" of the maquila movement, the experience of the first five years in Tijuana must have been rather disappointing. Nevertheless, something had been achieved. A small but expanding U.S.-owned industrial base was being established to stand beside, and sometimes to join in, ventures with domestic industry in Tijuana. From Tijuana, through San Diego and up to Los Angeles and beyond, groups of dedicated entrepreneurs were slowly beginning to realize that the maquila industry did have some very concrete benefits to offer, particularly in the needle trades and in electronics.

The most important private maquila facilitator in the Californias is Henry Esparza's company, Assemble in Mexico, which aggressively created a market for its shelter and subcontracting services all over the Californias and beyond. It has brought a large variety of industries and processes to Tijuana, and has actively involved itself in the training of the local work force. Its main competitor is IMEC, a company that has specialized mainly in the electronics field. Howard Boysen, who built it up to its present position, worked for Fairchild, the first U.S. electronics corporation to go into offshore assembly in the 1960s. Boysen opened the Fairchild factory in Tijuana in the late 1960s, and he saw clearly the great potential of the maquila program for the electronics industry. He eventually bought out his bosses and established IMEC (International Manufacturing, Engineering, and Consulting). IMEC, like most facilitators, strives to maintain a balance between a U.S. head and a Mexican managerial and technical team in each of its plants. To this end it has

---

[9] In 1988, 44 percent of maquilas but 75 percent of maquila jobs were located in specialized maquila parks (Ochoa in Lee 1988: 90).

trained and brought along many Mexican managers and technicians, which is no doubt good for Mexico and tends to be cheaper and more convenient than hiring U.S. citizens.

The Mexican input to the maquila industry in Tijuana has been considerable, but until quite recently in a rather less visible fashion than in other cities along the border. This is mostly due to the absence of proper industrial parks and to the other commercial opportunities available in, for example, tourist-related activities. In the 1980s several of the leading business families in the city began to take more interest in the maquila industry. The Grupo Bustamante added the provision of maquila sites to its involvement in utilities and hotels; the Lutherot group runs three maquila parks as well as various tourist ventures; and the Consorcio Tijuana under the direction of Jaime Bonilla has also added maquila site provision to its newspaper, construction, and tourist interests (see Salas-Porras 1987: 57).

Another influential maquila facilitator in Tijuana is Jorge Salman Hadad, a long-time apparel maquila operator. He is particularly important because he is a past president of the National Maquila Association and during his term of office he spoke up clearly and loudly for the importance of the maquilas in Mexico's effort to achieve economic progress.

Therefore, in these three centers of maquila development along the border, a recognizably transnational class has emerged over the past twenty years. This has brought together Mexican and U.S. capitalists, professionals, and officials, who see their own interests and the interests of their respective nations best served by promoting the maquila industry. On occasion, U.S. facilitators directly cause the loss of some U.S. jobs, and Mexicans forgo some economic opportunities to make a success of the maquilas. Therefore, this transnational capitalist class is genuinely putting other wider interests above their narrower national interests. My argument is that the transnational capitalist class along the border, like similar classes all over the world, is furthering the interests of global capitalism.

CONCLUSION

The tendency to transnationalization of the global capitalist system, visible since the 1950s, accelerated dramatically in the 1980s. One consequence of this trend has been the creation of an embryonic transnational capitalist class which is in the process of replacing the old compradors and swallowing up most of the new indigenous bourgeoisies in the Third World and, increasingly, what is left of the socialist world and the new Eastern Europe.[10] These tendencies do not entirely depend on the transnational corporations, but, as the recent experiences

---

[10] I argue this in detail in Sklair 1990, especially chaps. 3 and 5.

of the maquila industry along the Mexico-U.S. border illustrate, the implantation of foreign-operated factories stimulates the growth of transnational classes.

I have tried to show how the export-led developmental strategy, driven as it is from the outside by the demands of the global capitalist system, has created a local transnational capitalist class along the Mexico-U.S. border. But these local classes are not simply an effect of the system, for they also embody a history, a culture, and their own practices. They can turn the developmental strategies of global capitalism to their own purposes and even, on occasion, challenge those who wield central power in the system. In doing this they create their own contradictions, throw up opposing classes, provoke class struggles, set in train economic, political, and cultural-ideological changes. History, far from being at an end, has hardly begun!

REFERENCES

Ake, Claude, ed. 1985. *Political Economy of Nigeria*. London: Longman.
Baird, P., and E. McCaughan. 1975. "Hit and Run: U.S. Runaway Shops on the Mexican Border." *NACLA Report* 9 (July-August).
Bath, C. Richard. 1982. "Health and Environmental Problems: The Role of the Border in El Paso-Ciudad Juárez Coordination," *Journal of Interamerican Studies and World Affairs* 24:375–92.
Carrillo, Jorge, and Alberto Hernández. 1985. *Mujeres fronterizas en la industria maquiladora*. Mexico City: SEP/CEFNOMEX.
Evans, P. 1979. *Dependent Development. The Alliance of Multinational, State and Local Capital in Brazil*. Princeton: Princeton University Press.
Gibson, L.J., and A. Corona Rentería, eds. 1985. *The U.S. and Mexico: Borderland Development and the National Economies*. Boulder: Westview.
Gillespie, K. 1984. *The Tripartite Relationship*. New York: Praeger.
Hale, C. 1965. "Industrial Development Corporations in Texas," *Federal Reserve Bank of Dallas, Business Review*, Part 1 (February): 3–9; Part 2 (March): 3–9.
Herzog, Lawrence. 1990. *Where North Meets South: Cities, Space and Politics on the United States-Mexico Border*. Austin: University of Texas Press.
Ihonvbere, J., and T. Shaw. 1988. *Towards a Political Economy of Nigeria. Petroleum and Politics at the Semi-Periphery*. Aldershot: Avebury.
Jamail, Milton. 1981. "Voluntary Organizations along the Border." In *Mexico-United States Relations*, edited by Susan Kaufman Purcell. New York: Academy of Political Science.
Lee, Thomas P., ed. 1988. *In-Bond Industry/Industria Maquiladora*. Mexico City: Administración y Servicios Internacionales, S.A.
Mungaray L., Alejandro. 1983. "Contradicciones en el desarrollo de las maquiladoras en Tijuana," *Economía Informa* 107 (August): 25–31.

Prock, Jerry. 1983. "The Peso Devaluations and Their Effect on Texas Border Economies," *Inter-American Economic Affairs* 37 (Winter): 83–92.

Ross, Stanley, ed. 1978. *Views across the Border*. Albuquerque: University of New Mexico Press.

Salas-Porras, Alejandra.1987. "Maquiladoras y burguesía regional," *El Cotidiano*, Número especial 1:51–58.

Sklair, Leslie. 1989. *Assembling for Development: The Maquila Industry in Mexico and the United States*. Boulder: Westview.

———. 1990. *Sociology of the Global System*. London: Harvester.

Tocups, Nora. 1980. "City Growth and Cooperation along the U.S.-Mexican Border," *Georgia Journal of International and Comparative Law* 10 (Fall): 619–44.

Whiteford, Scott. 1986. "Troubled Waters: The Regional Impact of Foreign Investment and State Capital in the Mexicali Valley." In *Regional Impacts of U.S.-Mexican Relations*, edited by Ina Rosenthal Urey. Monograph Series, no. 16. La Jolla: Center for U.S.-Mexican Studies, University of California, San Diego.

5

The Mexican-Origin Population of the United States as a Political Force in the Borderlands: From Paisanos to Pochos to Potential Political Allies

Rodolfo O. de la Garza and Claudio Vargas

As U.S.-Mexico relations have become more salient and problematic to both countries, political leaders and scholars in Mexico and the United States have focused increasing attention on the U.S.-Mexico border region. In part this is because problems central to relations between these nations—ranging from immigration and pollution to drug smuggling and the consequences of uneven economic development—are so keenly felt there. Focus on the border region has also shifted attention to the Mexican-origin population that has lived in the area since the eighteenth century.

Because of the common historical origins of Mexican Americans, some observers conclude that they are culturally integrated, that is, that the political division separating Mexico and the United States is irrelevant to the culture and society of this population. This argument has two variants. One sees a homogeneous culture that is equally vibrant on both sides of the border, unique to the region and distinct from the respective mainstream societies. The other sees an essentially unintegrated Mexican society living on the U.S. side of the border. In this view,

---

We would like to thank Diana Solís of the *Wall Street Journal*, Jesús Tamayo of the Centro de Investigación y Docencia Económicas in Mexico City, Professor Sylvia Bernard of the Universidad Autónoma de Guadalajara, and Velma García of Smith University for their comments on an earlier version of this paper. This paper was prepared with the assistance of the Bilateral Commission on the Future of United States-Mexican Relations.

the Mexican-origin population is an irredentist threat to U.S. national unity (de la Garza and Flores 1986; J. García and de la Garza 1985).

This essay rejects both of these views. It argues instead that current and future relations between the Mexican-origin populations of the border can only be understood within the context of the historically evolving relationship between the United States and Mexico on the one hand, and between the Mexican-origin population of the United States as a distinct population and the Mexican government and Mexicans per se, on the other. The chapter begins, therefore, with a synthesis of the history of those relationships. The second section examines recent relevant developments through 1988 in the United States and Mexico, respectively. The final section analyzes the implications of these developments for the future of the relationship between Mexican Americans, Mexico, and Mexicans, as well as for U.S.-Mexican relations.

It should be noted that the Mexican-origin population of the United States includes Mexican Americans (citizens of Mexican origin), permanent resident aliens, and undocumented aliens. As U.S. citizens, Mexican Americans differ in their legal and political status and in their sociopolitical orientations from Mexican legal residents and undocumented aliens. Therefore, the term "Mexican" will refer to citizens of Mexico residing in Mexico or the United States.

Origins and Evolution of the Relationship

For heuristic purposes, it is useful to conceptualize four distinct stages in the relations between Mexican Americans, the Mexican government, and Mexicans that roughly correspond to the years 1848–1928, 1929–1970, 1971–1982, and a fourth stage that has been evolving since 1982. The distinctions among these reflect the transition in the status of Mexican Americans in U.S. society and the recognition of and response to those changes by Mexicans and Mexican officials. They also reflect the profound changes that Mexican government and society have experienced and which influence Mexican perceptions of the United States in general and of Mexican Americans in particular.

1848–1928

The relationship was most intimate early in the first stage. During those years there were no meaningful cultural distinctions between Mexicans and Mexican Americans, and Mexican officials did their best to protect the interests of their former citizens who had become "Americans" but who in cultural terms remained Mexicans for decades. They insisted that the Treaty of Guadalupe Hidalgo (1848) explicitly addressed the rights and privileges of this group, and through their diplomatic missions they protested on behalf of both these former Mexicans and more recent Mexican emigrants when their rights were violated.

Further strengthening these bonds was the treatment these first generations of Mexican Americans received at the hand of American society. Despite being U.S. citizens, they were almost immediately denied the rights inherent in their citizenship. Moreover, and perhaps more significantly, by the early twentieth century, as U.S. institutions took root across the Southwest, this abuse intensified, and southwestern society systematically and comprehensively segregated and discriminated against Mexican-origin citizens and immigrants alike. In effect, U.S. society treated all Mexican-origin residents and citizens as if they were undesirable aliens. Considered foreigners and lacking access to U.S. legal and political institutions, Mexican Americans turned to Mexican consuls for assistance. These officials nurtured the bonds between Mexican Americans, Mexicans, and the Mexican government (Gómez Quiñones 1976; Balderrama 1982).

1929–1970

The establishment of the League of United Latin American Citizens (LULAC) in 1929 signals the beginning of the second and most contentious stage in the relationship. LULAC, the American G.I. Forum, and other organizations created during this period were concerned with establishing the American identity of Mexican-origin citizens, providing them political access, and protecting the hard-won economic gains of a fledgling middle class. The extent to which a substantial segment of this population has come to think of themselves as Americans rather than Mexicans is indicated in that, with notable exceptions, they now gave their organizations English names (LULAC, American G. I. Forum, Mexican American Political Association, Political Association of Spanish Speaking Organizations) and, more significantly, opposed continued Mexican immigration. Rather than identify with the plight of Mexican immigrants, many Mexican Americans individually reported the undocumented to the U.S. Immigration and Naturalization Service and through their organizations lobbied against immigration and the Bracero Program (de la Garza 1980; Allsup 1982: 102–10).

Parallel patterns characterized developments in Mexico during this period. Influenced perhaps by the enactment in 1921 of a U.S. immigration law affecting Mexico, Mexican officials now also recognized the legal and political distinctions between aliens in the United States and Mexican Americans. They therefore continued to defend the rights of the former but no longer acted on behalf of the latter. To the contrary, Mexican officials were now uncooperative and antagonistic toward Mexican Americans who sought their assistance. For example, in 1956 they jailed and then expelled Reies López Tijerina when he sought Mexican support for the land rights struggle in New Mexico (Nabokov 1969: 216–17). During the 1968 Poor People's March in Washington, D.C.,

Tijerina again requested a meeting with Mexican officials, who once again refused on the grounds that he was not a Mexican. They finally met with him after Secretary of State Dean Rusk requested they do so. Secretary Rusk perhaps hoped the meeting would reduce tensions associated with the march. Whatever his reasons, he assured Mexican officials that the meeting would be peaceful because, unknown to Tijerina, U.S. officials were members of Tijerina's entourage (de la Garza and Schmitt 1986). In the 1980s, Mexican officials also refused to respond to petitions from a group of Texas Mexican Americans regarding payments that Mexico was to have made following a major claims settlement with the United States in 1941. The terms of that settlement required Mexico to distribute funds that had been allocated for the claimants it represented, the great majority of whom were Mexican Americans (Mexican informant, Fall 1987).

Mexican society gradually began to acknowledge the cultural transformations experienced by Mexican Americans, but the process incorporated misinterpretations and prejudices. An extreme example of these was the use of the term pocho to label Mexican Americans. A Chicano writer defined a pocho as "a Mexican slob who has pretensions of being a gringo sonofabitch" (Enrique Hank López, quoted in Madrid-Barela 1976: 51). In its initial formulation, this negative image, which is reflected in Octavio Paz's 1949 influential essay on the pachuco in *El laberinto de la soledad*, did not acknowledge that Mexican Americans were no longer Mexicans but were instead creating a distinct but absolutely authentic new variant of American culture. The continued development of that identity, combined with its political manifestations and a more tolerant attitude among Mexicans, attenuated these biases. Consequently, within Mexico, Mexican-Mexican American relations were reevaluated within the context of U.S.-Mexican relations.

The Mexican government's actions during these years probably reflected its recognition that Mexican Americans were American citizens. From the 1920s through the 1960s, Mexican officials sought to manage relations with the United States in ways that would prevent U.S. interference in the consolidation and institutionalization of political and economic changes being effected by Mexico's revolutionary regimes. Given that objective, responding to Mexican American concerns might have produced an angry U.S. response, the cost of which would have been excessive given the long-term benefits that relations with Mexican Americans could yield.

1971–1982

The third stage in the relationship was characterized by sporadic ad hoc efforts on both sides to reestablish relations. In the United States, this effort was led by Chicano activists and was the logical consequence of the Chicano movement's emphasis on cultural nationalism. It also reflected the movement's charge that Mexican Americans would never be allowed equal rights in U.S. society. Leaders such as José Angel Gutiérrez and Reies López Tijerina therefore looked to the Mexican government for assistance in implementing their domestic political strategies. This effort was principally about enlisting support from the Mexican state on behalf of Mexican American socioeconomic and political advancement within the United States. It enjoyed some minimal but noteworthy successes, especially in the area of higher education (de la Garza 1980: 573–74).

The Mexican government's support of those efforts and its increased oil wealth combined to stimulate a wider range of Mexican American interest in developing linkages to Mexico. Mexican American academics became involved because of their support of the Chicano movement and because of a genuine interest in Mexican-Mexican American relations. Also, while they were struggling to be recognized within their own academic environments, their work was being promoted by university programs and academic meetings in Mexico, some of which were government funded. Mexican American businesspeople joined the effort and developed proposals ranging from promoting Mexican theatrical performances and creating franchises for Mexican exports, to establishing Mexican American distributorships for PEMEX products. Rather quickly, leaders of mainstream Mexican American organizations also became involved in the effort and by the late 1970s took control of it with the creation of the Hispanic Commission (Gutiérrez 1986: 29, 32). It is noteworthy, however, that virtually no Mexican American elected or appointed officials participated in these efforts. This may be because Mexican American officials were primarily concerned with consolidating their recently won place in governing institutions and because American political officials would have looked askance at such behavior. The State Department's reaction to these types of contact indicates that these were well-grounded fears (de la Garza 1980: 574; 1986: 39).

1982–PRESENT

By 1982, these efforts had produced little more than what the Chicano activists had initially accomplished. Moreover, the onset of Mexico's economic collapse gave little reason to expect much from the relationship in the foreseeable future. Perhaps the most significant result of the contacts made during this period was their effect on the perception that Mexicans had of Mexican Americans.

Paralleling these events and to some extent influencing them was the improving political status of Mexican Americans. In 1970, Mexican Americans were as effectively excluded from the political process as they had been in 1900 (F. García and de la Garza 1977). By 1982, however, the historical legal obstacles to Mexican American political participation were tumbling down, and Mexican Americans had become a significant part of the electorate courted by both major political parties. Also, the number of Mexican American elected and appointed officials was increasing at almost all levels. These successes vitiated the argument that Mexican Americans would never have access to the political process, as well as the need for seeking Mexican assistance in order to address local problems.

In Mexico, the effort to improve relations with Mexican Americans began with President Echeverría in 1970, on the heels of the crisis of 1968. He personally met with Chicano activists on several occasions, providing them material and symbolic support. He also stimulated interest in emigration and supported Mexico's pathbreaking study of the issue, the Encuesta Nacional de Emigración hacia la Frontera Norte y a los EEUU. His efforts were expanded by President López Portillo, who met with Chicanos during his presidential campaign as well as after he took office. During his presidency, the number and range of contacts expanded so rapidly that officials established an Office of Chicano Affairs in the Labor Ministry to help manage them. Mexican Americans were troubled that the office was established there rather than in Mexico's Ministry of Foreign Relations; this placement indicated that the office would involve itself primarily with issues concerning Mexican workers in the United States. Mexican officials also encouraged Mexican Americans to establish the Hispanic Commission in the United States, which would function as a gatekeeper for Mexican American groups seeking access to Mexican officials (Gutiérrez 1986: 29, 32). These activities occurred while Mexico was relying on its newly discovered oil reserves to increase its independence vis-à-vis the United States.

According to José Angel Gutiérrez, the López Portillo regime also sought to formalize relations between the Mexican government and Mexican Americans. Gutiérrez and three other Mexican American leaders—Tijerina, Mario Obledo (former MALDEF official and California cabinet member), and Ed Peña (then LULAC president)—were invited to the celebration of the fiftieth anniversary of the Partido Revolucionario Institucional (PRI), Mexico's official political party. Gutiérrez observed:

> The Mexicans wanted us to establish an office like the Palestine Liberation Organization had. They would help us fund it. It would have political and cultural units. They wanted to know where we would place it. We didn't know how to respond. We screwed up. We were unable to respond at their level. They wanted us to grow in stature. They treated us with respect, even with our poor Spanish and *babosadas* [stupidities]. Look at

the seating arrangements during the formal state dinners. We were seated horizontally on a par with the U.S. and vertically on par with the superpowers (interview, Fall 1987).

It was during López Portillo's presidency that at least some Mexican officials first began to reevaluate systematically their relations with Mexican Americans. As a result of increased contacts with a wide diversity of Mexican Americans, Mexican government representatives, intellectuals, and society at large began to recognize the changing status of Mexican Americans in the United States. By the end of López Portillo's six-year term, there was a growing awareness among a number of Mexican officials that it was in Mexico's interests to promote among Mexican society a better understanding of and increased willingness to deal more seriously with Mexican Americans, whatever their feelings about them.

As of 1982, Mexican-Mexican American relations were on more solid footing, but the prospects for close political linkages seemed dim. The onset of the economic crisis caused the regime's support for Mexican American-oriented activities to decline dramatically. Nevertheless, by 1987 the Mexican government had produced its Program for Enhanced Relations between the Mexican Government and the U.S. Mexican American Community, calling for a systematic expansion and improvement of relations. The reasons for and implications of this initiative are reviewed in the following section.

A CHANGING RELATIONSHIP

THE MEXICAN CONTEXT

The Mexican government's attempt to institutionalize relations with Mexican Americans appears to be part of a new strategy for developing allies who will advance Mexican interests in the United States. U.S. pressures associated with the debt crisis, immigration, the drug trade, and the Central American conflict convinced Mexican officials that they needed such assistance. As Romeo Flores Caballero, chairman of Mexico's Chamber of Deputies' Committee on Border Affairs, said about his attempts to foster relations with Mexican Americans, "we need all the help we can get."

These efforts signal an important departure from the historical pattern of disdaining such activities on the grounds that they constitute violations of the Estrada Doctrine, Mexico's policy of nonintervention in the internal affairs of sovereign nations. According to Jesús Tamayo, a Mexican specialist on U.S.-Mexico border issues, however, that doctrine has been an excuse rather than a reason for avoiding relations with Mexican Americans.

Whatever the historic significance of that principle, Mexico's leaders no longer strictly adhere to it. For example, they viewed the Simpson-Rodino debate in the U.S. Congress as "strictly an internal U.S. matter with which the Mexican government could not interfere." This hands-off approach also "indicated contentment with the status quo and its 'escape valve' for Mexico's chronic unemployment" (interview with Adolfo Aguilar Zinser, December 1987). It may also have reflected the widely shared mistaken judgment that the legislation would not pass, and that it would have little effect on migratory flows even if it were approved.

Mexico's elites have behaved much differently since the Immigration Reform and Control Act (IRCA) was enacted in 1986. There has been extensive press coverage of IRCA-related matters. Labor leaders and senior public officials have held hearings on various aspects of the legislation and met with Mexican Americans to discuss the effects of IRCA. Mexican officials have also expressed their appreciation to those Mexican American groups that are working to protect the rights of Mexican immigrants.

Clearly, Mexican leaders perceive Mexican Americans as their most likely new allies, and they will no longer allow their prejudices to impede relations. As Tamayo said,

> Forget about how Mexicans used to view Chicanos. That's all over now. In the past, officials used the issue about noninterference in internal U.S. affairs as an excuse for not dealing with Chicanos simply because they did not want to deal with them (interview, November 1987).

Leonel Castillo, a nationally prominent Mexican American leader who met often with Mexican leaders, shares this view:

> In the old days they called us pochos. . . . No more. Now they are willing to overlook our mistakes. At a September 16 celebration, for example, a Chicano spokesman stood and gave a speech lauding Benito Juárez and the defeat of the French. The Mexicans applauded and said nothing—in public (interview, November 1987).

Obviously, Mexican elites recognize that Mexican American political influence continues to grow, and that there are issues such as immigrant rights and border development which concern Mexicans and Mexican Americans and which could serve as the basis for working together. The words of President de la Madrid and other elites illustrate how Mexicans are reinterpreting the Estrada Doctrine and how they see Mexican-Mexican American interests coming together:

> Mexico is morally and politically obliged to promote respect for the human and labor rights of Mexican-Americans and Mexicans, whether undocumented or not. —Miguel de la Madrid, *Mexico City News*, February 2, 1987.

> A new, more active Mexican [foreign] policy could start by reaching out to the Mexican-American community and with the many consulates here to ensure the rights of Mexicans under the new legislation [IRCA]. —Adolfo Aguilar Zinser, *Christian Science Monitor*, August 7, 1987.

> The Chicano community and the undocumented are, when all is said and done, a border beyond the border. Defending the second border north of the nation is an act of sovereignty and of mutual benefit. —*Uno más Uno*, February 13, 1987.

The effort to promote these relationships may also be related to the Mexican government's concern that independently established linkages may develop in ways that would threaten state interests if they are not monitored. Aguilar Zinser considers this as a principal reason for Mexico's newfound interest in Mexican Americans.

> There is a recognition that there are many initiatives developing spontaneously in the private sector and among governors and other officials on both sides of the border that are being carried out autonomously. The Gobernación Ministry is anxious about the possible political consequences of this, so they are trying to control it (interview, November 1987).

Mexican officials are known to be anxious about autonomous organizational developments (Craig and Cornelius 1980: 325–93; Stevens 1970), and relationships between Mexicans and Mexican Americans obviously have the potential to produce exactly this type of outcome. The Arizona Farm Workers Union, for example, organizes and distributes benefits among workers in Mexico. Once those workers are working permanently in Mexico, it is easy to envision them drawing on their experiences as members of a democratic union to make demands that will exceed the response capabilities of Mexican union and government officials.

Whatever its reasons, the Program for Enhanced Relations illustrates a change in the Mexican government's attitude toward Mexican Americans. Responsibility for the program is officially under Mexico's National Population Council, an agency of the Gobernación Ministry. Mexico's three most important ministries—Gobernación, Foreign Relations, and Planning and Budget—had a role in its final form, but it seems to have been developed at Gobernación in consultation with leading Mexican specialists on Mexican Americans and the border, under Secretary Manuel Bartlett's supervision. On August 10, 1987, Mexico's National Population Council hosted a major conference, entitled "Key Demographic, Social, Political, and Cultural Features of the Mexican American Community: The Simpson-Rodino Legislation," that was clearly intended to be the first step in implementing the Program for Enhanced Relations.

The program has six major sections: (1) the Mexican American population; (2) key problems between Mexico and the United States; (3) the political and economic importance of the Mexican American population; (4) efforts to strengthen identification and establish closer ties with Mexico; (5) efforts de enhance interaction with the Mexican government; and (6) program of activities.

Overall, the document evidences a good understanding of the Mexican American population. However, as is the case with all official position papers in Mexico or elsewhere, it overstates the government's case. In this instance, the objective is to emphasize the disadvantaged status of Mexican Americans, highlight their cultural loyalty and political clout, and thus implicitly show that Mexican Americans and Mexicans are likely to become close allies and that it is in Mexico's interest to foster these ties.

For example, the document states that the principal problem facing Mexican Americans is discrimination and that this has increased in recent years. Without in any way suggesting that discrimination has ended, there is no evidence that discrimination has increased. To the contrary, de jure discrimination is now unconstitutional and nonexistent, the Voting Rights Act of 1975 and 1982 eliminated most of the practices that had disenfranchised Mexican Americans, and discriminatory educational practices and financing methods across the Southwest are changing in ways that benefit Mexican Americans. No mention is made of these developments. The document also states that Mexican Americans have "great difficulty" receiving social security and unemployment benefits. There is no evidence indicating that Mexican American experiences with these programs differ in any way from the experiences of the majority population.

The Program for Enhanced Relations suggests that Mexican Americans will be the electoral majority in the border states within twenty years. Although the number of Mexican American voters will increase in the coming decades, they will not become the majority of the southwestern electorate.

The most significant statements the document makes about Mexican Americans concern their culture. Time and again, the document recognizes that Mexican Americans have created a distinct identity and it praises their cultural production. With this, the Mexican government has taken a major step toward officially burying "pocho."

The Program for Enhanced Relations calls for a variety of activities to be initiated or coordinated by the Ministries of Gobernación, Education, Health, Foreign Relations, Labor and Welfare, Agrarian Reform, Transportation and Communications, Commerce and Industrial Development, and Tourism. Included among the eighty proposed activities are:

- Meetings between key Mexican American leaders and governors of Mexican frontier states and states from which migrants come.
- The distribution in Mexico of films, novels, and news regarding Mexican Americans.
- The development of a historical awareness in Mexico of the Mexican American experience; summer seminars for Mexican American university students; agreements with state departments of education; Spanish language courses; and invitations to Mexican American professors to Mexican universities as visiting faculty.
- Establishment of the "Mexican American Prize for Arts and Sciences."
- Advising Mexican Americans regarding commercial exchange with Mexico.
- Advising the Mexican American business community regarding commercial and industrial projects of the Mexican government.
- Promoting economic development in the ancestral regions of Mexican Americans.
- Promoting Mexican American investment in their ancestral regions.

The context in which the Program for Enhanced Relations' initial event was staged is also important. It came toward the end of de la Madrid's presidency, suggesting that this type of activity had not been high on his agenda. The program notes, however, that relations with Mexican Americans had been a priority for him, but that the economic crisis prevented him from addressing them. Also, the event was held during the most intense phase of the campaign for the PRI's presidential nomination. This campaign is not waged openly within the PRI; instead, contenders traditionally use their government offices to develop political support through orchestrating events that would normally fall within the purview of their respective responsibilities. Efforts to develop relations with Mexican Americans follow this pattern, and it is therefore not surprising that the Program for Enhanced Relations was closely linked to the presidential aspirations of the minister of Gobernación.

Nevertheless, the fact that the program was part of a government initiative gave it a status beyond a mere electoral ploy, since it established a program commitment to work with Chicanos that would have to be honored by whoever became president. Thus, it is not surprising that, in general, those Chicanos who are invited to meet with government representatives are ones who either support the PRI or at least are not critical of it. Meeting with such individuals allows the PRI to claim that it enjoys harmonious relations with Chicanos even when that relationship is quite problematic. Rhetoric aside, it is not yet clear that Mexican elites have rid themselves of their prejudices, or that Mexican leaders would be tolerant of the give-and-take that such a relationship would require. As the following response to the suggestion that Mexico develop a Mexican American lobby suggests, some (many?) Mexican elites still harbor resentments and are unlikely to accept a relationship in which Mexican Americans would be less than blindly supportive:

> Of course, many Americans of Mexican origin show genuine concern for the well-being of Mexico and respect the historical project chosen for our country—the only country we have—by those of us who in spite of the cost involved decided to remain Mexicans. But to the extent that Hispanic Americans are primarily committed to the values and goals of American society, we cannot assume their authentic respect for the distinct historical goals, values, and worldview of the nation that failed to fulfill some of the legitimate ambitions of their ancestors and themselves (interview with Robert Huesca, September 1987).

Perhaps this attitude explains at least partially why, with very few exceptions, the Mexican Americans who are invited to participate in events such as the 1987 conference mentioned above are those who tend to be uncritically supportive of the Mexican government. Jorge Bustamante, Mexico's leading expert on migration, argues that this pattern is a coincidence and reflects only the limited contacts that Mexican officials have with Mexican Americans (in Alzati 1986–87). Leonel Castillo disagrees:

Mexicans know they are inviting only a small, unrepresentative group of Chicanos. They do this because they are cultivating friends and supporters they will be able to call on later. They want friends who will deliver, just like everybody else does. They hate Tony Bonilla, for example. He criticized the PRI. They wanted to lynch him. They distributed his speech to all the Mexican consulates in the United States. Then they invited him to an official function (interview, November 1987).

Supporting Castillo's assessment is the response that a high-ranking Mexican official (someone deeply involved in these activities and currently consul in a major U.S. city) gave to a question about his views of Mr. Bonilla: "He is an animal."

Regardless of the priority the Program for Enhanced Relations receives during the current administration, its existence and the way it was launched indicate that from Mexico's perspective, Mexican-Mexican American relations have entered a new stage. This new stage is more than a response to the improving status of Mexican Americans. It also seems linked to recent economic and political transformations in Mexico. The former include the ongoing economic integration of the U.S.-Mexico border region, the concomitant capital shift, and job creation experienced by both sides of the border. This has forced the Mexican government to make social issues in border communities a priority and has increased the saliency of emigration and relations with Mexican Americans.

On the political side, the strength of the opposition along the northern frontier has grown greatly since the mid-1970s. Mexican government officials have been concerned about the domestic and international implications of this pattern and have responded accordingly. An integral part of their reaction has been an effort to gain Mexican Americans' goodwill and political support, thus impeding overtures to form alliances with with opposition groups.

Finally, the government's strategy for overcoming the economic crisis calls for much closer ties to the United States. Therefore, the Mexican state, unions, and businessmen, in their attempt to expand contacts in the United States, are also reaching out to diverse sectors of Mexican Americans.

These developments, then, have created the conditions for expanding relations between Mexico, Mexicans, and Mexican Americans. The Program for Enhanced Relations is evidence that Mexican elites are much more informed about Mexican Americans than ever before. This knowledge can serve as a foundation for expanding and improving Mexican-Mexican American relations. Salinas de Gortari, the first Mexican president to take office in an environment of support among a variety of elites for reaching out to Mexican Americans, will likely pursue such a goal but he will move cautiously. During the 1988 campaign Salinas met with Cesar Chávez, a meeting which officials in the Mexican embassy cite as evidence that the Salinas administration is committed to implementing the Program for Enhanced Relations. Prior to the meeting, however, an adviser to Salinas consulted an American official to get his views on whether to schedule it. The meeting was held after the official strongly supported it (interview, January 1988).

Finally, whatever path the new administration takes, contacts between Mexico's private sector, state and local-level officials, and Mexican Americans will continue to grow. These can only be more productive because of Mexico's increased understanding of Mexican Americans.

THE U.S. CONTEXT

Trends that began in the 1970s had by 1982 become regularized patterns, indicating that the Mexican-origin population of the United States had changed in ways that have significant implications for the course of Mexican-Mexican American relations. These changes are evident in the composition of the Mexican-origin population, in Mexican American attitudes toward Mexican immigration, and in Mexican American political status.

By 1982, the Mexican-origin population contained a larger foreign-born sector than perhaps since early in this century. Of the 8.74 million Mexican-origin residents in the nation in 1980, 25 percent (2.199 million) were foreign born. Approximately 58 percent of these had arrived between 1970 and 1980, and only 20 percent had come before 1960 (1980 Census of Population, vol. 1, chap. D). This influx continued in the 1980s and may well have increased because of the continued deterioration of the Mexican economy. This heightened presence has had a variety of effects. It produced an ethnic economic enclave that benefits Mexican American businesses (Cárdenas, de la Garza, and Hansen 1986). In general, Mexican immigrants do not seem to displace Mexican American workers or lower their wages, although they may do both in specific local situations (Muller and Espenshade 1985: Bean, Telles, and Lowell n.d.; Rodríguez and Núñez 1986). Their presence has generated controversy in schools where Mexican and Mexican American parents have different views of the educational process (Romo 1986). In areas such as South Texas, Mexican American officials, including educators, have protested that Mexican immigrant students drain scarce local resources. At the same time, the need for bilingual education, a program Mexican Americans support, is justified in large part by the presence of Mexican immigrant children. Finally, although Mexican immigrants tend to reside within Mexican American barrios, their private lives are conducted within distinct social arenas, perhaps because of the traditional antagonisms between Mexicans and Mexican Americans (Rodríguez and Núñez 1986; Valdez 1986; Menchaca 1987).

The post-1970 wave of immigrants has included an unknown number of political dissidents who differ in important ways from most Mexican immigrants. The latter come for economic reasons, do not bring with them a tradition of political activism or involvement (Craig and Cornelius 1980), and do not become politically active after they are here (J. García and de la Garza 1985; Alvarez 1987: 345). The dissidents left Mexico because of their opposition to the rules that govern the Mexican polity. They are convinced that the regime is becoming increasingly authoritarian, and they point to recent elections such as those in Nuevo León and Chihuahua as examples of how unresponsive and corrupt the system has become. More important, they have developed organizations within the United States through which they are continuing and expanding their protests. Mexican officials are concerned about this development (interview with Adolfo Aguilar Zinser, December 1987).

Although there are claims that such organizations have been established in seven cities, the only active groups seem to be the American Coalition for Democracy in El Paso, the Asociación de Potosinos de Chicago, and Por un México en Acción (PUMA) in Los Angeles. Little is known about PUMA. The other two groups have small memberships and limited finances, and although these three groups maintain contact with each other, they do not coordinate their activities. The Asociación de Potosinos has a distinct right-wing orientation and is led by expatriate Sinarquistas and Panistas. It has established no contacts with Mexican Americans. The American Coalition for Democracy is more broadly based and has reached out to Mexican American groups. MECHA, an activist Mexican American student group at the University of Texas at El Paso, has joined their efforts but the local LULAC chapter would not.

According to a member of the American Coalition, the organizations differ in their tactics. PUMA's membership comes "from a different educational level. They like to protest. We move at a different level; we write letters and hold conferences. The Asociación de Potosinos does both."

A major objective of these organizations is to inform Americans about what is happening in Mexico so as to create pressures that will lead to reforms. The American Coalition claims to have written all U.S. House and Senate members, and the organization apparently was a factor in the decision of the mayor pro tem of Ciudad Juárez not to participate in El Paso's 1986 Christmas tree-lighting ceremony. The president of the American Coalition objected when the Juárez mayor was invited to the event, since he is a PRI member and the coalition views the PRI as an "illicit government." "We want the present administration in Juárez to know that they're not welcome in El Paso. By inviting them to participate in this civic event we are patronizing Mexico's corrupt government" (UPI Wire Service, November 26, 1986). The Asociación de Potosinos picketed President de la Madrid during his last visit to Washington, D.C., and it has demonstrated against Mexican officials in Chicago during September 16 celebrations. The organization also wrote to President de la Madrid protesting sending entourages to cities such as Chicago to celebrate national holidays, arguing that the consuls are competent to host such events and that the government's sponsorship of such expensive tours is proof of its venality.

The second major pattern that has become clear since 1982 is the change in Mexican American attitudes toward Mexican immigration (see de la Garza 1985). Although Mexican Americans are divided in their views of undocumented immigration, they are much more positive about it than are Americans generally. This new attitude may be interpreted as the recognition that Mexican immigrants have not been the cause of Mexican American poverty and subordination. Mexican Americans, therefore, no longer spend their time attacking Mexican immigration. Instead, they now direct their energies toward changing those aspects of American society that have always been the primary source of their problems.

Even though many Mexican Americans are not supportive of increased immigration or of undocumented immigration per se, no Mexican American organization has come out against Mexican immigrants as they did in decades past. Moreover, Mexican immigrants now find their strongest allies among Mexican Americans. It was Mexican Americans who led the efforts in Doe v. Plyer to have Mexican alien children admitted to Texas schools. The Mexican American Legal Defense and Education Fund (MALDEF), the National Association of Latino Elected Officials (NALEO), and other groups were very active in monitoring and influencing the implementation of IRCA. Also, some elected officials are supportive of Mexican immigrants, at least in part because they are an important part of their constituency. Román Martínez, a Texas state representative, acknowledges that his district "would not have been created if not for the undocumented" (*Wall Street Journal*, January 4, 1988).

A third pattern that has become evident since 1982 is the increased political status Mexican Americans now enjoy. The 1982 extension of the 1975 Voting Rights Act institutionalized the basis for continued Mexican American political advances. It supported legal challenges that produced a second Mexican American council district in Los Angeles and increased the number of Mexican American officials elected locally in Texas.

That legislation and successful litigation have combined with the mobilization campaigns of organizations like the Southwest Voter Registration and Education Fund and San Antonio's Communities Organized for Public Services to make Mexican Americans an important political force. Between 1973 and 1987, Mexican American elected officials had increased from 95 to 247 in Arizona, from 231 to 466 in California, from

366 to 577 in New Mexico, and from 565 to 1,572 in Texas (NALEO Report, September 17, 1987). The major political parties now are attentive to and solicitous of Mexican Americans. For example, there is a Senate Republican Conference Task Force on Hispanic Affairs, and the contenders for the 1988 Democratic presidential nomination eagerly accepted an invitation to debate in South Texas, the heartland of Mexican American political strength, in December 1987.

Together, these three patterns have produced an increased diversity within the Mexican-origin population that will both stimulate and hinder relations between Mexican Americans and Mexican officials and society. In the area of immigration, for example, the attention Mexican officials give to Mexican-origin contingents who are critical of U.S. immigration policy suggests that Mexican officials appreciate and will nurture relations with such groups. In February 1987, Diputado Flores Caballero arranged for such a group to meet with President de la Madrid, several members of his Cabinet, labor leader Fidel Velásquez, the president of the Chamber of Deputies, and deputies from leftist parties. They also had extensive interviews with radio, television, and newspaper reporters (Primitivo Rodríguez, personal correspondence, December 1987).

Other groups are equally concerned about immigration issues but do not necessarily support the Mexican government's policies on the issue. Antonia Hernández, MALDEF director, met with Mexican officials often before IRCA passed but refuses to participate in more visits to Mexico because she is tired of "symbolic trips." She considers such meetings unproductive, partly because Mexican officials will not discuss the domestic sources of emigration. Now she works with consular and diplomatic officials in the United States who share her concern with specific immigrant rights issues (interview, December 1987).

Rick Schwartz, the director of the National Immigration, Refugee and Citizenship Forum, has also noted divergences in how Mexican officials and Mexican American leaders deal with immigration issues:

> My overall impression is that there is more dialogue now than in the early 1980s, but it is not my impression that their [Mexican American] behavior is significantly affected by that dialogue. Very seldom do they put on the table ideas or perspectives from the Mexican government. The National Council de la Raza [a major Mexican American organization] is not particularly going out of its way to carry water for Mexico.

He adds that there are potential areas of conflict as well: "Chicanos are opposed to guest workers. Mexicans talk out of both sides of their mouths on this" (interview, November 1987).

The increased political status Mexican Americans enjoy may also work to promote and retard these relationships. As the number of Mexican American officeholders in southwestern states and border cities has increased, the opportunities for Mexican American and Mexican officials to draw on cultural goodwill and develop cooperative solutions to old problems have also increased. A Texas Mexican American legislator who meets regularly with Mexican officials, for example, used his contacts to link Mexican American businesspeople in his district directly to Mexican producers. He has also facilitated a deal that resulted in Mexican American businesspeople becoming distributors of a Mexican Petroleum Institute product that prevents corrosion on stored oil derricks. These activities help the Mexican economy, American consumers, and Mexican American businesses. They also helped the legislator politically: "Our economic activities support the efforts of Governor Bill Clements. Even the rednecks agree that we have to understand what is happening in Mexico. I have ambitions beyond this office. What I am doing in this area will help me later" (interview, October 1987).

Often, however, Mexican American interests will be incompatible with Mexican interests. In those cases, Mexican American officials will surely support their constituents. Illustrating this is the support Mexican American leaders in Texas are giving to an oil import fee. Such a fee could have severe consequences for Mexico's balance of payments. Nonetheless, Mexican American leaders strongly support it because of the positive impact it would have on the Texas economy and on their own local areas (Treviño 1988).

Also, Mexican American interests will vary from region to region. In El Paso, for example, organized labor that is composed primarily of Mexican Americans is opposed to the *maquiladora* (in-bond) industry. In South Texas, the Hidalgo County Commissioners Court, which is dominated by Mexican Americans, passed a resolution in favor of maquiladoras.

Mexican American officials, especially those in border areas, will also face cross pressures regarding internal Mexican political developments. Their desire to have good relations with Mexican officials will make them reluctant to comment on these issues. However, organizations such as the American Coalition will pressure them to speak out, and those pressures will intensify as Mexican Americans become openly critical of Mexican political practices.

Antonia Hernández has expressed frustration over the unwillingness of Mexican officials to deal with the social inequalities that stimulate emigration. Oscar Martínez, a respected community spokesman and professor from El Paso who specializes in U.S.-Mexico border issues, has moved beyond frustration to publicly denouncing these problems. Chicano leaders are more reluctant than ever to deal with the Mexican government. Chicanos look to Mexico for cultural identification, but they are ambivalent about a Mexican elite that is oppressing its people (*Houston Chronicle*, July 5, 1987).

Mexican American groups will also vary in the extent to which they are interested in fostering relations with Mexican officials and groups. Those that pursue these linkages include marginal activist groups that have particular interests, such as immigrant rights, in common with Mexican leaders. They have few alternatives within the United States. "The more we are ignored here, the more we are forced to turn outside" (quoted in *Wall Street Journal*, May 14, 1987). Some business groups are also interested in these linkages. The great majority of Mexican American leaders and organizations, however, are primarily concerned about issues and processes within the United States. According to a recent survey, for example, the issues concerning Mexican American state legislators included education, taxation, indigent care, and social services. Issues directly related to Mexico such as debt servicing and immigration reform went unmentioned (Pachón and Desipio n.d.; de la Garza 1982a).

CONCLUSION

Nineteen eighty-two clearly marked the beginning of a new stage in the relations between Mexicans, the Mexican government, and the Mexican-origin population of the United States. From the Mexican perspective, what distinguishes this stage is that Mexican officials now recognize that Mexican Americans may be useful allies. They have therefore initiated several activities designed to promote closer linkages. In the long run, perhaps the most significant of these will be the campaign to change the way Mexicans think about Mexican Americans. The effort is already producing positive results.

From the perspective of the Mexican-origin population in the United States, what distinguishes this period is its multifaceted response to the efforts of Mexican officials to create a "Mexican American lobby." If the effort is defined narrowly and limited to the issue of immigrant rights, there is no question that the Mexican government's initiative will be successful. There are no other significant foreseeable issues, however, on which there is likely to be so much agreement between Mexican Americans and Mexican officials. As has been noted, furthermore, it is not unreasonable to think that Mexican Americans and Mexicans will soon disagree even on this issue if there are attempts to reintroduce guest worker programs.

If the objective is to establish a broad-gauged relationship in which Mexican-origin groups present a united front on behalf of Mexican interests generally, the effort will have poor prospects.[1] As has been

---

[1] Ethnic lobbies have historically not been effective champions of home-country causes, and there is no reason to expect a Mexican American lobby to succeed where others have failed. See Mohammed 1987; de la Garza 1982b.

noted, there are not many issues where the interests of the two populations coincide. Also, there are general political impediments to the development of such a lobby that transcend disagreements over specific substantive issues. Mexico's recent political and economic problems have made the regime vulnerable to charges of authoritarianism and corruption, and organizations like the American Coalition have attempted to use these accusations to rally Mexican Americans to their cause. The gross irregularities during Mexico's 1988 presidential election solidified the hostility of important segments of the Mexican American community against the Mexican government. Mexico's leaders cannot assume that they will enjoy widespread respect or support among the Mexican-origin population of the United States. Like other segments of the population, most of what Mexican Americans learn about Mexico probably comes from the media and movies. As John Bailey (1989) and Carlos Cortés (1989) have shown, those sources teach very negative lessons. The additional information they gain from Mexican residents may be equally negative as the following statement of criticism of government officials by a Mexican immigrant illustrates: "They live in the best homes, drive the best cars and make the best salaries. Meanwhile, we have to leave the country to find opportunities here" (*Wall Street Journal*, January 4, 1988).

In conclusion, relations between the Mexican-origin population of the United States, Mexicans, and Mexican officials have become multilayered and very complex. The Mexican-origin population of the United States is now so diverse that, at any given moment, important segments of it may be aligned with or opposed to policies supported by the Mexican government. Similarly, Mexican society is so segmented that private organizations and even officials in the border area may engage in activities involving Mexican Americans that the federal government would prohibit or control if it were aware of them.

Nevertheless, two trends that began in the 1970s may become more important. The first concerns the role of nonstate actors in Mexico. A consensus is developing among Mexico's civil society that it is in its interests to autonomously expand its ties with Mexican Americans. As this evolves it will change the character of the relationship in ways that are unforeseeable. The second is that relations between Mexicans and Mexican Americans will continue to intensify as U.S. involvement in Mexican economic issues leads to further involvement in Mexican politics. Again, however, the consequences of this intensification are unclear.

As these trend evolve they will necessitate changes in perspective. Mexicans will need to abandon the idea that Mexican Americans are a natural and unconditional ally. They must also recognize the diversity of Mexican Americans. Maintaining the view of Mexican Americans as a homogeneous population that needs only to be rounded up at

Mexico's behest will impede developing the type of relations Mexicans now seek.

Mexican Americans will do well to consider developing relations with nongovernmental groups. They must recognize, however, that even those types of linkages have legal limits. Specifically, Mexican Americans must not intervene directly in Mexico's internal affairs. They may express their concerns and criticisms, but they must not assume that their rights of free speech also include the prerogative of intervention.

Thus, it seems safe to conclude that the relationship between the Mexican-origin populations on both sides of the border will not have a single impact on U.S.-Mexico relations; it will, instead, affect that relationship in multiple ways. Because its impact is so diverse and crosscutting, this relationship is unlikely to affect decisively the outcome of most, if any, major issues in the relations between the governments of Mexico and the United States for the foreseeable future.

REFERENCES

Allsup, Carl. 1982. *The American G.I. Forum: Origins and Evolution*. Austin: Center for Mexican American Studies, University of Texas at Austin.

Alvarez, Robert R. 1987. "A Profile of the Citizenship Process among Hispanics in the United States," *International Migration Review* 21:2 (Summer).

Alzati, Fausto. 1986–87. "A Mexican Response to Governor Babbitt's Remarks," *Journal of Hispanic Policy* 2.

Bailey, John. 1989. "Mexico in the U.S. Media, 1979–88: Implications for the Bilateral Relation." In *Images of Mexico in the United States*, edited by John H. Coatsworth and Carlos Rico. La Jolla: Center for U.S.-Mexican Studies, University of California, San Diego, for the Bilateral Commission on the Future of United States-Mexican Relations.

Balderrama, Francisco E. 1982. *In Defense of La Raza: The Los Angeles Mexican Consulate and the Mexican Community, 1929–1936*. Tucson: University of Arizona Press.

Bean, Frank D., Edward E. Telles, and B. Lindsay Lowell. n.d. "Perceptions and Evidence about Undocumented Immigration to the United States," *Population and Development Review*, forthcoming.

Cárdenas, Gilberto, Rodolfo O. de la Garza, and Niles Hansen. 1986. "Mexican Immigrants and the Chicano Ethnic Enterprise: Reconceptualizing an Old Problem." In *Mexican Immigrants and Mexican Americans: An Evolving Relation*, edited by Harley L. Browning and Rodolfo O. de la Garza. Austin: Center for Mexican American Studies, University of Texas at Austin.

Cortés, Carlos. 1989. "To View A Neighbor: The Hollywood Textbook on Mexico." In *Images of Mexico in the United States*, edited by John H.

Coatsworth and Carlos Rico. La Jolla: Center for U.S.-Mexican Studies, University of California, San Diego, for the Bilateral Commission on the Future of United States-Mexican Relations.

Craig, Ann, and Wayne A. Cornelius. 1980. "Political Culture in Mexico: Continuities and Revisionist Interpretations." In *The Civic Culture Revisited*, edited by Gabriel Almond and Sidney Verba. Boston: Little, Brown.

de la Garza, Rodolfo O. 1980. "Chicanos and U.S. Foreign Policy: The Future of Chicano-Mexican Relations," *Western Political Quarterly* 33:4 (December).

———. 1982a. "Public Policy Priorities of Chicano Political Elites." Working Paper 7, U.S.-Mexico Project Series. Washington, D.C.: Overseas Development Council, July.

———. 1982b. "Chicano-Mexican Relations: Framework for Research," *Social Science Quarterly* 63:1 (March): 115–30.

———. 1985. "Mexican Americans, Mexican Immigrants and Immigration Reform." In *Clamor at the Gates*, edited by Nathan Glazer. San Francisco: Institute for Contemporary Studies.

———. 1986. "Chicanos as an Ethnic Lobby: Limits and Possibilities." In *Chicano-Mexicano Relations*, edited by Tatcho Mindiola, Jr., and Max Martínez. Houston: Mexican American Studies Program, University of Houston.

de la Garza, Rodolfo O., and Adela Flores. 1986. "The Impact of Mexican Immigrants on the Political Behavior of Chicanos: A Clarification of Issues and Some Hypotheses for Future Research." In *Mexican Immigrants and Mexican Americans: An Evolving Relation*, edited by Harley L. Browning and Rodolfo O. de la Garza. Austin: Center for Mexican American Studies, University of Texas at Austin.

de la Garza, Rodolfo O., and Karl M. Schmitt. 1986. "Texas Land Grants and Chicano-Mexican Relations," *Latin American Research Review* 21:1:123–38.

García, F. Chris, and Rodolfo O. de la Garza. 1977. The *Chicano Political Experience: Three Perspectives*. North Scituate, Mass.: Duxbury.

García, John, and Rodolfo O. de la Garza. 1985. "Mobilizing the Mexican Immigrant: The Role of Mexican American Organizations," *Western Political Quarterly* 38:4 (December 1985): 551–65.

Gómez Quiñones, Juan. 1976. "Piedras contra la luna. México en Aztlan y Aztlan en México: Chicano-Mexican Relations and the Mexican Consulates, 1900–1920." In *Contemporary Mexico: Papers of the IV International Congress of Mexican History*, edited by James W. Wilkie, Michael C. Meyer, and Edna Monzon de Wilkie. Berkeley: University of California Press.

Gutiérrez, José Angel. 1986. "The Chicano in Mexicano-North American Foreign Relations." In *Chicano-Mexicano Relations*, edited by Tatcho

Mindiola, Jr., and Max Martínez. Houston: Mexican American Studies Program, University of Houston.

Madrid-Barela, Arturo. 1976. "Pochos: The Different Mexicans, An Interpretative Essay," *Aztlan* 7:1 (Spring).

Menchaca, Martha. 1987. "The Politics of Chicano-Mexicano Cultural Differences." Paper presented at the National Association for Chicano Studies, Northern California Regional Focus Conference, Berkeley, California, November.

Mohammed, E. Ahrari. 1987. *Ethnic Groups and U.S. Foreign Policy*. Westport: Greenwood.

Muller, Thomas, and Thomas J. Espenshade. 1985. *The Fourth Wave: California's Newest Immigrants*. Washington, D.C.: Urban Institute.

Nabokov, Peter. 1969. *Tijerina and the Court House Raid*. Albuquerque: University of New Mexico Press.

Pachón Harry, and Louis Desipio. n.d. "Preliminary Assessment of Latino Legislators and Legislative Issues in Six States." Unpublished report submitted to the IUP/SSRC Committee on Hispanic Public Policy, Center for Mexican American Studies, University of Texas at Austin.

Rodríguez, Néstor, and Rogelio T. Núñez. 1986. "An Exploration of Factors That Contribute to Differentiation between Chicanos and Indocumentados." In *Mexican Immigrants and Mexican Americans: An Evolving Relation*, edited by Harley L. Browning and Rodolfo O. de la Garza. Austin: Center for Mexican American Studies, University of Texas at Austin.

Romo, Harriett. 1986. "Chicanos, Transition and Undocumented Mexican Families: Perceptions of the Schooling of Their Children." In *Mexican Immigrants and Mexican Americans: An Evolving Relation*, edited by Harley L. Browning and Rodolfo O. de la Garza. Austin: Center for Mexican American Studies, University of Texas at Austin.

Stevens, Evelyn P. 1970. "Legality and Extra-Legality in Mexico," *Journal of Inter-American Studies* 12:1 (January): 62–75.

Treviño, Jesse. 1988. "Hispanics Favoring Oil Import Fee," *Austin American-Statesman*, January 11.

Valdez, Avelardo. 1986. "Residential Patterns of Chicanos, Undocumented Mexicans and Anglos in San Antonio (Bexar County), Texas: An Assessment of Recent Changes and Social Costs." In *Mexican Immigrants and Mexican Americans: An Evolving Relation*, edited by Harley L. Browning and Rodolfo O. de la Garza. Austin: Center for Mexican American Studies, University of Texas at Austin.

6

The Emerging Environmental Crisis along the United States-Mexico Border

C. Richard Bath

WATER QUALITY AND SUPPLY

Multiple resource and environmental issues come into play along the 2000-mile border shared by the United States and Mexico. Many of these relate to water, perhaps the most important resource in the borderlands and critical for borderlands development. The primary sources of water in the borderlands, largely a semi-arid desert region, are the Colorado and Rio Grande/Río Bravo river systems.[1]

The issue of water availability also includes the groundwater stored beneath the border in large subsurface aquifers, or bolsons. Groundwater is important along much of the border, but it is especially critical for the El Paso-Ciudad Juárez area, which relies heavily upon the Hueco Bolson to satisfy human consumption needs. Anticipating future shortages, El Paso has had to seek alternative sources of water. In 1980 the city applied for drilling rights in the Mesilla Bolson, most of which lies in New Mexico. New Mexico rejected the application, and the case—which involves basic water use issues such as farmer versus urban resident, water consumption patterns, and water conservation—has been in court since 1981.

Mexico—which shares the Hueco and Mesilla bolsons—is watching the case closely to determine how its interests will be affected, since at

---

[1] Two of the most contentious issues in bilateral relations—over the Chamizal and over salinity of the Colorado River—involved these river systems. The Chamizal dispute, involving the Rio Grande in El Paso, was eventually settled in 1964 but it took many years of bitter negotiations (Lamborn and Mumme 1988). The increased salinity of Colorado River water, stemming from the Wellton-Mohawk irrigation project in the United States, threatened crops in Mexico. This issue was resolved through Minute 242, signed by the U.S. and Mexican sections of the International Boundary and Water Commission in 1974.

present there is no international or binational agreement on aquifer sharing (Mumme 1988). Because water is essential for economic growth, Mexico is obviously concerned about its future supply. If the current pattern of increasing consumption continues in the desert region of the border, lack of water may be the single greatest constraint on its further industrialization. Much border industry now uses relatively little water, and that is likely to persist; however, if population continues to increase and if water consumption rates continue to rise, especially in Mexico, there will be real water shortages from El Paso to San Diego.

In the past, water quality has not been a major issue in U.S.-Mexican relations. Increasingly, though, water quality has become a key item on the bilateral agenda. In the Lower Rio Grande Valley, municipal and agricultural wastes threaten the estuaries and coastal zones of the Gulf of Mexico and pose a serious threat to marine resources. Moreover, the millions of gallons of raw sewage that Nuevo Laredo dumps into the Rio Grande jeopardize the health of residents living downriver.

In October 1989, the U.S. Justice Department filed suit against the City of El Paso for failure to meet water emission standards established under the Clean Water Act. Two industries are primarily responsible for the industrial wastes discharged into the city's treatment plants: one is involved in stone-washing jeans and the other in metal plating. The outcome of this case could determine what types of industries locate along the border in the future.

Another serious case is the New River in Calexico-Mexicali. The New River arises in the United States, flows into Mexico, and then returns to the United States, where it is used to irrigate crops in California's Imperial Valley. As the river flows through the rapidly industrializing city of Mexicali, Mexico, it picks up large amounts of raw sewage and, more importantly, of hazardous and toxic substances. These threaten the health of anyone coming into contact with river water and may well accumulate in crops grown on both sides of the border.

Untreated sewage is a major problem all along the border. Although Tijuana and Mexicali have treatment plants, they are totally inadequate. Ciudad Juárez, with a population of over one million, has no water treatment facilities at all. And the treatment facilities north of the border in the El Paso area frequently break down and dump wastes into the river. Perhaps the major success story is that of Nogales, Sonora/ Nogales, Arizona, where a unique method of financing helped construct a plant to treat sewage from both sides of the border (Mumme and Nalven 1988; Nalven 1986).

Perhaps the most celebrated case of water pollution is in the San Diego-Tijuana area, where untreated sewage flows north from Tijuana onto the beaches of San Diego (Mumme and Nalven 1988). Over twelve million gallons of untreated sewage flow into the Tijuana River each day, and the river contains substantial amounts of highly toxic chemicals. It flows into the Pacific Ocean and from there the wastes drift onto Imperial Beach, a valued estuary in the United States which pollution has closed for ten years. Public health officials have determined that the river carries bacteria for amoebic dysentery, vibrio cholera, staphylococcal disease, hepatitis, encephalitis, malaria, and even polio.

AIR QUALITY

With increased population and industrialization, air pollution has become a problem in the borderlands, especially in the copper-producing regions of Sonora and Arizona (Mumme 1984; Kamp 1985). The San Diego-Tijuana region also has air pollution problems although some of the exacerbating factors are being reduced as streets are paved and home heating converts to relatively clean natural gas (though wood-burning fireplaces continue to trouble local air pollution officials). In Ciudad Juárez the particulates that the city contributes to air pollution are visible, making it easy for officials in the United States to blame Mexico for air pollution problems in that region (Applegate and Bath 1986; Bath and Rodríguez 1983).

The real problem is vehicular emissions, and these are not likely to abate in the near future (Gray et al. 1989). The international boundary is itself responsible for violation of federal standards. The highest concentrations of carbon monoxide and ozone are the direct result of the time it takes to clear U.S. Customs; cars wait in line for an average of thirty minutes with their engines running. In recent years the problem has been exacerbated by an increase in the number of trucks transporting goods for the *maquiladora* (assembly plant) industry. In the summer of 1989, for example, between three and four hundred trucks typically waited in line for twelve to sixteen hours to cross the international bridge, contributing significantly to pollution levels. Changes in the hours and staffing of the border crossing have helped resolve this problem.

Another factor is an increase in the number of vehicles more generally. Ten years ago the number of vehicles in El Paso was roughly twice that of Ciudad Juárez; now the numbers are nearly equal. Since a change in Mexican law allowed the import of older automobiles without the large import taxes of the past, Ciudad Juárez has become a graveyard for older U.S. vehicles. These are precisely the kind of vehicles most likely to contribute the largest quantities of pollutants. Traffic patterns do not help matters. In Ciudad Juárez there are no freeways to speak of and traffic is of the stop-and-go variety, while in El Paso the public transportation system serves very few and the automobile remains the chief means of transportation. In neither city does there appear to be any plan for mass transit, nor for joint planning to handle international traffic.

Hazardous Materials and Hazardous Wastes

The newest environmental topic in bilateral relations is hazardous materials and hazardous wastes ("hazmats" and "hazwastes" in the current jargon). The issue burst on the scene recently and has already been the subject of a host of conferences. Underlying the issue is the creation of new chemicals that no one knows how to dispose of. The hazardous materials and wastes rubric covers several sub-issues (see Applegate and Bath 1985). One is the import and export of banned substances. For instance, the U.S. government may ban use of a chemical in the United States but permit its export to Mexico, where it may be used on a product, such as tomatoes, which is then exported to the United States.

Another is the health of farmworkers threatened by pesticides used in the fields. There is genuine concern, especially in the Lower Rio Grande Valley, that farmworkers suffer severe health problems. Former Texas secretary of agriculture Jim Hightower created a political storm by insisting on protecting the health of these workers. However, the nature of farm labor on the border makes it very difficult to track the actual impact on workers' health. Workers may be picked up in the morning at the border, work all day in the fields, then return to Mexico at day's end. If some took ill they would be nearly impossible to locate in Mexico, and they would be unlikely to show up on Mexican health statistics since medical practices in Mexico do not normally include testing for pesticide poisoning.

There seems to be general awareness that the maquila industry is generating hazardous materials but no one seems to know where these wastes are going. Certainly other types of industry are also producing large amounts of wastes, but there is generally no record of what happens to that waste either. Under law it is supposed to be returned to the United States if its point of origin was in the United States, but what evidence exists suggests that very little is actually returning.

An even more serious problem is the illegal dumping in Mexico of hazardous wastes produced in the United States. Such dumpings have been recorded in the past, and they can only become more common in the future as new regulations take effect in the United States. As landfills and incinerators come under increasing regulation, the costs of disposing of hazardous wastes will escalate, making illegal disposal outside the country even more attractive. Mexico is an obvious site choice.

A recent example illustrates the range of the problem. In October 1989, 175 barrels of PCBs were found abandoned on four trucks in an El Paso *colonia*, or makeshift settlement. The barrels were leaking and presented a definite health threat to residents. Subsequently it was disclosed that the trucks belonged to Adán Sigala, a Mexican citizen from Chihuahua City who had apparently picked up the barrels in

Denver and was waiting to cross them into Chihuahua. When the barrels were discovered, Sigala fled into Mexico. He was later identified as the state leader of the Marxist-oriented CDP party, which claims to represent the impoverished of Chihuahua State. Reporters questioned Sigala about his involvement in the shipment of PCBs, and he responded that the "gringos" were making too much of the incident and that the chemicals "are totally inoffensive." He added, "This substance has curative properties and therefore it is not the first time that I have brought it into Chihuahua. It is very good for rheumatism, and rheumatism sufferers benefit greatly from the PCBs" (*El Diario de Juárez*, October 25, 1989). One can only hope that innocent people did not ingest the PCBs as medication. The reporters later found PCB barrels being used in colonias in Chihuahua for water storage and garbage. (Such usage has also been found in colonias on the U.S. side of the border.) One environmental engineer, commenting on the incident, concluded that Chihuahua was becoming the chemical cemetery of the United States.

THE REGULATORY FRAMEWORK AND BORDER-AREA HANDICAPS

This brief review of water, air, and hazardous materials problems by no means exhausts the range of environmental issues in bilateral relations. Perhaps the basic point is that, with increasing population and urbanization along the border, environmental issues will become more evident and, most assuredly, more controversial. And with economic growth and industrialization, problems will require far more government attention than in the past.

Environmental policy in the U.S.-Mexico borderlands is determined by three different regulatory frameworks: the U.S., the Mexican, and the bilateral or international. Before looking at these three policy frameworks, however, mention should be made of two characteristics which have a tremendous impact on all three: namely, rapid population increase in the borderlands and the relative poverty of the region.

POPULATION GROWTH

A salient feature of the entire borderlands region is its truly phenomenal rate of population growth and urbanization. Population and urbanization rates began to rise during World War II, when major expansions of military and naval bases took place along the border. The Bracero Program, begun during the war, brought Mexican workers to work in the fields, and this also stimulated population increase. Today, partially because of migration and higher birth rates, the entire border remains a leading area of population growth for both countries. El Paso and San Diego are two of the fastest-growing cities in the Sunbelt, and other border cities are not far behind. But growth on the U.S. side is nothing compared with the growth of border communities in Mexico. Both

Ciudad Juárez and Tijuana have populations over 1 million; thirty years ago both were less than 200,000, and their rate of growth in the last twenty-five years surpasses 300 percent (Hansen 1981). Mexicali, a city of 60,000 in 1960, now has over 650,000 inhabitants. Although the rate of growth has slowed in recent years, the border still attracts new residents. The major draw, aside from proximity to the United States, is the supply of new jobs opening in the maquila industry.

The impact of population increase on border resources and the environment is quite evident. Indeed, it is the rapid rate of urbanization that is essentially responsible for both environmental deterioration and resource depletion. Obviously the number of people, as well as increased consumption rates, threatens water supplies all along the border. Air pollution is the direct result of an increase in the number of vehicles. Perhaps the biggest impact has been on sanitation facilities. Cities all along the border are hard pressed to upsize their sewage facilities, when they have them, on pace with population growth. Both Mexicali and Tijuana have built sewage facilities in recent years, but they are already inadequate. And as conditions in colonias on the U.S. side of the border indicate, the more developed United States is not much better off.

BORDER POVERTY

The second characteristic of the border which affects the policy framework is poverty (see Stoddard and Hedderson 1987). On the U.S. side, with the single exception of San Diego (which many argue is not really a border community because of its distance from the actual border), all border communities are characterized by poverty. The Texas border communities—El Paso, Laredo, Brownsville, and McAllen—all rank at the bottom among U.S. metropolitan regions on standards of wealth and income. And in unemployment, these cities rank higher than both state and federal averages. This poverty has important implications for successful resource and environmental management. First, those most likely to be concerned with environmental issues come from higher educational and income groups (see Mitchell 1984), and these groups are underrepresented in the border area. Second, other problems are (rightfully) given priority over environmental ones: employment, housing, education, nutrition, health, and the basic requisites of life are far more likely to receive attention than quality-of-life issues such as the environment. You are not likely to worry about air pollution if you are starving.

If the U.S. side of the border is poor relative to the remainder of the United States, the Mexican side is even poorer. Ironically, most of the border region is much better off economically than the interior of Mexico and therefore continues to draw population from within Mexico. It is easy to see how poverty can affect environmental and resource policy in this country as well. First, given Mexico's low level of economic development, it may be willing to forgo environmental management in favor of any kind of economic growth. Certainly this would appear to have been the case until very recently. Second, the perceived difference in level of economic development between the two countries may hinder certain types of cooperation for successful environmental management. Mexicans, operating within a framework of dependency, are likely to be extraordinarily suspicious of U.S. actions. Given historical relations between the two countries and frequent interventions by the United States, these Mexican perceptions may be justified. It certainly makes the problem of costs on mutual efforts difficult to handle. Third, since the economic crisis hit Mexico in 1982, there is no money available to support effective environmental policy. Government agencies are operating on budgets barely adequate to cover salaries. Until the economy rebounds, as it is showing early signs of doing, there is little possibility that the public sector, operating under IMF guidelines to restrict such expenditures, can fund necessary environmental protection measures.

The resulting environmental deterioration in the borderlands is producing a terrible loss of human capital essential for economic growth and industrialization. For example, polluted water is causing intestinal disease on both sides of the border, especially among children: intestinal disease is the leading cause of death on the Mexican side of the border (Bath 1982), and it is rampant in colonias on the U.S. side (GAO 1988; U.S. Congress 1988). Students in one El Paso County colonia spend an average of only nine years in the school system. It is possible that many of these students drop out because intestinal ailments caused by contaminated water undermine their academic potential. In turn, their lower level of education condemns them to low-paying jobs. Society thus loses workers who otherwise would take better jobs and contribute the higher level of taxes needed to alleviate the situation which caused the problem in the first place. Maybe we should approach the entire problem of environmental management from the point of view of how much poor environmental management costs in terms of losses in human capital.

THE U.S. REGULATORY FRAMEWORK

Perhaps the outstanding characteristic of the U.S. regulatory framework is federalism. Federalism has all sorts of impacts for border environmental policy. First, the national government may pass environmental laws, but it leaves enforcement largely to the states. States, in turn, often turn enforcement over to local government, in a loose chain of command that results in all sorts of problems. For example, state and local governments may lack the resources or political will for effective enforcement. This would appear to be the case for air pollution policy in Texas, where the state government has shown little enthusiasm for effective air pollution control. In fact, efforts to implement federal laws in Texas led to a virtual war between the Environmental Protection Agency and the Texas Air Control Board, impeding policy development for many years.

Federalism may also produce discrepancies between states over policy implementation. Pesticide use, for instance, is strongly regulated in California and barely regulated at all (until recently) in Texas. Federalism may contribute to confusion about policy responsibility; that is, which agency is suppose to handle which problem. A case in point is the confusion—perhaps because of a plethora of laws—about who is responsible for regulating hazardous materials and wastes.

Another difficulty presented by federalism regards water policy. Water policy in the United States is essentially left to the individual states unless it involves one of the big river systems such as the Colorado or Rio Grande. Here the federal government plays the role of water developer and allocator by interstate compact (Hundley 1966; Reisner 1986). But in the case of groundwater there is no federal policy. While the courts may eventually resolve this issue, at present there is no legal way to divide groundwater between states, leaving the legal basis for international aquifer sharing questionable.

Federalism creates a good bit of confusion for Mexico, where the federal system is poorly understood. States in Mexico rarely act independently of the central government in Mexico City, and it is difficult for Mexicans to understand states' powers in the United States. In the Mexican system the president directs policy with little attention to state or municipal concerns. The U.S. president has no such power, especially for border issues, which are likely to fall under separate policy communities and government agencies.

THE MEXICAN REGULATORY FRAMEWORK

Perhaps the major problem with the regulatory framework in Mexico is the level of the administration's determination to pursue effective environmental management (Mumme, Bath, and Assetto 1988). Mexico jumped on the environmental bandwagon in the early 1970s, passing new laws and creating a government agency (the Under Ministry for Improvement of the Environment) to handle environmental policy. From the start, however, there was a serious question about how much the government would actually do, since environmental policy could conflict with economic growth. And, in fact, industrialization has taken precedence over environmental concerns, especially in Mexico City, the heartland of industrialization.

It was not until the middle class, especially in Mexico City, became concerned with quality-of-life issues that the Mexican government took serious interest in environmental policy. The first president to place environmental issues on the federal agenda was Miguel de la Madrid.

Unfortunately, this concern for the environment surfaced just as the Mexican government went broke. De la Madrid created a new cabinet-level agency, the Ministry of Ecology and Urban Development (SEDUE) to handle environmental policy, but from the outset the agency was handicapped by lack of funds even for basic equipment or technical training.

THE BINATIONAL REGULATORY FRAMEWORK

Despite the weak policy framework existing within each nation-state, the binational or international policy framework has enjoyed some recent successes. Since 1973 there has been a series of meetings of government representatives, scholars, and others concerned with environmental issues in the borderlands. Several conferences have focused exclusively on environmental issues (see Applegate and Bath 1974; Ross 1983; Sepúlveda and Utton 1984), and most conferences on bilateral relations now include a section on environmental problems. Environmental issues place high on the working agenda of the U.S.-Mexico Border Public Health Association, which operates under the auspices of the Pan American Health Organization.

This combined community of interests keeps environmental issues at the forefront of the bilateral agenda when the two countries' presidents meet, as in August 1983, when Presidents Reagan and de la Madrid signed the Agreement between the United States of America and the United Mexican States on Cooperation for the Protection and Improvement of the Environment at La Paz, Baja California. The La Paz agreement, as it is commonly called, is important for several reasons. First, it specifies which agencies are to handle border environmental issues: the Environmental Protection Agency (EPA) in the United States, and the Ministry of Ecology and Urban Development (SEDUE) in Mexico.[2] Second, the La Paz agreement involves state and local officials in the negotiating process, recognizing that, at least theoretically, they have the best knowledge of most border issues. Third, the agreement defined the border region for environmental management as extending one hundred kilometers on either side of the boundary line, since many border-area environmental problems do not originate at the boundary itself. Fourth, the La Paz agreement endorses coordination of national programs, scientific and educational exchanges, environmental monitoring, environmental impact assessment, and periodic exchanges of information and data. This latter provision may facilitate data gathering, since Mexican officials have sometimes been reluctant to release their accumulated data. An interesting provision in the La Paz agreement calls for a

---

[2]Because the two sections of the International Boundary and Water Commission are housed respectively in the U.S. Department of State and Mexico's Ministry of Foreign Relations, there is still a possibility of IBWC intervention.

"special modality of financing" for the training of personnel, transfer of equipment, and construction of installations, which might provide a means to sidestep the Mexico's shortage of economic resources.

The La Paz agreement established three major working groups—to deal with water, air, and hazardous substances—with smaller subgroups under each one to handle local problems. The agreement can also incorporate annexes to deal with specific problems. Five annexes have been signed to date. The first of these deals with the persisting problem of sewage in the Tijuana-San Diego region, which reportedly will also be the subject of Annex 6 (Metzner 1989). In early October 1989, Presidents Bush and Salinas de Gortari signed an agreement for a joint treatment plant to handle Tijuana River water, with the details to be worked out by the IBWC. Interestingly, the United States agreed to pay about half the costs of the plant, but a suit filed by the EPA against the city of San Diego over its Point Loma treatment plant has impeded forward movement on the project.

The Working Group on Air Quality initially focused on problems in the Douglas-Nacozari-Cananea region. Annex 4 addressed this problem, but it is not yet fully resolved and is likely to remain a source of friction in the future. In 1986 the El Paso-Ciudad Juárez Air Quality Task Force was established to deal with air pollution in that area. It represents a more cooperative effort among federal, state, and local officials, and four major training sessions held by EPA officials for their SEDUE counterparts have put international cooperation on the upswing as well. This includes assistance provided to Mexican officials for an inventory of pollutants and for the inauguration of a vehicle inspection and maintenance program (Applegate and Bath 1989).

Another important addition to the La Paz agreement, signed by Presidents Bush and Salinas in October 1989, is Annex 5, a general agreement which provides a legal framework for dealing with air pollution along the border. An appendix to the annex identifies El Paso and Ciudad Juárez as the immediate targets of concern and obliges these two urban centers to identify the magnitude, type, and source of each pollutant within their respective territories. Each country also agrees to identify the control requirement for each stationary source of pollution and bring it into compliance with federal emission standards, and to monitor pollutants and use state-of-the-art mathematical air modeling analysis.

Annex 5 handles only stationary pollution sources—PM-10 or particulates and perhaps sulfur oxides and others associated with industrial sources—and does not cover the serious problem of vehicular emissions. A major stumbling block is that Ciudad Juárez does not have the technical means to monitor pollution and must depend on the United States for a monitoring inventory. The U.S. Congress allocated monies for this purpose and EPA officials adopted a plan for such monitoring, but the bureaucracy remains a major impediment to successful implementation of Annex 5 because of conflicts between EPA and SEDUE and between their respective foreign ministries. Annex 5 was to have been signed in October 1988 but was delayed because of opposition first from the U.S. Department of State and later from Mexico's Ministry of Foreign Relations. The joint monitoring program was eventually approved in 1990 and is now in effect in Texas. However, bureaucratic turf battles of this kind will always make it difficult to implement such agreements.

The Hazardous Materials and Waste Management Working Group has also addressed important issues under its rubric. Annex 2 to the La Paz agreement calls for a joint contingency plan to handle spills of hazardous materials. The primary aim was to prevent another disaster such as the blowout of the Ixtoc I oil well in the Gulf of Mexico in 1979. A pilot program was established in Calexico-Mexicali under Annex 2, and a joint response team was formed to inventory "hazmats" and "hazwastes" along the border. If local emergency planning committees could be made more effective or if the Emergency Planning and Community Right to Know Act were actually working along the border, significant advances could be made in this problem area.

Annex 3, the Agreement of Cooperation between the United Mexican States and the United States of America Regarding the Transboundary Shipments of Hazardous Wastes and Hazardous Substances, was signed on November 12, 1986. It was part of a larger concern on the part of the EPA that controls over exports of hazmats outlined in provisions of the Hazardous and Solid Waste Amendments of 1984 were not working. On November 8, 1986, the EPA enacted new regulations to cover such exports by requiring that it be notified of the intent to export within sixty days and that written consent be obtained from the receiving government prior to shipment. These amendments to the Resource Conservation and Recovery Act (RCRA) were to provide "cradle to grave" tracking of hazmats. These procedures will raise the costs of legal disposal and therefore make illegal disposal such as dumping in Mexico far more likely.

Further complicating the picture is a genuine puzzle about bureaucratic responsibility for oversight of hazmats and hazwastes (see Kamp and Gregory 1988). On both sides of the border, there is confusion over the laws covering various substances. For example, in the United States hazardous wastes fall under RCRA provisions but toxic chemicals are covered by the Toxic Substance Control Act (TSCA) and pesticides are under yet another law, FIFRA, making the reporting and tracking of chemicals exceedingly complex. Whenever hazardous materials are exported, the EPA, the Department of Transportation, and U.S. Customs are to be notified. The system works like this: a truck carrying hazmats deposits a manifest in a mailbox just before crossing the border; U.S. Customs then picks up the manifest and sends it to the Department of Commerce in Washington where, one supposes, information is disseminated to other governmental agencies. In practice, as in the El Paso case of the barrels of PCBs discussed earlier, the procedures for hazwastes are different and go through the EPA back to the Texas Water Commission, which is really responsible for enforcement of RCRA. Moreover, the FBI becomes involved because this may be an illegal shipment in interstate commerce.

The situation is not much better on the Mexican side, but no one paid much attention until 1989 when Mexico's 1988 environmental law and Annex 3 caught the attention of the maquila industry. Annex 3 defined hazardous waste as any waste which, if improperly dealt with, might result in health or environmental damage. Hazardous substances are similarly defined as substances, including chemicals or pesticides, that may produce effects harmful to public health, property, or the environment, and are banned or severely restricted in use. The signatories to Annex 3 pledge that their respective domestic laws will apply to any transboundary shipment of such materials. Each party also promises to cooperate in monitoring and spot-checking transboundary shipments of hazmats and hazwastes. Annex 3 calls for specific information about the shipper, the material, and the destination. The recipient country has forty-five days to reject the material after notification of its intended shipment. One country must also notify the other if it bans or severely restricts the use of hazmats. One provision deals explicitly with the maquila industry, stating that any hazardous waste generated during economic production, manufacturing, processing, or repair for which raw materials were utilized and temporarily admitted must return to the country of origin of the raw materials.

One of the most important provisions of Annex 3 in the view of Mexican officials is that whenever a violation is discovered, the "country of export shall take all practicable measures and initiate and carry out all pertinent legal actions." This includes: (1) returning the hazardous waste or hazardous substance to the country of export; (2) restoring as far as practicable the status quo ante of the affected ecosystem; and (3) compensating the damages caused to persons, property, or the environment. The country of export is also to inform the affected country of all measures and legal actions undertaken.

It is almost impossible to determine the impact of Annex 3 on the regulation of hazmats and hazwastes in the border community. However, researchers in the Border Ecology Project in Agua Prieta-Douglas found that few maquila managers knew Annex 3 existed and they were also unaware of the Mexican laws that regulate hazardous materials. It is also doubtful that much hazardous material is returning to the United States. The return of such material requires notification to the EPA, but an EPA spokeswoman for Region IX, covering California and Arizona, admitted that her office had received only ten such requests in five years prior to 1988 (Shimmer 1988). A spokesperson for the AFL-CIO, a harsher critic of the maquila industry, looked into records available for Region IX and found that only two of the one hundred maquiladoras in Mexicali filed notice of sending hazmats back into the United States (Kochan 1989). Data obtained from the Texas Water Commission for the four hundred maquiladoras operating along the Texas border indicate that only eleven returned waste to the United States in 1987, and ninety in 1988. Two privately owned disposal firms in El Paso contend that between them they disposed of wastes from 110 of the 362 maquiladoras operating in the El Paso region in 1988 (although officially there were only 262 maquiladoras in Ciudad Juárez at that time). The interesting question is what happened to the wastes generated by the remainder.

Mexico's 1988 environmental law, the General Law of Ecological Equilibrium and Environmental Protection, has yet to be effectively enforced due to a shortfall in funding. Other regulations announced in November 1988 aimed to force all generators of hazardous wastes into compliance with regulations by May 26, 1989. It was this deadline that sparked maquila industry interest in hazmats and hazwastes.[3] Under the provisions of the new laws, each facility must register with SEDUE, list the chemicals it uses and generates, and provide detailed plans for either recycling or disposing of its wastes. All maquiladoras must maintain accurate records and report twice a year to SEDUE on the volume and type of hazardous wastes generated. Wastes can be recycled by transferring them to a third party within Mexico. However, if the chemicals were imported from the United States or elsewhere, they must be returned to their country of origin. (This last provision may prove to be a point of dispute because of the large influx of Japanese plants in recent years.)

Many of the new provisions appear to accord well with the framework established by Annex 3 of the La Paz agreement. Nonetheless, there are some problems. One is that the classification of hazardous materials includes wastewater treatment sludges from electroplating operations, solvents used as cleaners, and acids and bases used in etching baths, which means that the new regulations will have a profound effect on the entire maquiladora industry. One outcome is that they are likely to stimulate the growth of the Mexican waste management industry and, in fact, this is already occurring. A second economic impact may be to encourage the production of chemicals within Mexico itself, and the maquila industry does seem to be moving toward local rather than foreign supply. If this is indeed the case, in the future Mexico will have to handle waste management largely by itself.

Another problem is that recycling and disposal of hazwastes is practically nonexistent in Mexico. There are as yet few qualified recyclers in the country and these are mainly small operations. The maquiladoras,

---

[3] Lawyers seem to have taken over analysis of the impact of Mexican laws on the maquila industry. See Alexander and Jacobs 1989, and the Fall 1989 issue of the *Lorman Letter*, published by the law firm of Gray, Cary, Ames, and Frye, in San Diego, California.

legally prevented from recycling, could turn hazwastes over to a Mexican firm if one were available. This situation could encourage unscrupulous entrepreneurs to form companies without the necessary expertise to adequately recycle or dispose of wastes. As for disposal sites, there is one located near Mexico City and one that is soon to come into operation near Monterrey. There are no sites along the border, which means that wastes generated in the border region should be transported to existing sites. However, transport facilities are sadly lacking and the attractions of "midnight dumping" are obvious.

If a maquila opts to send hazwastes back to the United States, it finds obstacles here as well. The maquiladora must locate a transporter in Mexico, a transporter on the U.S. side, and a disposal company on the U.S. side. And there is a possibility that the Mexican truck will be denied entry to the United States if it fails to meet U.S. safety standards. Moreover, each state has different rules, and disposal sites are generally lacking. California has none and Texas has only one licensed disposal site. All of these considerations increase the costs of disposal for the individual plant and for the entire industry, creating the possibility that such costs could drive production costs in Mexico higher than those found in other Third World countries and undermine the entire logic of maquiladora development.

The effectiveness of the La Paz agreement depends on SEDUE's regulatory efforts. From early on there was some doubt about SEDUE's regulatory capability. Mexico has a shortage of people trained to handle and assess hazmats and hazwastes, and this lack of personnel handicaps SEDUE's effectiveness. SEDUE has only five employees to handle all environmental problems for Ciudad Juárez and its three hundred maquilas; they would have to work long days indeed just to visit all the plants. Some personnel training is now taking place in the United States under EPA auspices, so the situation is likely to improve but it will be a long time before staffing in Mexico is adequate.

In late October 1989, the head of the SEDUE office in Ciudad Juárez was interviewed about regulation of the maquiladoras (*El Paso Times*, October 19, 1989). She stated that 30 percent of the industries were complying with the new regulations and that more than 30 percent were actually disposing of their waste properly but were simply failing to submit the required paperwork. Every effort was being made to train personnel, but for the moment SEDUE would depend on surprise inspections by the four available inspectors.

SUMMARY

Both increasing population and rising rates of urbanization have created severe environmental problems along the United States-Mexico border. Population pressures on the region's limited resources have produced substantial environmental deterioration. Water, a very scare resource along most of the border, poses problems in terms of both quantity and quality. It is questionable whether certain urban complexes, including El Paso-Ciudad Juárez and Calexico-Mexicali, have sufficient water for current populations, let alone future ones. Water availability may prove to be a major constraint on economic growth in parts of the border region. In terms of water quality, untreated sewage is perhaps the most critical problem, but other water pollution deserves immediate attention. Air pollution also plagues some of the twin cities along the border, especially Ciudad Juárez-El Paso, which has a severe air pollution problem and an almost insurmountable problem in effective pollution control. Hazardous materials and hazardous wastes are the newest in a succession of threats to the health and environment of all border residents.

The regulatory framework for successful environmental management along the border comprises three policy arenas: the U.S., the Mexican, and the binational. In the United States the major impediment to effective policy would appear to be federalism, which creates a fragmented and disjointed policy approach. In Mexico an initial lack of commitment to environmental management was replaced by serious government concern, but a scarcity of resources for effective policy implementation persists. At the binational level, a policy community has emerged which plays a key role in securing a place for environmental issues on the bilateral agenda. The signing of the 1983 La Paz agreement provides a legal and administrative framework that could eventually lead to successful environmental management. The annexes signed under the La Paz agreement affirm the willingness of all concerned to come to grips with environmental threats along the U.S.-Mexico border.

REFERENCES

Alexander, Douglas W., and Patricia Ann Jacobs. 1989. "Hazardous Waste Regulation of the Maquiladora Industry: Legal Framework and Practical Guidelines for Compliance." Austin, Tex. Mimeo.

Applegate, Howard G., and C. Richard Bath, eds. 1974. *Air Pollution along the United States-Mexico Border*. El Paso: Texas Western Press.

———. 1985. "Hazardous and Toxic Substances as a Part of United States-Mexico Relations." In *The U.S. and Mexico: Borderland Development and the National Economies*, edited by Lay James Gibson and Alfonso Corona Rentería. Boulder, Colo.: Westview.

———. 1986. "Air Pollution in a Transboundary Setting: The Case of El Paso, Texas and Ciudad Juárez, Chihuahua." In *Transboundary Air Pollution*, edited by C. Flinterman, B. Kwiatkowska, and J.G. Lammers. The Hague: M. Nijhoff.

———. 1989. "Air Pollution in the El Paso-Ciudad Juárez Region," *Transboundary Resources Report* 3:1 (Spring): 1–2.

Bath, C. Richard. 1982. "Health and Environmental Problems: The Role of the Border in El Paso-Ciudad Juárez Coordination," *Journal of Inter-American and World Affairs* 24:3 (August): 373–92.

Bath, C. Richard, and Victoria E. Rodríguez. 1983. "Comparative and Binational Air Pollution Policy in El Paso, Texas and Ciudad Juárez, Chihuahua," *Borderlands Journal* 6:4 (Spring): 171–97.

GAO (United States General Accounting Office). 1988. *Health Care Availability in the Texas-Mexico Border Area*. Washington, D.C.: GAO, October.

Gray, Robert, et al. 1989. *Vehicular Traffic and Air Pollution in El Paso-Ciudad Juárez*. El Paso: Texas Western Press.

Hansen, Niles. 1981. *The Border Economy*. Austin: University of Texas Press.

Hundley, Norris. 1966. *Dividing the Waters*. Berkeley: University of California Press.

Kamp, Richard. 1985. "The Smelter Triangle: An Overview of U.S.-Mexican Negotiations." Testimony before the United States Senate Committee on Environment and Public Works, Denver, Colorado, August 12.

Kamp, Richard, and Michael Gregory. 1988. *Hazardous Material Inventory of Agua Prieta, Sonora Maquiladoras with Recommendations for U.S.-Mexico Transboundary Regulations*. Naco, Ariz.: Border Ecology Project.

Kochan, Leslie. 1989. *The Maquiladoras and Toxics: The Hidden Costs of Production South of the Border*. Publication No. 186. Washington, D.C.: AFL-CIO.

Lamborn, Alan C., and Stephen P. Mumme. 1988. *Statecraft, Domestic Politics, and Foreign Policy Making: The El Chamizal Dispute*. Boulder, Colo.: Westview.

Metzner, Clifton G., Jr. 1989. *Water Quality Issues of the San Diego-Tijuana Border Region*. San Diego: Institute for Regional Studies of the Californias, San Diego State University.

Mitchell, Robert Cameron. 1984. "Public Opinion and Environmental Politics in the 1970s and 1980s." In *Environmental Policy in the 1980s: Reagan's New Agenda*, edited by Norman J. Vig and Mitchell E. Kraft. Washington, D.C.: Congressional Quarterly, pp. 51–74.

Mumme, Stephen P. 1984. "The Cananea Copper Controversy: Lessons for Environmental Diplomacy," *Inter-American Economic Affairs* 38 (Summer): 3–22.

———. 1988. *Apportioning Groundwater beneath the U.S.-Mexico Border*. Research Report Series, no. 45. La Jolla: Center for U.S.-Mexican Studies, University of California, San Diego.

Mumme, Stephen P., C. Richard Bath, and Valerie J. Assetto. 1988. "Political Development and Environmental Policy in Mexico," *Latin American Research Review* 23:1:7–34.

Mumme, Stephen P., and Joseph Nalven. 1988. "National Perspectives on Managing Transboundary Environmental Hazards: The U.S.-Mexico Border Region," *Journal of Borderlands Studies* 3:1 (Spring): 39–68.

Nalven, Joseph. 1986. "Transboundary Environmental Problem Solving: Social Process, Cultural Perception," *Natural Resources Journal* 26:4 (Fall): 793–818.

Reisner, Marc. 1986. *Cadillac Desert*. New York: Penguin.

Ross, Stanley R., ed. 1983. *Ecology and Development of the Border Region*. Mexico: ANUIES/PROFMEX.

Sepúlveda, César, and Albert E. Utton, eds. 1984. *The U.S.-Mexico Border Region: Anticipating Resource Needs and Issues to the Year 2000*. El Paso: Texas Western Press.

Shimmer, Kathleen. 1988. Conference on Hazardous Waste Management, Tijuana, November 15.

Stoddard, Ellwyn R., and John Hedderson. 1987. *Patterns of Poverty along the U.S.-Mexico Border*. Las Cruces, N.M.: Joint Border Research Institute.

U.S. Congress. House. 1988. *Inadequate Water Supply and Sewage Disposal Facilities Associated with "Colonias" along the United States and Mexican Border."* Hearings before the Subcommittee on Water Resources of the Committee on Public Works and Transportation, House of Representatives, 100th Cong., 2d sess. Washington, D.C.: U.S. Government Printing Office.

CENTRAL AMERICA

7

Managing Resources across Borders: The Case of the United States-Mexico and Mexico-Guatemala Boundaries

Stephen P. Mumme

The adjustment of sovereign claims is the fundamental challenge in managing transboundary natural resources. To this end various institutional arrangements have been tried, the most common being some variant of an international commission. The character and role of these commissions in managing transboundary resources are contingent on a great many variables, including the number of nations sharing a common frontier, the resource ecology of the frontier zone, the political and administrative structures of the contiguous states, levels of economic development in the contiguous countries, and the chronological age of the agency, among others.

These international commissions have increasingly attracted the scrutiny of scholars, policymakers, and environmentalists interested in their strengths and limitations as vehicles for advancing toward comprehensive resource management along international boundaries (see Willoughby 1979; Asiwaju 1989). Even so, systematic comparisons of international commissions' organizational structures, jurisdictions, and functions are few in number.

This essay compares the structure, jurisdiction, and functions of two commissions involved in transboundary resource management along North American borders, the International Boundary and Water Commission, United States and Mexico (IBWC), and the Comisión Internacional de Límites y Aguas, México y Guatemala (CILA). This comparison is useful for three reasons. First, it allows us to consider the character and role of international commissions along two very different frontiers, joining distinctive political systems, and among nations at different levels of development. Second, it allows us to consider the question of the effectiveness of these commissions as instruments for managing transboundary resources along these boundaries. Third, it enriches our understanding of the ways geographic patterns, political systems, and levels of development affect the capacity of the commissions to absorb new functions as these contiguous nations move in the direction of improving environmental and resource management along their common frontiers. While we shall not attempt broader generalizations concerning the character or capacity of international commissions in managing transboundary resources, it is hoped this study will contribute to the more systematic analysis of these specialized agencies.

The International Boundary and Water Commission, United States and Mexico

As one of the world's oldest institutions devised for the purpose of managing transboundary resources, the International Boundary and Water Commission, United States and Mexico (IBWC), established in 1889, has often been used as a model for the design of similar agencies around the world. Like all such commissions, the IBWC was established to address problems related to a particular geopolitical setting. While it has changed over the years, its formal structure, jurisdiction, and functions are embedded in a unique set of conditions that are not readily generalizable to other transboundary resource management situations.

The IBWC is the principal actor overseeing resource management along the 1965-mile U.S.-Mexico boundary, a role it shares with various domestic institutions in both countries. Originally constituted in 1889 as a boundary demarcation and management agency, the commission has since grown to embrace a wide range of functions falling under the aegis of water management. Like most other transboundary commissions, it is composed of national sections—representing each member country—which are accountable to their national governments for policy authority.

The IBWC's functions, jurisdiction, and structure as a resource management agency derive mainly from the geographic characteristics of the boundary region and basic political structures in each country. The geography of the U.S.-Mexican border is a definitive factor shaping the commission's functions. The border traverses a highly arid region in which water is the critical resource governing potential for economic development. While rainfall varies in the border region, nowhere does precipitation exceed 600 millimeters annually. Rivers, too, are in short supply. Much of the region's drainage takes the form of intermittent or ephemeral streams.

Control over the region's scarce water resources has been a major issue between the two countries and among domestic users. The major watercourses—the Rio Grande (which forms the boundary for 1,254 miles), the San Juan, the Río Conchos, the Colorado, and Tía Juana rivers—are presently fully apportioned and heavily burdened by multiple uses. Dramatic seasonal variation in watershed along these rivers complicates boundary delimitation and requires intensive management to avoid flooding.

Demographic growth and economic development are additional factors affecting IBWC's functions. Since the turn of the century, when human settlement along the border was sparse, population in the immediate border region has rapidly grown to approach a level in excess of twelve million inhabitants. Since World War II, the border economy has become increasingly industrialized on both sides of the border, spurred most recently by the boom in border assembly operations in Mexico (Jamail and Gutiérrez 1990). These trends have generated a host of problems, ranging from sewage, sanitation, and air pollution to illegal commerce in hazardous and toxic substances along the border (see Bath, this volume).

The problems the IBWC was created to solve derive from these geographic conditions. Historically, the commission's principal functions entailed water apportionment, boundary maintenance, flood control, and putting water to beneficial use in the service of borderlands development. A number of treaties in the first half of the twentieth century enlarged the IBWC's functions,[1] culminating in its current charter, the U.S.-Mexico Water Treaty of 1944. Under this document, which apportions the waters of the lower Rio Grande and Colorado rivers, the IBWC has responsibility for administering the terms of the water apportionment agreements, for constructing and operating several major water storage and flood control dams and operating associated hydroelectric facilities, for maintaining the river and land boundaries, and for constructing and operating sanitation and sewage facilities where such problems have an international character (IBWC 1975). The commission also collaborates with other agencies in addressing binational problems which abut upon its jurisdiction.

Just as the physical and demographic features of the U.S.-Mexico border region have set much of the IBWC's functional agenda, so too have the political structures of the two countries shaped its formal organization, jurisdiction, and functions. The United States and Mexico, while bearing some formal similarities in constitution and political structure, are in practice quite dissimilar political systems. The most salient difference for purposes of understanding the IBWC is that of federalism, or domestic intergovernmental relations. In the United States, federal-state relations are relatively decentralized, with states

---

[1] Among the principal treaties are the 1889 Boundary Treaty, the 1906 Water Treaty, and the 1933 Boundary Rectification Convention. For a list of the IBWC's international agreements, see IBWC 1981: 30–40.

assuming a substantial part of the fiscal and operational responsibility for policy implementation across a wide range of issue areas. In Mexico, this relationship has been historically centralized, dominated by national government.

Under its 1944 charter, the IBWC is structured as a binational agency comprising separate national sections. Each section is headed by a single commissioner who, by charter, must be a licensed engineer. The commissioners are each supported by a legal adviser, principal engineer, and secretary, who fill out the section's diplomatic delegation. Both the commissioners and their staffs are invested with diplomatic credentials and may travel across boundaries at will in the discharge of their binational responsibilities (IBWC 1975).

This arrangement is functionally derivative of the systemic differences between the two countries. Historically, Mexican presidents have exercised strong central control over both foreign relations and domestic affairs. Representative institutions and other federal bodies have functioned as dependencies of national administration under presidential management. In the United States, on the other hand, border states were interested in an administrative system that would enhance the authority of the commission and its responsiveness to their own interests. In this political and administrative milieu the design of more autonomous or collective decision-making procedures as agents of transboundary resource management was simply not politically feasible; hence the single-headed structure of the IBWC's national sections may be viewed as a necessary adaptation to prevailing political conditions.

Systemic differences are likewise reflected in the functions of the national sections. Since the IBWC's creation, the U.S. border states have been influential in shaping policy toward the commission in the United States, whereas in Mexico the border states have a highly restricted role in policy making. As a result, the U.S. section of the IBWC has acquired operational powers not enjoyed by the Mexican section.

To better appreciate how this has been accomplished it is necessary to examine the IBWC's formal jurisdiction. Under the 1944 Water Treaty, the IBWC, operating in its international capacity, is endowed with a very limited formal jurisdiction which extends only to boundary and water issues directly engaging the boundary. Concerns not engaging the boundary, though located in the border region, are the province of the domestic agencies of each government. This limitation, however, does not extend to the operational capabilities of the respective national sections of the commission, which may be related to the commission's narrow sphere of jurisdiction. Insofar as they are strictly domestic, additional functions may be added to each national section at the discretion of its member government.

On this basis the U.S. section has acquired control over a standing construction division and attained considerable policy leeway vis-à-vis the Department of State. It has done so by carefully cultivating an elite constituency of border-state politicians at the state and national levels and nurturing an image of itself as a regionally oriented agency that is responsive to the needs of U.S. communities along the border (Mumme 1984).

The Mexican section, on the other hand, functions within a far more centralized administrative and political structure. Its organizational functions are limited to the technical and diplomatic roles narrowly assigned to the IBWC under charter. Other strictly domestic functions that are instrumental to fulfilling the terms of Mexico's international agreements are assigned to appropriate domestic agencies of the Mexican government under the administrative oversight of the Mexican section. Given the organizational dependence of the Mexican section on the Mexican Foreign Ministry's Department of International Boundaries and Waters, and the limited political power of Mexican states, the commissioner of the Mexican section has little need to cultivate a border-state constituency. He must, however, maintain effective working relations with his CILA superiors and the chiefs of other federal departments.

The effectiveness of the IBWC as a transboundary resource agency has been a matter of dispute. From a strictly technical perspective, the agency has acquired an exceptional reputation for efficiency and solid management which rivals the best of both countries' domestic agencies with similar mandates (Mumme 1986). From a functional perspective, however, the commission's jurisdiction is quite narrow. Within this jurisdiction, its functional range has grown since 1944 and now incorporates a range of boundary and water management responsibilities. Such activities include an expanding sphere of binational sewage and sanitation operations, oversight of groundwater pumping near the boundary reach of the Colorado River, monitoring of salinity levels on the Colorado River, and adjusting boundary meanders along the Rio Grande River.

Despite this expansion, the IBWC falls far short of functioning as a comprehensive resource management agency. Rapid development along the U.S.-Mexican border has generated a range of problems and introduced new pressures on borderlands' resources. Since the mid-1970s, for example, the IBWC has been the object of various initiatives to address problems like hazardous waste and air pollution.

It is in this context of amplified environmental concern that the IBWC's management approach has been subject to some criticism since the mid-1970s. Critics have argued that the IBWC has failed to respond to a range of issues, including air pollution, nonhazardous and hazardous waste, water quality, apportioning groundwater, and other issues, which might best be managed within its operational framework (Bath 1982; Utton 1982; Jamail and Ullery 1979). Criticism from the U.S. side of the border has also argued that the commission is not sufficiently open to public influence and input, and that it has monopolized information on transboundary resources (Jamail and Ullery 1979; Bradley and DeCook 1978).

To some extent this criticism is justified. The IBWC has been reluctant to insert itself into questions which plainly lie outside its formal jurisdiction. Air pollution, hazardous waste, and managing fauna and flora clearly fall beyond the scope and reach of its treaty authority. To reach into these areas would inevitably encroach on functions currently exercised by other agencies, something the IBWC, mindful of its unique role, is reluctant to do. In other areas—water quality or groundwater apportionment, for example—the commission has putative foundation within the scope of its charter, but it is careful not to move ahead of the interests of border-state constituencies in the United States, whose support is an essential political precondition for the IBWC's efforts.

It is also true that the IBWC has resisted expanding the scope of public participation in its activities. The binational management of border resources has frequently depended on careful diplomacy, and IBWC diplomats have been keenly concerned lest their operations become politicized in this binational environment. Under the U.S. National Environmental Policy Act, however, IBWC projects have been subject to Environmental Impact Statements which invite public participation. Thus, since the mid-1970s, the commission has functioned under an increasing level of public scrutiny and become responsive to a wider range of public interests than in the past, at least on the U.S. side of the border (Jamail and Mumme 1982).

Even so, the broadening of environmental concern along the border to incorporate a range of new issues has led to efforts to circumvent the IBWC and develop alternate arrangements for managing border resources. In 1983, driven in part by public frustration with efforts to push the two countries to address problems through the commission mechanism, the United States and Mexico entered into a new agreement on a framework by which to cope with mounting concerns (*International Legal Materials* 1983). Under this agreement the two countries have reached a number of specific agreements, or annexes, which address problems both within and beyond the commission's jurisdiction.

Within the context of the new environmental accord, the IBWC's function and role remain much the same as in the past, limited, that is, to boundary and water-related concerns. The 1983 agreement has, in fact, strengthened the commission's functional claim to this domain by expressly acknowledging its policy preeminence in these issue areas (*International Legal Materials* 1983). In other areas, however, the IBWC's functions are confined to supporting other domestic agencies in transboundary environmental management. The big gainers in transboundary environmental management have been the Environmental Protection Agency (EPA), on the U.S. side, and the Ministry of Ecology and Urban Development (SEDUE) in Mexico. Each of these agencies is designated by the 1983 agreement as the respective national coordinator for transboundary environmental policy (*International Legal Materials* 1983).

To better appreciate this maturing role of the IBWC in transboundary resource management, a brief review of its role and functions under the new agreement is warranted. By 1990, five bilateral agreements, or annexes, under the 1983 accord had been signed. Of these, four involved areas tangential to the IBWC's competence, including an agreement to manage hazardous and toxic substances emergencies along the border (Mumme 1988), a related agreement to manage flows of toxic substances along the border (Mumme 1988), an agreement to manage air pollution in the vicinity of the "smelter triangle" along the Arizona-Sonora boundary (Mumme 1988) and, most recently, an agreement to cooperate to reduce air pollution in the El Paso, Texas-Ciudad Juárez, Chihuahua urban area (*International Legal Materials* 1990).

In each case, the IBWC's role in implementing the agreement is marginal. In the case of managing hazardous emergencies along the border, a joint response team organized under the authority of the national coordinators would include the IBWC along with other agencies if a potential threat to water quality was involved.[2] With respect to agreements on regulating transboundary hazardous waste flows and air pollution, the IBWC has no formal role in implementation. As a participating agency under the 1983 agreement, however, it is kept informed of the status and activities of other agencies engaged in implementing these accords.

Thus the amplification of environmental concern along the border has brought about an expansion of the number of institutions engaged in environmental management. Under the 1983 agreement, an increasing number of domestic agencies have acquired responsibilities for managing transboundary resources. The IBWC's role in transboundary resource management has substantially broadened, but only within a radius that can be justified within the language of its 1944 Water Treaty charter.

Within these limits the IBWC remains a major player in managing border resources. The growth of human populations along the international boundary and greater public sensitivity to the environmental impacts of industrial and agricultural practices have placed water quality concerns at the top of the commission's agenda (Dillon 1989). The IBWC has recently concluded negotiations for a new joint international sewage facility at San Diego, California-Tijuana, Baja California Norte, as well as

---

[2]Such a situation occurred in February 1990 when the ASARCO smelter at El Paso accidentally spilled 37,000 gallons of diesel fuel into the Rio Grande, threatening at least five hundred Mexican farmers downstream. See *Excélsior* 1990b, 1990c.

projects that will reduce the impact of sewage discharged into the lower reach of the Rio Grande River (Mydans 1990). Intensified appropriation of groundwater along the U.S.-Mexican border, currently not apportioned by any treaty, represents significant potential for conflict between the two nations (Rohter 1989). The IBWC will inevitably play a major role in the negotiation of any forthcoming agreement on groundwater.

In sum, the IBWC remains the most visible and best institutionalized component of binational resource management along the U.S.-Mexican border. Changing conditions along the boundary and the emergence of a broad range of environmental concerns on the bilateral agenda have both led the commission to absorb new functions and generated new institutional arrangements for transboundary resource management. Within this contemporary milieu, the IBWC has been pressured to innovate and to accommodate to a range of nontraditional issues and a wider array of agencies and actors engaged in resource management. Political limitations restrict its capacity for innovation, however, and account in good measure for the entrance of alternative domestic agencies in this issue area.

The Comisión Internacional de Límites y Aguas, México y Guatemala

Along the Mexico-Guatemala boundary, another international commission, the Comisión Internacional de Límites y Aguas, México y Guatemala (CILA), plays an important role in tranboundary resource management. CILA, established in 1961, is still in its infancy in terms of institutional development. Although an international commission to manage boundary affairs was authorized as early as 1882, it is testament to the delayed development of the Mexico-Guatemala border that such an international arrangement had to wait seventy-nine years.

As in the case of the IBWC, CILA's functions, jurisdiction, and structure are embedded in the geography of the boundary region and in basic political structures in the two contiguous countries. The Mexico-Guatemala boundary traverses an irregular course 598 miles long, proceeding from Belize's western border on the east to the Pacific coast on the west. From east to west, the boundary at various points follows the course of the Usumacinta, Salinas, and Suchiate rivers, elsewhere following a series of parallel, meridian, and geodesic lines (United States Department of State 1976). Unlike the U.S.-Mexican border, the Mexico-Guatemala border traverses a very humid, tropical landscape. Annual rainfall along much of the border varies between two thousand and five thousand millimeters (Guatemala National Water Commission 1967: 422). Human settlement along the border remains sparse, but it has increased substantially in recent years due to land pressures in Mexico and Guatemala.

The abundance of water has meant few conflicts over water apportionment, despite the fact that numerous rivers intersect the land boundary or join the boundary rivers. This situation is underscored by the absence of any water apportionment treaties between the two countries.[3] Water abundance has generated its own problems, however, including flooding and meandering river boundaries. It has also generated resource opportunities. Both Mexico and Guatemala are interested in exploiting the region's largest rivers, the Río Suchiate and the Río Usumacinta. In the case of the Usumacinta, for example, the two countries have entered into a cooperative agreement to do so (*Excélsior* 1989b). They have also studied ways to better exploit the Suchiate's water resources (Acuerdo para la Creación 1991). Other resources are also potential sources of conflict. The border cuts across a number of rich ecological zones, including the fertile Lacandon jungle of Chiapas, Quintana Roo, and Petén. This region, which remained isolated until the late 1960s, has suffered adverse impacts arising from recent migration and commercial timber and cattle operations.[4] The Mexico-Guatemala border has also been a zone of strategic concern for both countries as insurgency and domestic politics in Guatemala have pushed thousands of refugees into Mexico.[5]

The structure and functions of CILA also derive from political conditions in both countries. Administratively, both Mexico and Guatemala are quite centralized. While Mexican federalism in constitution and practice limits the autonomy of its subordinate political units, Guatemala's 1985 constitution provides for a unitary system under strong central governance. These formal constraints on the political power of administrative dependencies ensure that local constituencies play almost no effective role in the crafting of national boundary management policies. The formal limitations are reinforced by the fact that this border region is the among the least developed areas in either nation, with low levels of literacy, skills, and social organization: in short, the very resources which are most conducive to political mobilization and participation in national affairs.

In this context, CILA and its national sections have little policy and administrative independence from their respective foreign ministries. Under the 1961 charter, which drew heavily on the precedent of the

---

[3] Preliminary discussions aimed at a treaty on the utilization of boundary waters are presently underway. See *Excélsior* 1990d.

[4] As much as 70 percent of the original Lacandón forest has been destroyed. Population in the Lacandón region alone has increased from 12,000 in 1965 to 200,000 in 1989. See *Excélsior* 1987, 1989a; *Uno más Uno* 1988, 1989; *News* 1989; Buswell 1990.

[5] Since the early 1980s, close to 50,000 refugees have fled into southern Chiapas from Guatemala. Increased incidences of malaria, measles, dengue fever, and other maladies have been attributed to the influx of immigrants in the border zone (*Coloradoan* 1990; *Excélsior* 1989c, 1990f). Recently the situation has been aggravated by a major outbreak of cholera in the Río Suchiate region (*Uno más Uno* 1991).

IBWC, each section of CILA is constituted of a commissioner, who must be a licensed engineer, a principal engineer, a legal adviser, and an administrative assistant. The commissioners are each endowed with diplomatic privileges (Ordóñez Ochoa and Cabrera Cosío 1989; Acuerdo para la Creación 1961).

As in the case of the IBWC, CILA's official jurisdiction is quite narrow, limited to functions directly affecting the international boundary. Until recently, CILA's functions were correspondingly limited to traditional boundary and water operations. Today, CILA's basic functions fall into six general areas; first, surveying and maintaining land and water boundaries; second, researching the water resources of the border region; third, providing technical advice to its member governments regarding water resources along the border and recommending projects which would put these resources to beneficial use for both countries; fourth, conducting research and providing advice to member governments aimed at demarcating the maritime boundary in the Pacific Ocean; fifth, cooperating with other agencies in efforts to conserve, protect, and utilize natural resources in the border area, to include environmental protection and improvement; and sixth, cooperating with other agencies in developing contingency plans for natural disasters in the frontier area (Ordóñez Ochoa and Cabrera Cosío 1989).

As evident from this list, the burden of CILA's functions, more so than with the IBWC, are of a technical and advisory nature. This role is both developmentally and politically determined. As a practical matter, sparse settlement along the international boundary and the absence of binational cities of any size make sanitation and sewage management a low priority. CILA's national sections are also dwarfed by larger domestic agencies in both countries with operational responsibilities for developing and operating water and sanitation projects and other public works. Hence neither section of CILA has been delegated much operational power. To a significant degree, however, its technical and advisory mission has been dictated by conditions along the international boundary, where delayed development was reflected in a dearth of hydrological and resources data. As late as the mid-1970s, a Guatemala National Water Commission report to the United Nations cited "an absolute lack of flood flow records" as a major factor behind the lack of flood management programs throughout the country (Guatemala National Water Commission 1967: 430). As a consequence, CILA has been engaged in collecting flooding data along international river drainage basins, as well as developing an inventory of natural and environmental resources along the border. In this connection, one of CILA's first assignments, finally completed in 1988, was the development of the landmark *Physical Atlas* of the international river basins on the Mexico-Guatemala border (Ordóñez Ochoa and Cabrera Cosío 1989; Szekely 1988).

Within this context, CILA plays an important role in developing and protecting border resources. For example, in conjunction with the respective water resources agencies of its member governments, CILA has been instrumental in developing the basic hydrological and engineering data requisite for development of a large hydroelectric dam on the Usumacinta River (*Excélsior* 1989b). CILA has also overseen the channelization of the lower Suchiate River (Ordóñez Ochoa and Cabrera Cosío 1989: 2). The feasibility of other projects is currently under investigation.

CILA's data generation and advisory role might well be construed as lending the agency a wholly extractive orientation. Recently, however, growing environmental concern, both international and domestic, has placed environmental protection on its functional mandate. In 1988, Mexico and Guatemala reached an agreement to cooperate in protecting environmental resources in the border region (*Política Exterior* 1988: 85–86). Under this agreement environmental criteria are to be factored into CILA studies of drainage basins along the international frontier. Specifically, CILA is charged in Article 4 of the agreement with: (1) organizing working groups to study environmental problems along the border, to include threatened and endangered species of fauna and flora; (2) implementing necessary actions to conserve protected natural areas along the border; and (3) coordinating the efforts of respective government agencies, including those of local communities, to prevent illegal commerce in protected species of fauna and flora (Szekely 1988: 7–8). Interestingly, this new agreement, which is to be given force by follow-up annexes, makes CILA, subject to the broad policy oversight of Mexico's SEDUE and Guatemala's Ministry of Foreign Relations, the lead agency for environmental conservation in the border zone, significantly broadening its functional mandate beyond the traditional domains of boundary and water concerns. In this respect, CILA's functional range now extends beyond the more limited scope of the U.S.-Mexico IBWC.

While the new agreement has yet to be given specific effect, it potentially opens a wide functional panorama for CILA. The Mexico-Guatemala border region is presently the object of keen interest because of its rich biodiversity. The rapid development of the border region in the last decade has generated a new sense of urgency that many plant and animal species are being permanently extinguished.[6] Unfortunately, both Mexico and Guatemala have been slow to act in defense of such resources. In Guatemala in particular, institutional commitment to environmental conservation has been so negligible that a review of the environmental situation in the early 1980s reported, "there is no effective

---

[6] While the Guatemalan government still has no central environmental ministry, it has recently created an intersecretarial Environment Commission to coordinate policy and enter into bilateral discussions in this area (*Excélsior* 1990a; Comisión Nacional del Medio Ambiente, 1988).

commitment to environmental protection on the part of government. . . . The emphasis is on economic development at all costs" (Cooley et al. 1981: 43).

Recently, however, under pressure from the international community, both Mexico and Guatemala have begun to take conservation measures. In Mexico, the administration of Carlos Salinas de Gortari has made conservation of the Lacandón a priority, restricting commercial forestry in the region (*Uno más Uno* 1989; *Excélsior* 1989a). Guatemala, in a surprising about-face, established a nationwide network of protected zones in February 1989, to be administered by a new National Council for Protected Areas (Cohn 1989: 53). Guatemala's new president, Jorge Serrano Elías, has also declared a logging ban for the border region and cracked down on contraband traffic in hardwoods (Perera 1991: 56; *Excélsior* 1991).

On the bilateral front, international environmental groups like the Nature Conservancy, Conservation International, and World Wildlife Fund have lobbied extensively for the creation of additional nature preserves and protected zones along the border. In January 1990, the Mexican and Guatemalan governments simultaneously announced the formation of two new, semi-contiguous biosphere reserves abutting the international boundary in the El Petén region: Mexico's Calakmul Biosphere Reserve and Guatemala's Maya Biosphere Reserve (Houseal 1990: 20).[7] The two nations hope to capitalize on the new wave of eco-tourism as well as conserve national resources (*Excélsior* 1990g). While it is yet unclear just what role CILA will play in implementing these new policies, it seems certain that its role will broaden in the future.[8]

In sum, CILA's role in transboundary resource management along the Mexico-Guatemala boundary has, like its northern counterpart, been shaped by the geographic and political realities affecting the border region. Modeled after the IBWC and operating within a political context of administrative centralism, CILA has largely been confined to a limited technical and advisory role aimed at exploiting the region's hydrological resources. Recently, under the 1988 agreement, the potential range of its functions has significantly broadened to engage CILA in the conservation of natural resources along the border. It is too early to appraise its performance in this policy area, but recent bilateral cooperation in the environmental area and expansion of biospheres along the

---

[7]Mexico apparently took the initiative in moving toward these agreements (*Excélsior* 1988). It should be emphasized that despite these measures, which have potential for conserving the region's resources, exploitation of forests and wildlife continues unabated. The Guatemalan military, which controls the Petén region, is directly implicated in illegal trade in hardwoods and fauna and flora. See *Excélsior* 1990e; *Times of the Americas*, September 19, p. 5.

[8]Recently the two countries have concluded a new agreement to cooperate in regulating the illegal traffic in wildlife and protected species. It is unclear as yet whether CILA has an active role in implementing this agreement (*Excélsior* 1990a).

boundary suggest that CILA has the potential to become an important agency in managing border resources outside the traditional zones of boundary maintenance and water resource development.

CONCLUSION

As evident from our review of these two transboundary resource management agencies, the structure and capacity of such commissions are heavily determined by the character of the boundary regions under their jurisdiction and the nature of the political systems in which their national sections are embedded. The level of economic development and urbanization along the boundary, as well as the age of the commission itself, also play a role in determining its functions.

In considering the character of these two commissions it is important to note that while both are important actors in managing transboundary resources, neither has a monopoly in this sphere and neither enjoys comprehensive jurisdiction. While they are the only agencies with a predominantly international mission, they are joined by other domestic agencies in discharging their mandates.

Of the two cases reviewed above, the IBWC's role and functions on the U.S.-Mexico border have been shaped by the aridity of the border region, the policy decentralization of federal-state relations in the United States, and rapid urbanization and industrialization along the border since World War II. Its principal functions lie in the traditional domains of boundary and water management. Given the policy influence of the border states, however, the U.S. section has acquired operational functions and a level of policy autonomy which allow it to exercise an unusual degree of independence in shaping its policy agenda. The IBWC's age and greater maturity as an international commission contribute to its involvement in a wide range of functions within the province of boundary and water management.

CILA's character and functions, on the other hand, are directed to problems associated with a tropical, water-rich frontier which has been heavily stressed by the pressures of development in the past two decades. Levels of urbanization and industrialization are still low. Population growth and extractive demands have nevertheless dramatically altered the region's ecological balance, amplifying demands for more effective resource management.

Given the character of Mexican and Guatemalan public administration, CILA's administration and operations are also more centrally determined. As a young agency in a developing region, CILA's primary functions have been aimed at developing technical data on border water resources to enable both countries to harness the region's resources for purposes of development.

Both agencies have demonstrable weaknesses and strengths. The IBWC, due in good measure to the limits imposed by its state and local constituencies in the United States, has been unable to extend its functional range beyond the traditional domains of boundary and water management. On the other hand, it is a highly competent, influential agency with a near monopoly on developing solutions to transboundary problems within its special province. Alternatively, CILA's youth and administrative dependence are reflected in its largely technical data-gathering functions along the border. Its lack of an independent political constituency limits the extent to which it controls its own agenda, as well as its ability to compete with larger domestic agencies for actual operational functions and resources. But as the 1988 environmental agreement shows, CILA has been able to extend its functional range beyond the traditional scope of boundary and water concerns. This is so precisely because national governments in Mexico and Guatemala are not as constrained by local constituencies in developing their functional agendas along the border. It may also be related to the fact that there are fewer competing institutions in Mexico and Guatemala to which environmental management functions can effectively be assigned or which might compete within the administrations of either country for the discharge of such functions.

In sum, the two commissions are and will continue to be important players in the management of transboundary resources along their respective boundaries. In view of developments along both international frontiers, each commission has strong potential for functional development. We can expect to see the IBWC taking on new functions in the area of water quality, groundwater management, and recreation. On the Guatemala border, rapid development and growing international and domestic preoccupation with preserving the region's cultural and biological diversity portend a very large docket for CILA in the future, one extending beyond boundary and water management to include fauna and flora, archaeological sites, industrially generated pollution, and other functions. On both borders, the commissions' functional development entails sharing responsibility with other domestic agencies. Thus, the future of transboundary resource management on both borders is bound to involve the commissions in a more pluralistic milieu of agencies and interests than in the past. Within this context these international commissions are uniquely situated to settle bilateral resource disputes at their common boundaries and to manage regional resources in a sustainable and cooperative manner.

REFERENCES

Acuerdo para la Creación de la Comisión Internacional de Límites y Aguas entre los Estados Unidos Mexicanos y la República de Guatemala. 1961. Exchange of Memorandums: November 9–December 21. Copy provided to the author by Arq. Andreas Lehnhoff Femme,

Secretario Ejecutivo del Consejo Nacional de Areas Protegidas, January 8, 1991.

Asiwaju, Anthony. 1989. "National Boundaries Commissions as Problem Solving Institutions: Preliminary Research Notes on Nigeria, Niger, and Mali." Paper presented at the Conference on International Boundaries, International Boundaries Research Unit, Geography Department, University of Durham, England. September.

Bath, C. Richard. 1982. "U.S.-Mexico Experience in Managing Transboundary Air Resources: Problems, Prospects, and Recommendations for the Future," *Natural Resources Journal* 22:4 (October): 1147–69.

Bradley, Michael D., and Kenneth DeCook. 1978. "Ground Water Occurrence and Utilization in the Arizona-Sonora Border Region," *Natural Resources Journal* 18:1 (January): 29–68.

Buswell, Jackie. 1990. "Dramatic Loss of Mexican Forests and Jungles," *Voices of Mexico* 14 (July–September): 42–47.

Cohn, Jeffrey P. 1989. "A Will to Protect," *Americas* 41:2:46–53.

Coloradoan. 1990. "Mexico Faces Own Border Problem." July 20.

Comisión Nacional del Medio Ambiente. 1988. Decreto No. 68-86, Ley de Protección y Mejoramiento del Medio Ambiente. Guatemala: Presidencia de la República.

Cooley, James L., et al. 1981. *An Environmental Profile of Guatemala*. Washington, D.C.: U.S. Department of State, Agency for International Development.

Dillon, John. 1989. "Pollution Seeps from Mexico to U.S.," *Christian Science Monitor*, December 28.

Excélsior. 1987. "Si continúa la destrucción de la selva lacandona, graves consecuencias para el país," June 6.

———. 1988. "Propuso Camacho Solís crear reservas ecológicas entre México y Guatemala," May 27.

———. 1989a. "Decreto CSG veda forestal de 3 meses en la Lacandonia," February 14.

———. 1989b. "A petición de Guatemala, suspendió México un proyecto hidroeléctrico," May 26.

———. 1989c. "15 millones de dls. para refugiados," May 31.

———. 1990a. "Pactan México y Guatemala frenar el contrabando de flora y fauna," February 14.

———. 1990b. "Derramó Asarco 140 lts. de diesel en el Río Bravo," February 14.

———. 1990c. "Afecta a 500 labriegos el derrame de diesel en el Río Bravo: CNC," February 17.

———. 1990d. "México y Guatemala concertaron convenios y acuerdos sobre cooperación fronteriza," April 4.

———. 1990e. "Descubren cinco depósitos de madera contrabandeada desde Guatemala en la frontera con México: SARH," May 29.

———. 1990f. "Cordón sanitario en la frontera de México con Belice y Guatemala," June 10.

———. 1990g. "Se firmarán acuerdos con Belice y Guatemala para difundir la ruta maya," August 11.

———. 1991. "Protección militar en la frontera de México y Guatemala," April 8.

Guatemala National Water Commission. 1967. "Guatemala." In *Water for Peace*, vol. 1, Proceedings of the International Conference on Water for Peace. Washington, D.C.: U.S. Government Printing Office.

Houseal, Brian. 1990. "Maya Riches," *Nature Conservancy* 40:3 (May/June): 16–21.

IBWC (International Boundary and Water Commission). 1975. United States Section Manual, Vol. 1, Organization, Laws, and Procedures. El Paso, Texas: United States Section of the IBWC.

———. 1981. *Joint Projects of the United States and Mexico through the International Boundary and Water Commission*. El Paso, Texas: United States Section of the IBWC.

International Legal Materials. 1983. "Mexico-United States: Agreement to Cooperate in the Solution of Environmental Problems in the Border Area," 23:5 (September): 1025–33.

———. 1990. "Annex V (Agreement on Cooperation Regarding International Transport of Urban Pollution) to the Agreement to Cooperate in the Solution of Environmental Problems in the Border Area," 29:1 (January): 26–29.

Jamail, Milton H., and Margo Gutiérrez. 1990. *The Border Guide: Institutions and Organizations of the United States-Mexico Borderlands*. Austin: University of Texas Press.

Jamail, Milton H., and Stephen P. Mumme. 1982. "The International Boundary Water Commission as a Conflict Management Agency in the U.S.-Mexico Borderlands," *Social Science Journal* 19:1 (January): 45–62.

Jamail, Milton H., and Scott J. Ullery. 1979. *International Water Use Relations along the Sonoran Desert Borderlands*. Arid Lands Resource Information Paper No. 14. Tucson: Center of Arid Lands Studies, University of Arizona.

Mumme, Stephen P. 1984. "Regional Power in International Diplomacy: The U.S. Section of the International Boundary and Water Commission," *Publius* 14:4 (Fall): 115–36.

———. 1986. "Engineering Diplomacy: The Evolving Role of the International Boundary and Water Commission in U.S.-Mexico Water Management," *Journal of Borderlands Studies* 1:1 (Spring): 73–108.

———. 1988. "La Paz Agreement: Progress and Problems in Managing the Border Environment," *Transboundary Resources Report* 2:1 (Spring): 1–3.

Mydans, Seth. 1990. "U.S. and Mexico Agree on Border Sewage Plant," *New York Times*, August 22.

News. 1989. "Group of 100 Decries Destruction of Mexico's Jungles." July 9.

Ordóñez Ochoa, José Luis, and Luis Cabrera Cosío. 1989. *Comisión Internacional de Límites y Aguas entre Guatemala y México*. Mexico: Secretaría de Relaciones Exteriores.

Perera, Victor. 1991. "The Last Preserve: Guatemala Guards Its Rain Forests," *Nation*, July 8, pp. 54–56.

Rohter, Larry. 1989. "Canal Project Sets Off U.S.-Mexico Clash Over Water for Border Regions," *New York Times*, October 1.

Szekely, Alberto. 1988. "Mexico-Guatemala Transboundary Resources and Environmental Accord," *Transboundary Resources Report* 2:1 (Spring): 6–8.

United States Department of State. 1976. *International Boundary Study No. 175: Guatemala-Honduras*. Issued by the Geographer, Bureau of Intelligence and Research. Washington, D.C.: U.S. Department of State, July 23.

Uno más Uno. 1988. "Se comprometió el presidente Salinas a proteger las selvas lacandonas," December 9.

———. 1989. "Combate frontal a la corrupción en la selva Lacandonia, dijo Salinas de Gortari," January 1.

———. 1991. "El cólera va a llegar a México y la población puede estar tranquilo: estamos preparados para controlarlo," June 11.

Utton, Albert E. 1982 "Overview," *Natural Resources Journal* 22:4 (October): 735–48.

Willoughby, William R. 1979. *The Joint Organizations of the United States and Canada*. Toronto: University of Toronto Press.

8

The Integration and Disintegration of Regionalism in Central America, 1950–1990

Mitchell A. Seligson and Ricardo Córdova Macías

Regional economic integration affects border relations between neighboring nations. The dramatic success of the European Economic Community in rebuilding the war-torn economies of Western Europe and in stimulating unprecedented economic development among those countries has overshadowed similar attempts at regional economic integration in other parts of the world. Efforts at regional economic integration outside of Europe have been unable to achieve the same degree of success; indeed, most other regional common markets have failed and have been abandoned. Yet there is at least one case, the Central American Common Market (CACM), in which a considerable amount of progress was made in a relatively short span of years although the early success was not sustained over the long run. The case is one which is all but forgotten by analysts of regionalism, having been overshadowed by an international war, a civil war, a revolution, and a protracted guerrilla war. Despite the difficulties that emerged in the Central American case, there is hope even at this juncture that the nations in the region might resume their former efforts at economic (and indeed political) integration, and, as a result, that boundary relations might improve. This chapter examines the case of integration and disintegration in Central America from a historical perspective, tracing its early success, its later decline, and the prospects for its eventual resurrection.

BACKGROUND

Central America, comprising Guatemala, El Salvador, Honduras, Nicaragua, and Costa Rica, emerged from colonial rule under Spain as the Central American Federation, founded in 1824.[1] The individual units in the federation shared many features. As a result of some three hundred years of Spanish colonial domination, Spanish was spoken throughout the region, almost all residents were at least nominally Catholic, and the legal systems of the five countries reflected the Spanish tradition. Moreover, even though there are differences in size among the nations (with Guatemala having the largest population and Costa Rica the smallest), when compared to the great diversity in population and physical size of countries both north and south of Central America, these five countries appear practically indistinguishable. These similarities would seem to have boded well for the development of common interests and the emergence of a single political and economic unit. Such was not the case, however, and the federation proved to be ephemeral, collapsing entirely by 1839. From that point until the early 1950s, repeated efforts were made to reunite these countries.

Two examples are the Chinandega Plan to form a Central American Confederation in 1842 and the 1849 effort to form the National Representation of Central America. Both aimed to restore political unification of the region; the latter focused on matters such as conflict mediation and the implementation of foreign policy. Since these and similar efforts were directed toward forming a political union, they met political opposition from nationalistic leaders of the region. President Carrera of Guatemala, for example, was able to block both of the movements for unification mentioned above. Throughout the nineteenth century and up until the middle of the twentieth, all attempts at union met with failure. The sad history of unsuccessful union is perhaps best summed up by Thomas L. Karnes (1961):

> For one hundred thirty-five years these little states have tried to unite, federate, or confederate under numerous forms of government and have failed unconditionally, even though they apparently possess more bonds of similarity than any other small group of nations in the world (p. 3). . . .
>
> On at least twenty-five different occasions formal and official steps were taken to reconstitute the states into

---

[1] Geographically, Panama and Belize are also part of Central America. Panama, however, formed part of Colombia until the early years of the twentieth century, when it was split off as part of the arrangements to build the Panama Canal. Belize, formerly known as British Honduras, remained a British colony until the beginning of the 1980s. Most Belizians speak English and consider themselves part of the Caribbean rather than Central America.

some single form of government. No attempt lasted more than a few months, nor included all five of the nations. There has never been anything resembling success (p. 243).

After World War II, Central American visionaries once again took up the cause of regional integration. This time, however, they limited their immediate goal to economic as opposed to political integration. The argument used by the proponents of a move toward integration was strictly pragmatic; individually the economies were simply too small to sustain significant industrialization, whereas united in a common market they could achieve the benefits of economic development.

The key institution that promoted the new integration program was the United Nations Economic Commission for Latin America (ECLA). A new ECLA subcommittee—the Central American Economic Cooperation Committee (CCE), formed to handle Central America's program—was able to draw on the technical resources of the United Nations as it planned a program of development for the region. The period from the establishment of the CCE in 1951 until 1958 was spent largely in planning and culminated on June 10, 1958, with the signing of the Multilateral Treaty of Central American Free Trade and Economic Integration. This treaty was the first step toward reducing the tariffs that had obstructed intra-Central American trade. However, the treaty was highly cautious, freeing only a few of the many items listed in the Standard Central American Tariff Nomenclature (NAUCA). In this respect there is some similarity between the Central American treaty and the Montevideo treaty that established the Latin American Free Trade Association (LAFTA). As is the case with the Montevideo treaty, the free items were those which were not manufactured in the region anyway; thus, in terms of trade creation the effects were not substantial. The situation was to change drastically on February 6, 1960, when El Salvador, Honduras, and Guatemala signed a far-reaching agreement (the Treaty of Economic Association) eliminating tariffs on a much larger number of goods. Later that year, on December 13, the General Treaty on Central American Economic Integration was signed. The General Treaty took a different tack from that of the Multilateral Treaty, by freeing all goods produced in Central America, with a small number of stipulated exceptions. The General Treaty was initially signed by four countries, and Costa Rica signed on July 23, 1962.

The data in table 8.1 show the rapid growth in both total trade and regional trade in the region. The impact of the common market on regional trade was dramatic, as these data suggest. Beginning in 1962, regional trade skyrocketed, helping to spur industrialization and economic development.

TABLE 8.1
CENTRAL AMERICA: INTRA-REGIONAL EXPORTS (FOB), 1960–1986
(MILLIONS OF U.S. DOLLARS)

Year	Amount
1960	30.3
1961	36.2
1962	44.7
1963	68.7
1964	105.3
1965	132.1
1966	170.3
1967	205.6
1968	246.9
1969	250.1
1970	286.3
1971	272.7
1972	304.7
1973	383.3
1974	532.5
1975	536.3
1976	649.2
1977	785.4
1978	862.7
1979	891.7
1980	1129.2
1981	936.8
1982	765.5
1983	766.6
1984	706.9
1985	538.2
1986	420.5

Sources: SIECA and CEPAL.

In July 1969 harsh political reality, in the form of nationalism, was to overcome economic success. In that year a long-festering dispute between Honduras and El Salvador surfaced in the so-called Football War. This short but bloody conflict delivered the first major shocks to the CACM. Trade between Honduras and El Salvador halted, and the Inter-American Highway, the major road link among the five countries, was blocked. Trade within the region began to fall and special arrangements had to be made to keep the market from collapsing entirely.

As a consequence of the Honduras-El Salvador war, the Economic and the Executive Councils—chief institutions for the integration framework—stopped functioning and the legal system that regulated economic integration fractured.² In 1970 a meeting of Central America's economic ministers took place, in an important effort to reactivate the CACM. The ministers reached an agreement in principle, but the results had limited positive impact.

During the remainder of the 1970s, the normalization of Central American integration was not possible, due to the border dispute between Honduras and El Salvador. A peace treaty was finally signed in 1981 which initiated at lower levels the commercial relations between the two countries. But just as the CACM appeared finally to be overcoming the impact of the 1969 war, Nicaragua was in flames. The Sandinistas, fighting to overthrow the Somoza dictatorship, succeeded in July 1979. However, although the dictator was gone, the problems of economic development were far from resolved; indeed, they worsened in the years to come, in part as a consequence of the U.S.-supported Contra war.

By 1980 the Central American panorama was grim and getting worse. The international debt crisis—in which developing nations began to default on loans made earlier when banks in the United States, Europe, and Japan were awash with petro-dollars—hit the region as Costa Rica, struggling to repay foreign loans, was plunged into its most severe economic crisis of the century.

The Central American crisis was characterized by the following features during the 1980s:

- The existence of three armed conflicts (in Guatemala, El Salvador, and Nicaragua). Although each displays its own characteristics, together they produced a process of militarization in the entire region (Benítez Manaut 1986). The budgetary impact of this militarization has been enormous (Córdova Macías 1987). Moreover, war generated an enormous migratory movement of refugees and internally displaced citizens (Torres-Rivas 1985).

- Deterioration of the economies of the region, which can be seen in the behavior of macroeconomic indicators such as GNP growth, GNP per capita, inflation, unemployment, currency devaluation, foreign debt, etc. (see CEPAL 1988, 1989b). This economic picture has affected all the countries and all social sectors, but undoubtedly the sectors with fewer resources have been more affected. For 1980, at the start of the conflict, ECLA estimated that about 63.7 percent of the Central American population lived below the poverty level; that is to say, nearly two-thirds of the population did not have sufficient income to buy the basic basket of products and services (CEPAL 1983: 18). This is the social sector most affected by the economic crisis and the war.

---

²By 1971 Central America had signed twenty-nine multilateral agreements of economic integration. Twenty-eight were in effect for three countries at least, and twenty for all countries.

- In this context of militarization, war, and economic crisis, the volume of intra-regional commerce fell. In 1985, intra-Central American commerce had the same value in current dollars as ten years before; just 15 percent of the total exports of Central America were sent to other Central American countries (Fuentes 1987: 16–17). Since 1981 there has been a decrease in transactions realized through the Central American Chamber of Compensation. According to the Instituto para la Integración de América Latina (INTAL 1986: 112) intra-regional exports fell by 6.1 percent in 1984 and Central American imports experienced a reduction of 10.7 percent. Regional exports fell from U.S. $936.8 million in 1981 to $413.2 million in 1986.

The political and economic crises clearly have impacted the growth of regional trade, and stagnation and decline have been a persistent pattern in recent years. From the perspective of these data, one might conclude that regional integration is a lost cause. Nevertheless, at this critical juncture in Central American history, integration is drawing much attention as a possible means for solving the most serious crisis in the region's history.[3] The crisis itself seems to have generated new possibilities for the emergence of an even stronger regional unit. Integration can be a means for economic recovery (CEPAL 1985), and it can contribute to the search for a political settlement to the armed conflicts. An understanding of the challenge of and prospects for regional integration demands a review of the evolution of the conflicts themselves and the possibilities of resolving them.

CENTRAL AMERICAN INTEGRATION IN THE CONTEXT OF WAR AND MILITARIZATION, 1979–1990

Our working hypothesis is that the crisis of the 1980s was conducive to a search for political accommodation and the promotion of regional integration, on the basis of two principles that have increasingly gained prominence: multilateralism and pluralism.[4] By multilateralism we understand the process of accommodation and political negotiation that emerged in the region, examples of which are the Contadora and Esquipulas peace processes, and the economic negotiations with the

---

[3]Menjivar (1988) notes the integrationist desires present in Central American history since the last century and argues that there have been cyclical movements, alternating trends of crisis/bilateralism and prosperity/integration. Nevertheless, in the 1980s, as a consequence of the magnitude of the crisis, the two trends co-occurred. The bilateral approach sought better understanding with the United States—and more aid—while proponents of the second trend stressed the need for integration. This point is discussed throughout this paper.

[4]This is not to ignore conflict and confrontation in regional negotiations. However, our interest lies in accommodation and agreement, despite existing conflicts. For a view on the relationship between conflict and negotiation in the Central American crisis in the 1980s, see Aguilera 1989.

European Economic Community. In all of these cases the Central American governments negotiated as a bloc, rejecting isolationist or divisionist approaches that seek better treatment or a more advantageous position for a given country, or that admit principles of conditionality or exclusion.[5] The second principle is pluralism, understood as an acceptance of the political realities with which the countries of the region have had to coexist, such as the Nicaraguan revolution. Pluralism implied recognition of the Sandinista regime by its neighbors and the admission of Nicaragua as a negotiating partner. The acceptance that Central America is not a homogeneous region but one exhibiting different economic models and political regimes has been a significant achievement.[6] The way in which these principles came to predominate will be examined below, in a review of the forums and proposals for resolution of the conflict, as well as of programs and initiatives for Central America's economic recovery.

The nature and content of future regional integration models will differ from those of the immediate past. A first difference that becomes readily apparent is the political dimension of the current process, which requires a solution to conflict based on the principle of a nonmonolithic and nonhomogeneous region. In the past, integration was articulated at the economic level, under conditions of similar political regimes and without a dynamic of militarization and war.

Second, with regard to the debate on similarities and differences within the region, the strictly political elements of the crisis have accentuated the differences, while economic elements have highlighted the similarities even more. There are, of course, variations in degree, but there is a common economic problematic clearly expressed in the similar behavior of macroeconomic indicators.

The political process throughout the 1980s highlighted the need to view Central America as a region. In addition to shared structural, historical, and geopolitical elements, the events of the 1980s evidenced the interdependence of the Central American countries and underscored the need to search for a joint solution to the crisis.

The need to overcome the crisis by accepting pluralism and multilateralism has enabled Central America to "become a region" and to come together as an interlocutor to negotiate the terms of international cooperation. The impossibility of finding individual national solutions will continue to be a key factor as Central America faces the future. As one Central American scholar asserts: "a regional geopolitics of increasing diversification, sovereignty, self-sufficiency, and regional comple-

---

[5] This approach of discrimination and conditionality in aid has surfaced in bilateral relations between the United States and the governments of Central America, excluding Nicaragua from aid. It was also present in the Caribbean Basin Initiative, a regional proposal in the early 1980s which functioned on the basis of discrimination.

[6] For an explanation of Nicaragua's differences with its neighbors, see Gorostiaga 1983.

mentarity is necessary as the basis for a far-reaching alternative for the peoples of the region" (Gorostiaga 1984: 27).

SIMULATING SCENARIOS

An important element in this discussion is the relationship between continuity and/or intensification of armed conflict and the problem this poses for economic recovery. As former Colombian President Belisario Betancur noted in 1984, "without peace there can be no development, and without development there can be no peace. We must break this vicious circle" (in Fagen 1987: 3). The problem lies in the impossibility of economic recovery and the promotion of development without a solution to military conflict. This situation has been particularly complicated by U.S. policy in the region, which has favored military instruments over political negotiations, applying its strategy of "low-intensity warfare."

However, important efforts have been undertaken to seek a political alternative of demilitarization and negotiation. Especially noteworthy is the economic model simulated by the Policy Alternatives for the Caribbean and Central America (PACCA) for the period 1986–92, which contrasts two scenarios of Central America's potential for economic growth and for attracting the external aid necessary to fulfill this potential. The first scenario is the continuation of the "low-intensity war," and the second is negotiated demilitarization of the region (Fagen 1987).

The model's findings are illustrative of the complexity of the situation: economic growth for the region as a whole could average 2–4 percent per year between 1986–92 under peace conditions, and less than 2 percent if the military track is maintained. Per capita economic growth under the demilitarization scenario could recover and grow by a total of 4 percent over the entire period, but if the conflict continues it could decline by 4 percent.

These results show clearly that no development or economic recovery is possible under conditions of continuing war. With regards to Betancur's dilemma, peace is a pre-requisite for development, and without development there cannot be long-term stability:

> Thus the cycle closes: without negotiations and demilitarization, there can be no reconstruction of the economies and societies of the region; without reconstruction, there can be neither economic growth nor enhanced political participation, . . . there can be no lasting peace and no political stability (Fagen 1987: 6).

THE CONTADORA PROCESS

The Contadora Group began with an invitation that the Panamanian chancellor extended to the foreign ministers of Colombia, Mexico, and Venezuela to meet on January 8 and 9, 1983, to examine the complex Central American panorama. The group derived its name from the island where this meeting was held. The presidents of the four member countries met again in July 1983 to discuss the general guidelines for a peace negotiations program to be proposed to the Central American governments. Two months later they made public the Documento de Objetivos, an outline of goals containing the twenty-one points to be pursued through regional negotiations. These included aspects of regional security as well as issues of socioeconomic development. Finally, in January 1984, the Contadora Group announced the rules for implementing the commitments to items in the Documento approved by the governments of the region. The norms of immediate application referred to security, political, and socioeconomic issues.

The Contadora Group continued to work with the Central American governments and in August 1984 presented a first draft of a peace agreement, the Acta de Contadora para la Paz y la Cooperación en Centroamérica. This agreement provoked objections from the governments of El Salvador, Guatemala, Honduras, and Costa Rica, and was initially accepted only by Nicaragua. This gave way to a process of negotiations and discussion of several revised versions of the Contadora agreement. None received the backing of the U.S. government and they were rejected by almost all Central American countries (Benítez Manaut and Córdova Macías 1989).

An important feature of the Contadora initiative was that it emerged outside of the framework of the Organization of American States, largely because of the inefficiency and crisis affecting this institution. Subsequent efforts by other Latin American countries, such as the Support Group composed of the governments of Argentina, Brazil, Peru, and Uruguay which was created on August 25, 1985, shared this characteristic.

One of the Contadora Group's main contributions was bringing the different governments of the region to the negotiating table. The dynamics of regional negotiations, from the creation of the group to the signing of the Esquipulas II agreement, was a contributing factor in the development of pluralism and multilateralism. Even though the Contadora initiative did not result in the adoption of any of the peace proposals advanced, it paved the way for the signing of Esquipulas II (Bagley and Tokatlian 1988). The weakness of the negotiations promoted by the Contadora Group lay in the fact that they could not advance beyond the political will of the Central American governments.

The Esquipulas II Agreements

On May 24–25, 1986, the presidents of the Central American countries held a meeting in Guatemala. The most important product of this meeting was the Esquipulas Declaration, in which they agreed to sign the Contadora agreement and announced their decision to "formalize the meetings of the presidents as a necessary and convenient mechanism for the analysis of the problems [of the region]."

A second regional peace process, parallel and complementary to Contadora, began in February 1987, when Costa Rican President Oscar Arias convened a meeting of the Central American presidents and presented his peace proposals. The presidents agreed to discuss them at a future meeting in Esquipulas, Guatemala. There, on August 7, 1987, the Central American presidents signed the Procedure for the Establishment of a Firm and Lasting Peace in Central America, better known as the Esquipulas II agreement. The accord establishes a commitment to work for the achievement of peace, and it sets a time frame for the promotion of measures to that end. President Arias's proposal was successful in part because the scope of the negotiations was less ambitious than that of the Contadora initiative, and also because the actors in this process were the presidents themselves, that is, the highest decision-making political power (Córdova Macías and Benítez Manaut 1989).

Esquipulas II expounded "national reconciliation" in societies experiencing profound divisions, on the basis of three measures to be undertaken simultaneously: a dialogue between the "unarmed political opposition" and the respective governments, a declaration of amnesty, and a cease-fire to coincide with the beginning of negotiations. In addition, the agreement recognized the need to "initiate an authentic democratic process, pluralist and participatory." Although an exhaustive analysis of the evolution of and adherence or nonadherence to the Esquipulas agreement is beyond the scope of this essay, we can at least note its repercussions. From our viewpoint, the political dynamic generated in the region, which promoted the development of the principles of multilateralism and pluralism, is more important than the fact that the agreement by itself has not completely resolved any of the region's armed conflicts.

The inter-state character of the Nicaraguan conflict, and the fact that Nicaragua's political regime and economic system differ from those of the rest of the region, made this country the "test case" for the Esquipulas II agreement. Presidential meetings in El Salvador, Honduras, and Nicaragua between 1989 and 1990 revolved around the Nicaraguan case. The Sandinista government implemented the measures contained in the Esquipulas II agreement and agreed to negotiate with the domestic opposition and the counterrevolutionary forces, signing the Sapoa

Accords in March 1988. In February 1989 the Nicaraguan government pledged to hold presidential elections in February 1990, and the commitment to hold free and fair elections became the key factor in the political negotiations. In exchange for these concessions, the Sandinistas gained recognition from the other governments of the region, as well as a political solution to the Contra problem. This success led to another at the presidential summit in August 1989, where a joint plan for the demobilization and repatriation or relocation of counterrevolutionary groups based in Honduras was approved.

Moreover, the process of negotiation and verification of the Esquipulas II agreement, together with parallel negotiations toward international cooperation with Central America, were key factors in the emergence of propitious conditions for the development of multilateralism and pluralism as the basis for promoting Central American integration. As early as the May 1986 presidential meeting, the intention to "promote and foster joint positions to confront common economic problems" was reaffirmed, and the decision was made to "reinforce institutionally and financially the organizations of Central American integration." Subsequently the Nicaraguan presidential declaration of April 3, 1990, stated that "the consolidation of democracy, once the obstacles in the way of peace have been overcome, demands a resolute confrontation of the economic challenge." With this in mind, it was proposed that the next presidential summit take up the following issues:

- The restructuring, strengthening, and reactivation of regional economic integration.

- Evolution toward a productive system integrated at the regional level.

- Reconsideration of the problematic of the external debt.

- A better distribution of the social costs inherent in the necessary adjustment of the region's economies (*La Prensa Gráfica* [San Salvador], April 6, 1990).

An important aspect of the negotiating process generated by Esquipulas II is the institutionalization of summits as a forum for debate and political agreement among the presidents of the region (see table 8.2).

THE CENTRAL AMERICAN PARLIAMENT

The creation of a Central American Parliament was approved at the presidential summit of May 1986, as part of the effort toward political understanding, peace, and integration in Central America. The drafting of a proposal began in August 1986, and in October 1987 the Treaty for the Creation of the Central American Parliament and other Political

TABLE 8.2
SUMMITS OF CENTRAL AMERICAN PRESIDENTS

Summit	Place	Date
1	Esquipulas, Guatemala	May 24–25, 1986
2	Guatemala, Guatemala	August 6–7, 1987
3	San José, Costa Rica	January 16, 1988
4	San Salvador, El Salvador	February 13–14, 1989
5	Tela, Honduras	August 5–7, 1989
6	Montelimar, Nicaragua	April 2–3, 1990

Mechanisms was officially presented (Córdova Macías and Benítez Manaut 1989). It has since been ratified by the legislatures of Guatemala, El Salvador, Honduras, and Nicaragua, though paradoxically not by Costa Rica's; hence, the treaty is not yet in effect.

The importance of a Central American Parliament lies in the need to have a political mechanism to promote, support, and strengthen regional integration, as well as a forum for high-level regional communication and accommodation. Gloria Abraham (1989: 44) has suggested that "this mechanism be the only instrument established in the framework of the peace plan," which would make it the only permanent institutional legacy of the Esquipulas II process.

An important limitation of the project for a Central American Parliament is its conception as a regional organization for the presentation and analysis of—and recommendations about—political, economic, social, and cultural matters of common interest. In other words, the parliament would be a deliberative body only, since the governments would not be bound by its agreements or recommendations. Nevertheless, by its very nature the parliament might provide a base for a gradual enhancement of its powers.

Additionally, a Central American parliament would, for the first time in the history of Central America, give political parties an important role in regional integration. Representation in the parliament would not be based on nationality but on ideological tendencies. This would open unprecedented avenues and horizons to political parties and contribute to the consolidation of political parties and political pluralism and to the development of ideological debate. Nevertheless, there is an inherent contradiction in this arrangement, for even though the deputies would be elected to the parliament in fair and free elections, in accordance with the laws of each country,[7] the parliament's powers would be extremely limited (Aldecoa Lazarraga 1989: 39).

---

[7]This applies exclusively to the twenty deputies from each country. The rest of the members of parliament—former presidents and vice presidents—are not elected.

INTERNATIONAL COOPERATION

The final contributing factor in revitalizing the regional integration project on the basis of multilateralism and pluralism is international cooperation, for it has forced Central American governments to act as a bloc despite existing political polarization. This basic regional consensus at the economic level has great relevance for the future of Central American integration. We will review in this section the main initiatives and negotiations on international cooperation.

In November 1985, at the Second Conference on Political Dialogue and Economic Cooperation in Luxembourg, the European Economic Community and the Central American countries, including Panama, signed an Agreement of Cooperation. This agreement was the culmination of negotiations begun at a conference of ministers of the EEC, its member states, the nations of Central America, and the countries of the Contadora Group, in San José, Costa Rica, on September 28–29, 1984. The Agreement of Cooperation establishes most favored nation status for both imports and exports and gives preferential treatment to Central America "in the framework of the programs [that the EEC] reserves for nonassociated developing countries" (Fuentes 1987). In addition to any advantages which the Agreement of Cooperation provides in terms of economic and commercial cooperation, the negotiating process itself had a major important outcome: the fact that the Central American governments had to hold prior meetings to hammer out common positions on development issues before beginning negotiations with the EEC was a powerful factor in strengthening regional integration. The Agreement of Cooperation also established the Mixed Commission, which has held three meetings—in Brussels, June 1987; Managua, June 1988; and Brussels, June 1989—to review the evolution of commercial exchange, to identify problems and obstacles that have emerged since the Luxembourg agreement (see CEPAL 1989a), and to make recommendations on improving relations and commerce between the EEC and countries of Central America (see CEPAL 1989c).

In 1987 the United Nations General Assembly passed two resolutions to prepare a Special Plan of Economic Cooperation for Central America (SPEC), which would promote the pacification and development of the region and serve as a channel for funding from the international community. The General Assembly approved the plan on May 12, 1988.

Reacting to these initiatives from the international community, Central American governments have worked together to set priorities for international cooperation. At a January 1988 conference, vice presidents, ministers of foreign affairs and planning, and individuals responsible for implementing economic integration approved the Plan for Immediate Action. This plan forms part of a regional development strategy whose short-, medium-, and long-term objectives are to identify and direct international aid to priority areas and sectors in the Central American region, framing these efforts to accord with regional criteria of economic rationality and efficiency (SIECA 1988). The plan was incorporated into the Special Plan of Economic Cooperation, and it served as a general framework for the proposals presented to the European Economic Community.

Both the Plan for Immediate Action and the Special Plan of Economic Cooperation for Central America:

> give priority to the so-called Emergency Program which includes five points: food aid, an emergency fund for economic revitalization in Central America, energy security, foreign debt, and aid to refugees and displaced persons (INTAL 1989: 79).

While it is not yet possible to conduct a thorough assessment of the United Nations' Special Plan of Economic Cooperation for Central America, the plan does suffer from one apparent weakness: given the level and severity of the region's needs, there is concern that the resources outlined in the plan (roughly U.S. $4 billion) will be insufficient.

On November 29, 1987, the Acapulco Commitment to Peace, Development, and Democracy was signed by eight Latin American presidents during their first summit (in Acapulco, Mexico). The eight countries represented were the members of Contadora and its Support Group: Argentina, Brazil, Colombia, Mexico, Panama, Peru, Uruguay, and Venezuela. The presidents agreed to implement an emergency program for Central America which contains "measures to promote Central America's interregional commerce and to facilitate access by the exports of member countries of the Common Market to the countries of the Group of Eight."

CENTRAL AMERICAN INTEGRATION IN RETROSPECT

In this paper we have outlined the benchmarks in the evolution of regionalism in Central America. We have shown that despite many similarities in history, size, culture, and economic development, prior to World War II all integration efforts met with failure. The Central American Common Market, formed in the 1960s, proved to be the most successful effort to date, but it too succumbed to nationalist pressures.

Despite the failures of the past, we believe that regional integration offers a great opportunity to overcome problems of economic underdevelopment. Moreover, we see reactivation of the CACM as a distinct possibility. We are particularly encouraged by the democratic elections that have taken place in all five Central American countries. For the first time, all of Central America is ruled by civilian governments. We are also encouraged by the winding down of the Contra war and evidence that the armed conflict of El Salvador is drawing to a close. In the 1990s and beyond, we expect to see a reactivation of the CACM and a move toward greater regional unity.

REFERENCES

Abraham, Gloria. 1989. "El Parlamento Centroamericano: Su incidencia en el desarrollo futuro de la región," *Polémica*, segunda época, 8 (May–August): 41–46.

Aguilera, Gabriel. 1989. Centroamérica. Concertación y conflicto, una exploración, *Nueva Sociedad* 102 (July–August): 33–40.

Aldecoa Lazarraga, Francisco. 1989. "El Parlamento Centroamericano: A la luz de la experiencia europea," *Polémica*, segunda época, 8 (May–August): 35–40.

Bagley, Bruce Michael, and Juan Gabriel Tokatlian. 1988. *Contadora: The Limits of Negotiation*. Washington, D.C.: Johns Hopkins Foreign Policy Institute.

Benítez Manaut, Raúl. 1986. "La militarización de Centroamérica. Problemas de interpretación," *Polémica* 21 (October–December).

Benítez Manaut, Raúl, and Ricardo Córdova Macías. 1989. *México en Centroamérica. Expediente de documentos fundamentales (1979–1986)*. Mexico: Universidad Nacional Autónoma de México.

CEPAL (Comisión Económica para América Latina). 1983. "La crisis en Centroamérica: Orígenes, alcances y consecuencias." Mexico: CEPAL, September. Mimeo.

———. 1985. "Centroamérica: Bases de una política de reactivación y desarrollo." Mexico: CEPAL. Mimeo.

———. 1988. "Centroamérica: La evolución de la economía en 1987." Mexico: CEPAL, September. Mimeo.

———. 1989a. "Informe sobre la cooperación de la Comunidad Europea a los países del Istmo Centroamericano." Mexico: CEPAL.

———. 1989b. "Centroamérica: Situación actual y perspectivas de la economía y la integración." Mexico: CEPAL, June.

———. 1989c. "Evolución reciente del intercambio comercial entre los países del Istmo Centroamericano y la Comunidad Económica Europea." Mexico: CEPAL.

Córdova Macías, Ricardo. 1987. "Los efectos económicos de la militarización en la región centroamericana (1979–1986)." Occasional Papers Series, 20. Miami: Latin American and Caribbean Center, Florida International University.

Córdova Macías, Ricardo, and Raúl Benítez Manaut. 1989. *La paz en Centroamérica: Expediente de documentos fundamentales, 1979–1989*. Mexico: Universidad Nacional Autónoma de México.

Fagen, Richard. 1987. *Forging Peace. The Challenge of Central America*. New York: Basil Blackwell, for PACCA.

Fuentes, Juan Alberto. 1987. "La integración económica centroamericana. Nuevas perspectivas a partir de la turbulencia," *Polémica*, segunda época, 1 (January–April): 15–34.

Gorostiaga, Xabier. 1983. "Dilemmas of the Nicaraguan Revolution." In *The Future of Central America*, edited by Richard R. Fagen and Olga Pellicer. Stanford, Calif.: Stanford University Press.

———. 1984. "Geopolítica de la crisis regional." Cuadernos de Pensamiento Propio. Managua, Nicaragua: CRIES.

INTAL (Instituto para la Integración de América Latina). 1986. *El proceso de integración en América Latina en 1985*. Buenos Aires: INTAL-BID.

———. 1989. *El proceso de integración en América Latina en 1988*. Buenos Aires: INTAL-BID.

Karnes, Thomas L. 1961. *The Failure of Union: Central America 1824–1960*. Chapel Hill: University of North Carolina Press.

Menjivar, Rafael. 1988. "Centroamérica: Hacia una integración para la paz," *Polémica*, segunda época, 4 (January–April): 14–27.

SIECA (Secretaría Permanente del Tratado General de Integración Económica Centroamericana). 1988. Carta Informativa No. 316. Guatemala: SIECA, February.

Torres-Rivas, Edelberto. 1985. "Report on the Condition of Central American Refugees and Migrants." Occasional Paper Series. Washington, D.C.: Hemispheric Migration Project, Georgetown University.

SOUTH AMERICA

9

The Transformation of South America's Borderlands

William H. Bolin

BACKGROUND

There are more than 18,000 miles of boundaries separating the countries of South America—nearly twice the length of the internal land borders in Europe, Scandinavia, and the Balkans west of the Russian Empire, and over ten times the length of the U.S.-Mexico border. The South American borders separate countries that differ not only culturally and racially, but even more in their levels of economic and social development. Theoretically, this provides the possibility for complementary trade, and also for regional conflict. Historically, however, most South American frontiers have experienced little trade or cross-border flows of people, and for the most part they have also been conflict free relative to other world regions.

If one compares international conflict among the independent nations of South America with those occupying Western Europe since the end of the Napoleonic Wars, the results are illuminating. Notwithstanding many more miles of boundaries and high levels of diversity, since the middle of the nineteenth century South American countries have had relatively few conflicts and have developed surprisingly little economic interdependence compared with post-Napoleonic Europe. The reasons for this must go far beyond linguistic or tribal differences between European peoples and the basically two-language population of the South American continent. There are even greater cultural differences, for example, between the largely indigenous population of Bolivia and the European-descended Argentines than there are between any two European countries. The contrasts between largely black Portuguese-speaking northern Brazil and mainly mestizo Spanish-speaking Venezuela are almost as great.

While Europe was torn by over a century of wars costing millions of lives, in comparative terms South America has had a few infrequent skirmishes. The War of the Pacific in the 1880s and the Chaco War of the 1930s are the main exceptions. More people died at Stalingrad alone in World War II. While intra-European trade and European economic interdependence have grown substantially in spite of major European wars every generation or so, South American countries, with few exceptions, historically have neither traded nor invested to a significant extent with each other.[1] For centuries, the emptiness of South America's border regions worked to insulate the nations of the continent from both trade and conflict.

Given the original settlement patterns of the colonial period and the ways in which those patterns physically limited cross-national economic integration, one would expect that South American border regions would be largely undeveloped and marginal. This was certainly the case until the last three decades, when a number of South American national border zones suddenly began experiencing dramatic growth and development in transportation, communications, agriculture, industry, and mining production. This development has been accompanied by increasing human settlement in border regions. At the same time, contact between settlements along South American borders—both direct or through electronic communications—has grown enormously, generating both new opportunities for cooperation and new threats of friction.

Overall population growth in South America has been impressive over the last three decades. While much of this growth was directed at urban areas through internal migration, it is less well known that some of the border provinces are the fastest-growing regions in individual countries. In Argentina, for example, while greater Buenos Aires grew 17 percent between 1970 and 1980, the growth of three border subregions was even greater: Tierra del Fuego territory, 87.7 percent; Santa Cruz Province, 36 percent; and Neuquen Province, 57.8 percent. In Brazil, the Rio de Janeiro metropolitan area grew 26.1 percent during the 1970–1980 period, but border provinces expanded even more rapidly: Amazonas, 50.6 percent; Roraima, 96.7 percent; and Rondonia, 331.4 percent. Obviously these regions still remained sparsely populated. For example, Rondonia State, nearly half the size of France, still only had about two persons per square kilometer in 1980, but its string of uncontrollable towns and settlements along rivers and new roads gave it an overall population of nearly one-half million with important economic, social, and political impact compared with a decade before. The Brazilian city

---

[1] In spite of major efforts to increase them, intraregional Latin American exports as a percentage of total exports rose only from 8.8 percent in 1960 to 16 percent in 1975 and then declined to 12.8 percent in 1987 (J. Wilkie and Pertal 1990: table 2609).

of Porto Velho, about 150 miles from the Bolivian border (and over 1,600 miles from Rio) grew from 64,522 in 1970 to 134,621 in 1980. In Venezuela, Caracas grew 48 percent from 1961 to 1971, but in the same period some boundary regions expanded even faster: Bolívar State, 83.4 percent, and Amazonas Territory, 84.5 percent (R. Wilkie 1984: 98, 150, 420).

The expansion of transportation and communications has hastened the spread of population and development toward boundary zones. There are now several flights each day between Buenos Aires and the town of Río Grande on remote Tierra del Fuego. The Trans-Amazon and other highways in Brazil have reached Bolivian, Peruvian, and Venezuelan borders. In Venezuela, computers regularly transmit data between Puerto Ordaz on the Orinoco River and Caracas. Television signals are easily received by Argentines and Chileans from each other's stations along the border, and by Brazilians and Venezuelans along their common boundary. All now are being reached by satellites from transmitters inside and outside the continent.

Still, the historic "unresolved border questions" on the continent have not entirely disappeared.[2] On the contrary, as each previously uninhabited forest, desert, swamp, or offshore island becomes more populated or has its resources developed, the nearby boundary becomes more strategic in economic and political terms. It is worth noting that nitrate deposits in the Atacama Desert and potential oil reserves of eastern Bolivia were significant factors in the Chaco and Pacific wars. Such boundary resources could create territorial conflict between neighboring nations in various parts of the continent.

Even boundary regions once thought to be distant from national capitals and human contact are rapidly becoming integrated into national development, modernization, and domestic politics. In just the past two years there has been a resurgence of interest in continental economic integration based on reduction of trade barriers—a trend reinforced by more freely functioning domestic markets. All this is likely to keep borders in the public mind more than in the past. Minor incidents of border friction will be more noticed in capital cities when the border is developed.

BOUNDARIES, CONTINENTAL STABILITY, AND
ECONOMIC DEVELOPMENT

The pace of change along various borders of the continent has been so dramatic that an understanding of the frontier situations of South America is now important to any analysis of the long-term outlook for continental peace and economic development.

---

[2] Ireland 1938 and Burr 1955 provide a good perspective on historical border disputes and their origins.

Scholars have long recognized borders as pressure points. The global importance of frontier pressure for foreign affairs was reflected in a series of lectures at UCLA in 1940 as World War II began to be felt in its full dimensions. The lectures were published in 1941 a few months before Pearl Harbor. Reading them now provides valuable perspective. Malbone Graham, who chaired the lectures, writing the preface to their publication on July 19, 1941, said it very clearly: "it is precisely in proportion as states become integrated, rub shoulders more closely, that frontiers rise in importance because they are the media through which and across which the modern world passes" (Graham 1941: viii). Writing in the same volume, Roland Hussey, referring specifically to frontier questions in the Americas, looked forward from 1940 and concluded, "There is probably no method which will assure the avoidance of the dangers of frontiers. But at least, we of the Americas may thank our fates for space in which still to grow" (p. 139).

One only has to overlay a population map of South America in 1940 on a topographic map of the continent to see what Professor Hussey had in mind. In cultural and economic terms South America had been an archipelago of "population islands" separated by deserts, jungles, mountain ranges, or simply vacant territory. South American peoples appear to have neither fought nor traded with each other, largely because there was little cross-border communication. Navigable water would have brought greater contact (and probably more conflict) than any interaction along their physical land borders, which were mainly vast uninhabited lands.

These border spaces were not all impenetrable, even in 1940. In the few decades since then, boundary territory has indeed been penetrated at an accelerating pace. Roads—from high-speed highways to dusty truck and bus routes—now link all major cities in South America. A large part of the Amazon jungle, the Andes, the Chaco, and Patagonia—nearly all of the huge regions historically perceived as remote—now can be reached by scheduled bus, truck, or airplane service. New agricultural development zones have been created in frontier regions while others are being utilized more intensively. Hamlets and trading posts of the 1940s turned into towns with rotary clubs and chambers of commerce.[3] Some have become major cities. Dams and factories have been erected and, above all, people are settling in frontier areas which hardly anyone on either side of the border even noticed a few decades ago.

Exactly to what degree and where has Dr. Hussey's "space still to grow" been filled by development? What have been the economic, political, social, and ecological impacts of this expansion? To what extent

---

[3]For example, Rio Branco (on the Rio Acre) and Porto Velho (on the Rio Madeira) near Brazil's western border had rotary club memberships of over thirty businessmen each by 1985. (Westwood Village, California, had 125 members in the same year). See Rotary International 1985.

will borderland development pose new threats for peace, development, or cultural progress for a quarter-billion people? What lessons can be drawn from other frontier situations which have been more extensively studied? What are the implications of these phenomena for U.S. policy and U.S. welfare?

These questions suggest a rich arena of inquiry for scholars of international relations and economic development in the Americas. The recent emergence of borderlands research as an academic subfield reflects the need for scholarly answers to changing boundaries in all of the Americas. New techniques and approaches to interdisciplinary border studies have been developed in the study of the U.S.-Mexico boundary. There is potential to build significantly on that experience with regard to similar evolving frontiers in the rest of the hemisphere. In South America one fruitful approach might involve gathering data on a number of commonly agreed indices of economic growth and cultural contact in frontier areas. These could cover information as diverse as population, number of telephones, reported border trade, agricultural production, number of automobile club members, number of schools, number of scheduled buses per week, number of post offices, etc. This kind of information could monitor the degrees of development and cross-border contact in each boundary region to permit more precise tracking of development trends and projection of their social impact.

Analyzing a large number of indices of growth in border provinces for the past four decades appears worthwhile in spite of the intrinsic problem of gathering information on historically unimportant areas. The construction of a statistical matrix of border areas with various indicators of growth or contact would allow the more precise establishment of priorities for the study of South American frontiers by showing exactly where and to what degree each frontier is being transformed by human contact. Meanwhile, the recent acceleration of events in a few zones makes their importance evident.

SOME EXAMPLES OF BORDERLAND DEVELOPMENT IN
SOUTH AMERICA

Among the many boundary zones in South America that were isolated and undeveloped forty years ago, four regions in particular have displayed striking levels of economic growth. They include the lower Orinoco Valley, the Itaipu/Paraná River zone, the extreme southern borders of Argentina and Chile, and the Amazon Basin/eastern Andes frontier.

THE LOWER ORINOCO VALLEY

The first region of transformation was the lower Orinoco Valley, opened to development by a spectacular mitigation of malaria when DDT became available after World War II. The conquest of the malaria threat, followed by systematic development efforts under each successive postwar Venezuelan government, resulted first in the opening of one of the world's richest iron ore deposits on the lower Orinoco. This would be followed by subsequent development of important bauxite deposits. As part of a long-term national effort to use petroleum income to diversify the economy, vast amounts of cheap hydroelectric power were created on the Caroni River, leading from the highlands of the Brazilian border north to the Orinoco.

By the 1980s, the Caroni River had a hydroelectric capacity of some ten million kilowatts. This power was used to establish a new iron and steel industry (based on the Orinoco iron mine), which by 1983 was employing 16,000 workers, while reportedly creating another 160,000 indirect jobs (Sidor n.d.).

The availability of low-cost power in the lower Caroni River, combined with good access to overseas markets via ports on the Orinoco River, also gave rise to the development of a major aluminum industry in the same region. Cheap power and transport were first used in the 1960s to fabricate imported aluminum, then to manufacture aluminum from imported bauxite. The discovery of bauxite deposits in the Orinoco watershed allowed direct integrated production of aluminum from mine to finished product. The whole process was aided by extremely low-cost energy available from both hydroelectric dams and natural gas, all in the same region.

The steel mills, aluminum factories, and a wide range of secondary processors now are in full operation and monitored by a multistory computer center. There are large plantings of pine forest on previously unusable land—all superimposed over a major gas and oil field and arrayed around an ocean port (Puerto Ordaz) with modern bulk-handling facilities. In 1949 Puerto Ordaz consisted of an iron ore dock and a camp for miners near a small village of some four thousand persons at San Félix. The Puerto Ordaz-Ciudad Guayana urban complex and the administrative center of Ciudad Bolívar (colonial Angostura) combined by 1985 to form an urban population on the lower Orinoco of over 400,000 people, complete with supermarkets, theaters, world-class hotel facilities, and a university campus.

Meanwhile, that huge jump in population and surge in productivity have resulted in vastly improved communications and have caused roads to be built—and in the past few years, paved—all the way down to the Brazilian border through a zone which could not even be visited legally without a special permit from the authorities as recently as ten years ago. Now in the dry season one can take a bus from Manaus on the Amazon to Boa Vista on the Rio Branco via Tumaremo, Venezuela, to Ciudad Guayana on the Orinoco and on to Caracas. The paved portion of the road passes within fifty miles west of Mount Roraima, where Conan Doyle set his 1912 novel, *The Lost World*. It passes even closer to Indian tribes about whose exact location and culture little was known in 1940, when Roland Hussey was writing about "space still to grow" in Latin America.

The Brazilian and Guyanese governments in 1989 announced plans for building a road to link Georgetown, Guyana, and Manaus (via Boa Vista). This would, in effect, also connect Guyana's main population center by land with Venezuela for the first time (*Caribbean Insight* 12:4:11).

Large-scale clandestine gold mining has been going on in the southern Venezuela state of Bolívar and in Amazonas Territory for more than five years, generating uncontrolled immigration, lawlessness, and river pollution from hydraulic mining and use of mercury (*Wall Street Journal*, August 4, 1988: 1; *New York Times*, May 3, 1990). Forest clearing has taken place to enhance local food supply and gain mining access. Trucks and buses pass regularly between Venezuela and Brazil over this suddenly important border. The increasing gold production has been matched by similar activity on the Brazilian side of the Sierra Pacaraima and elsewhere down the Rio Branco system, often with supplies brought in from Ciudad Guayana rather than far-off Rio de Janeiro.[4]

Inevitably and tragically, these new developments have endangered the Yanomama Indians who span the frontier (*New York Times*, May 3, 1990). New airstrips, authorized and unauthorized, are scattered throughout the entire region of both countries. Venezuela and Brazil have both enhanced scheduled air service to the border, including a service inaugurated in 1989 between Georgetown, Guyana, and Boa Vista, Brazil, by Cruzeiro do Sul, the Brazilian airline. Along airstrips and rivers there is a new and alarming traffic in drugs en route from Colombia to the United States and Europe via Venezuela and Guyana.

Many Venezuelans now perceive Ciudad Guayana as a key strategic zone from the standpoint of national defense and internal stability. Hence, a modernized Venezuelan air base has been built in Tumaremo.[5] Brazil has long maintained a military presence at Boa Vista and this apparently has been given additional importance by Brazil for both internal and external reasons. Among other considerations, the potential foreign exchange income from much of the gold mining in the entire region still escapes return to the central banks of the two countries.

Malaria, once almost extinct in the border state of Bolívar, Venezuela, is now back in the area in a particularly virulent form, the

---

[4]When excessive flooding occurred in 1986, cutting off Boa Vista (the long-established town near Brazil's frontier with Venezuela) from the nearest Brazilian city (Manaus), the governor of Roraima State, Brazil, flew to Ciudad Guayana, Venezuela, instead of Brasilia, for emergency supplies. Author's interview with President Figuereido of Corporación de Guayana. S.A. (the government entity charged with overall development of the region), Ciudad Guayana, Venezuela, September 18, 1986.

[5]Author's interview with Senator (retired General) Alfonso Ravard, in Caracas, Venezuela, September 19, 1986. General Ravard was the first president of Corporación de Guayana and first president of Petróleos de Venezuela, S.A.

product of uncontrolled population movements and inadequate health facilities.[6] At the same time, the importance of the state in Venezuelan foreign trade, domestic economy, and domestic politics continues to expand.

THE ITAIPU/PARANÁ RIVER ZONE

Another frontier in the process of transition is the Itaipu area on the Paraná River system where Argentina, Brazil, and Paraguay meet. Over the past fifteen years, the world's largest hydroelectric project[7] has been built at a place where previously there were only a few sleepy towns and two hotels for the small number of tourists who came to view the famous Iguaçú Falls. The building of the dam was accompanied by new highways through southern Brazil and Paraguay, accelerating the linkage of Paraguay to the Atlantic Ocean. This relieved the country's dependence on the unpredictable Paraná-La Plata River system, which historically inhibited its exports, and shifted the focus of its foreign relations from Argentina toward Brazil. New transport and communication facilities have turned Paraguay and southwest Brazil into one of the world's leading sources of soybeans, while the sale of power by Paraguay to Brazil adds another major potential export for the former country.

The Itaipu Dam near the intersection of the borders of the three countries is now functioning and, as the steadily increasing availability of cheap power takes effect, a series of industrial projects are planned and being executed on the same basis as in the lower Orinoco region. Puerto Stroessner, once a modest settlement on the Paraguayan side of the Paraná, became a boomtown during the construction of the dam and has now grown to the size of a city. The movement of people and goods back and forth across the river is little controlled and this is leading to new problems: increasing public health disorders, smuggling, lawlessness. If not given attention, such problems will continue to grow as productivity in the border region rises (*New York Times*, June 6, 1988: A7). Meanwhile, farther down the Paraná in Argentina's Misiones Province, over 200,000 tons a year of wood pulp began to be produced in 1985, and new forest plantings continue (IDB 1986a: 4–5). Still another hydroelectric plant has been under construction for many years on the Paraná system at Yacyrita on the Argentina-Paraguay border. This dam is still incomplete, but the several billion dollars invested in the construction thus far have already transformed the surrounding area. Orders for twenty turbines to be financed by the Inter-American Development Bank were placed in late 1987, but there is rising doubt about their need (IDB 1987: 5).

---

[6] Author's interview with Dr. Arnaldo Gabaldón, Universidad Central de Venezuela, Caracas, September 19, 1986. (Dr. Gabaldón led the antimalaria efforts in the 1940s.)

[7] Its eventual capacity will reach 12.6 million kilowatts (Ministerio de Minas 1985).

The control of the flow of water in the Paraná River system has, of course, been a major transnational agenda item in the planning and construction of the Itaipu and other dams on the system. It is still one with potential for controversy among the several countries touched by the river. The key issues have been river transport, flood control, and ecological management.[8]

THE FAR SOUTH, ARGENTINA AND CHILE

A third evident zone of borderland development and potential confrontation has been the "Far South" region of the continent—including Patagonia, the Straits of Magellan, Tierra del Fuego, and the Beagle Channel. Only a decade ago, Argentine and Chilean tanks faced each other on the low saddle over the Andes at Río Turbio—to the alarm and astonishment of local residents on both sides who, when they were very few, got along together remarkably well for more than a century. Behind those 1980 bilateral tensions lay the very rapid development of resources—oil, gas, coal, fish, wood products, and chemicals—on the southern tip of the continent, as well as programs of conscious industrial expansion to populate the far south of both countries. By 1985 such government-subsidized programs had created over thirty small factories on Argentine Tierra del Fuego and a commercial-industrial free zone on the outskirts of Punta Arenas, Chile.

Today the development continues as confrontation has been largely replaced by cooperation. Exported forest products from southern Chile tripled from 1974 to 1986 (Secretaría Regional 1987: 22). Between Puerto Natales and Punta Arenas there is a new open-pit coal mine, which began to produce in 1988—at the rate of over 800,000 tons a year. Local commercial use of natural gas doubled from 1974 to 1986 in the extreme southern region of Chile. In 1988, on the Straits of Magellan north of Punta Arenas, the world's largest methanol plant, dedicated entirely for export, went into production, based on steadily increasing natural gas availability. For several decades both Argentina and Chile have produced oil and gas on both sides of the Straits of Magellan. In fact, in a little-noticed program of cooperation, the two state oil companies extract gas from the same field, which lies directly under the straits and spans the border. This program operated even during the period of bilateral tension between the two countries from the late 1970s through the mid-1980s.[9]

---

[8] Author's interviews with members of the Braun-Menéndez family and with Coronel Gustavo Delfor González Sass in Buenos Aires, Argentina, November 1987. The Braun-Menéndez family are owners of large sheep ranches in the far south of both countries. Coronel González commanded a tank regiment at Río Turbio during the confrontation with Chile.

[9] Author's interview with Major General Claudio López Silva, Intendente, Region XII, at his office in Punta Arenas, Chile, and personal visit to gas installations on Straits of Magellan, December 3, 1987.

Other opportunities for cooperative development exist in transport, cross-border labor movement, and tourism. With the resolution of the Beagle Channel dispute these are now being addressed. Seafood exports, including cultivated fresh chilled salmon from the Puerto Montt-Chiloe area, have expanded rapidly. By 1988, sixty-five firms (mainly Chilean) were operating in one hundred different locations and were projecting annual exports of ten thousand metric tons.[10] All registered seafood shipments from the extreme south of Chile doubled from 1980–86 (Secretaría Regional 1987: 22). No one knows the amount of open-sea fish being taken offshore by the huge Russian, Asian, Spanish, and Norwegian factory ships that refuel regularly at Ushuaia on the Beagle Channel. In December 1988 the territorial governor there stated that there was almost always one of those ships refueling or resupplying at the small Ushuaia dock.[11]

The total population of the southernmost cities of Chile grew from 77,000 to 119,000 from 1970 to 1982, according to official estimates, and growth appears to be continuing at the same pace. "Roll-on/roll-off" ship service through southern Chile and Argentina's southern frontier is expanding.[12]

Under arrangements of the past few years, trucks and buses, under customs and immigration "seals," can now go from central Chile to Punta Arenas, Chile, on the Straits of Magellan via the Argentine roads. However, long-standing border tensions between the two countries convinced Chile of the need to build its own internal land connection. The first "all land-all Chile" road connection between the far south of Chile and the rest of the country has been under construction for years. This extraordinary road, called the Carretera Austral, cuts across high elevations of the Andes, over glaciers and along dangerous mountain slopes, to its present terminus south of Puerto Montt. The project is not without detractors; the Austral road project has been criticized as unnecessarily expensive compared with improvement of Chilean ocean transport facilities or expanded use of underutilized Argentine roads.

Interestingly, during the very same period in which the Carretera Austral was under construction, populations along the Argentina-Chile border were forming local binational committees to deal with border concerns, with no opposition from the central governments on either side of the border. Committees sought to deal with such border prob-

---

[10] Author's interview with Pablo E. Aguilera Marín, Sub-Gerente of Unilever affiliate, Pesquera Mares Australes Ltda., in the course of a visit to production facilities near Puerto Montt, Chile, November 27, 1987.

[11] Author's interview with Territorial Governor Alfredo Alberto Ferro at his office in Ushuaia, Argentina, December 11 1987.

[12] Author's interviews with businessmen of both ports and the captain of M.S. *Evangelistas* en route from Puerto Montt to Puerto Natales, Chile, November 27–30, 1987.

lems as improved transport for tourism, pest control for local livestock, and immigration control for workers crossing the border daily between work and home. There have also been attempts to create cooperative arrangements over the use of roads and the transboundary movement of regional commodities such as lumber.

On the Argentine side, in southern Patagonia, informed local government and business people in 1987 estimated the growth of border area settlements as follows: Río Gallegos (Santa Cruz Province), from 42,000 to 75,000 since 1980; Ushuaia/Río Grande (Tierra del Fuego), from 15,000 to 50,000 since 1980.[13] The growth has come mainly as a result of petroleum exploration and duty-free assembly plants. Although there is no way to verify the above estimates until the next census, there is clear evidence of rapid growth in the amount of new construction, which is placing a strain on local infrastructure. The growth figures on the Argentine side of Tierra del Fuego roughly match recent Chilean government estimates concerning the same Argentine towns.

THE AMAZON BASIN/EASTERN ANDES FRONTIER

A fourth area of rapid development along previously empty borders lies in the often-rich alluvial plain on the eastern slope of the Andes leading down into the Amazon Basin, Mato Grosso, and the Chaco. Santa Cruz de la Sierra, now a major city for oil production, agriculture, and narcotics transshipment, had one semi-paved street and no buildings over two stories high forty years ago. It was linked to Cochabamba and La Paz by a new road, progressively improved into a major highway since then. Bolivia thus opened a huge zone of cattle, cotton, and food production in an effort to create a new and more productive life for the Indians living on the bleak, depleted lands of the Andean Altiplano. Oil and gas production and exports led to further economic expansion, and soon long-known iron deposits were further explored. More recently, Beni Province has seen steady clearing of forests and grazing of cattle closer and closer to Brazil, with dangerous implications for unique wildlife and tropical forests in the area.

Similar road-building efforts over the Andes in Peru and Ecuador have opened up new lands for development, including oil and gas exploration. All this has attracted populations into areas along the Brazilian border that were previously virtually empty. Ecuadorian and Peruvian army patrols had minor border clashes in the 1980s. Iquitos, Peru, a long-existing port on the Amazon, has boomed. Drugs form only part of the explanation for this growth, although enhanced transporta-

---

[13] Author's interviews in Río Gallegos, Ushuaia, and Río Grande, Argentina, with local businessmen, foreign oil exploration executives, and church officials, December 1987. Also, 1987 interviews with the territorial governor of Argentine Tierra del Fuego, Ushuaia, and the governor of Chilean Zone XII, Punta Arenas.

tion and communications facilities have expedited coca production, and cocaine dealers have added their own networks all along the eastern borderlands of Peru, Ecuador, Bolivia—and Colombia.

Brazil, meanwhile, in a high-priority national program, has pushed its own roads, communications, and agricultural development—some planned, some unplanned—westward to its frontiers. All along Brazil's western borders the forces of change, in the form of agricultural expansion and livestock production, have been accelerating in recent years. Uncontrolled forest burning and lumber cutting in western Brazil—first in Mato Grosso, then Rondonia, and later Acre—have caught the eye of the world press, mainly because of the ecological damage these developments are imposing on the Amazon region. Important new oil and gas discoveries since 1986 in the western Amazon near Peru and Bolivia have already resulted in proven production and pipeline construction (*New York Times*, November 16, 1990: C1). South of the Amazon, in the once empty western Pantanal swamp of western Mato Grosso, a new uncontrolled gold rush is affecting that wetland area significantly and swiftly (*New York Times*, August 12, 1991: A4). Rondonia State has a serious new problem with the passage of drugs from Peru and Bolivia, which is bringing with it the usual lawlessness, corruption, and wild spending (*New York Times*, August 20, 1991: A4). These problems cry out for borderland cooperation between Brazil and its neighbors and are now attracting Brazilian government attention. Such concepts of border cooperation are beginning to take practical shape among the Andean countries themselves (see Ganster 1990).

Bolivia, Peru, and Argentina tentatively agreed in 1987 to open their border areas by connecting their national rail systems. This plan would offer continuous transcontinental rail service from the Atlantic to the Pacific oceans for the first time (*La Nación* 1987: 1, 6). As of mid-1991, the financing required for this project remained uncertain. However, a major topic in the September 1990 visit of Argentine President Menem to Chile was the potential use of Chilean ports for the export of fruits and vegetables from Mendoza and other western provinces of Argentina. This idea has been promoted for years by Argentine producers in Mendoza and by Chilean export merchants in Santiago, but in the past it generated little interest among central government authorities in either nation. It might now proceed, against the background of new free trade negotiations all over the continent.

CONCLUSION

South America's borderlands are no doubt in a state of rapid transition, spurred by improved physical access, communications, population movements, and recent accelerating movements to remove trade barriers. Their future will inevitably involve the continuous weighing of costs of ecological threats and social distortions against the advantages of economic growth. The reality is that the borderlands offer opportunities for enhanced incomes among poor South Americans, something few elected leaders will seek to block. But there are also multiple dangers in the rapid development of border frontier areas. They include ecological destruction as well as crime, deteriorating public health, and increased potential for international conflict. There are many opportunities for joint environmental planning, for rational development of natural gas and minerals, for improved law and order, for cheaper communications, for better public health, and even for drug control. However, conflict resolution and cooperative effort will demand both more attention in the capital cities of South American countries and more systematic gathering of information about border areas. The task is made difficult by the very fact that, historically, border zones have been regions of marginal national importance.

Interest in South American borderlands in the past has been centered in such international entities as the Organization of American States (OAS), the Economic Commission for Latin America (ECLA), and the Inter-American Development Bank, through its Institute of Latin American Integration in Buenos Aires.[14] There has also been ongoing interest in borders among the military of most South American countries.[15] In Washington there has been a recent escalation of interest, not so much motivated by border regions themselves as by the fact that drug smuggling and environmental destruction happen to intersect there, in what are still very empty spaces despite recent growth. In the end, in the broad sweep of both national and international affairs, the meaning of borderland development has received relatively little attention, even where the effects have been obvious.

Now, with the dramatically increased discussion of free trade throughout the hemisphere, interest in South American border questions can be expected to rise. More freely functioning domestic markets in South America, resulting in more internationally competitive exports, lead logically to reduction of artificial barriers for intracontinental trade. This in turn points to great importance for those borders across which increased trade can pass.[16] The Andean countries (minus Chile) have entered into the initial stages of new free trade negotiations. Brazil, Uruguay, Paraguay, and Argentina are in serious negotiations concerning the formation of another free trade zone on the southern continent. Chile is studying both projects while continuing in practice the active

---

[14] Various Organization of American States regional studies are summarized in OAS 1984. See also the series of four OAS studies on the Tratado de Cooperación Amazónica (reports of seminars and meetings), 1985 and 1986; IDB 1988: 79–80; IDB 1986b.

[15] Londono 1977 is a representative military study and provides a short review of studies at military institutes of other Latin American countries.

[16] For a short summary of these developments see IDB 1991: 3.

expansion of trade with neighbors through various agreements for expediting border movement of goods and people.

Thus, improved transport, expanded communications, frontier settlement, and efforts to expand cross-border trade are all likely to focus more attention on various South American borderlands, catapulting these regions and the issues that affect them out of a past in which they received remarkably little interdisciplinary study.

REFERENCES

Burr, Robert. 1955. "The Balance of Power in Nineteenth Century South America: An Exploratory Essay," *Hispanic American Historical Review* 35 (February).

Ganster, Paul. 1990. "Andean Border Integration: Report on a Seminar in Lima, Peru, 3–6 July 1989," *Journal of Borderlands Studies* (Spring): 95–153.

Graham, Malbone W., ed. 1941. *Frontiers of the Future*. Berkeley: University of California Press.

IDB (International Development Bank). 1986a. "A Harvest of Cellulose on the Paraná River," *IDB News*, July.

———. 1986b. "La frontera como factor de integración," *Integración Latinoamericana* 118 (special issue). Washington, D.C.: IDB, November.

———. 1987. *IDB News*, September.

———. 1988. *Economic and Social Progress in Latin America*. Washington, D.C.: Inter-American Development Bank.

———. 1991. "Latin Economies Opening Up," *The IDB*, May.

Ireland, Gordon. 1938. *Boundaries and Conflicts in South America*. Cambridge: Harvard University Press.

La Nación (Buenos Aires). 1987. "Argentina-Bolivia Rail Link," 118, no. 417003 (November 4).

Londono, Julio. 1977. *Geopolítica de Suramerica*. Bogotá: Imprenta y Publicaciones de las Fuerzas Militares.

Ministerio de Minas y Energías. 1985. *Annual Report of ELETROBRAS-Centrais Electricas Brasileiras S.A.* Brasilia: Ministerio de Minas y Energías.

OAS (Organization of American States). 1984. *Integrated Regional Development Planning*. Washington, D.C.: Department of Regional Development, OAS.

Rotary International. 1985. *Official Directory of Rotary International*. Evanston, Ill.: Rotary International.

Secretaría Regional de Planificación y Coordinación. 1987. *Exposición de Intendente Mayor General Don Claudio López Silva a S.E., El Presidente de la República Capitán General Don Augustino Pinochet Ugarte*. Punta Arenas, Chile: Secretaría Regional de Planificación y Coordinación, XIIa Región, Magallanes y Antártica Chilena.

Sidor. n.d. "Briefing Paper, Puerto Ordaz, 1984." Sidor Institutional and Public Relations Office, obtained in course of visit to installations, September 18, 1986.

Wilkie, James W., and Adam Pertal, eds. 1990. *Statistical Abstract of Latin America*, vol. 24. Los Angeles: Latin American Center, University of California, Los Angeles.

Wilkie, Richard W. 1984. *Latin American Population and Urbanization Analysis 1950–1982*. Los Angeles: Latin American Center, University of California, Los Angeles.

10

National Security and Politics: The Colombia-Venezuela Border

John D. Martz

As two of the more durable democracies in the Latin America of the late twentieth century,[1] Colombia and Venezuela have also played important roles as regional powers in the conduct of hemispheric affairs.[2] The first of these Grancolombian states was a prime mover in the Contadora Group, which has labored on behalf of Central American peace in recent years. The latter, which had been internationally vigorous during much of the 1970s, has progressively increased its own exercise of leadership over the course of the last three decades.[3] At the same time, the two neighbors have often proceeded individually without undertaking collaborative action. Among other reasons, this has notably reflected historic disagreements concerning their common frontier. In modern times, a new set of problems has further complicated the relationship and aggravated relations between Bogotá and Caracas. Such intimidating questions as drug trafficking, smuggling, and guerrilla insurgencies have heightened the difficulties.

As a consequence, disputes revolving about the border have become more controversial as well as potentially divisive. Periodic arguments and angry exchanges are not uncommon. For Colombia, there are

---

This chapter was previously published in the *Journal of Inter American Studies and World Affairs* 30:4. Reprinted by permission of the journal.

[1] For a useful comparative analysis, see Peeler 1985.

[2] Useful discussions for Colombia include Silva Lujan 1985; Vázquez Carrizosa 1986. For Venezuela, see Ameringer 1986.

[3] The point was developed at length for the first two decades of Venezuela's democratic era in Martz 1977.

concerns that Venezuelan diplomatic intransigence is encouraging a military buildup. Venezuela, on the other hand, fears that Colombia's severe security problems are about to spill across the border. The currency of drugs, smuggling, and corruption has presented an array of political and socioeconomic challenges that is stubbornly resistant to resolution. Domestic political controversies in both countries have also mitigated against effective negotiations, although the exchange of diplomatic communications has been maintained through the years. Indeed, many points of dispute have become directly relevant to domestic politics in both countries.[4]

Typically, tradition in both countries follows customarily universal patterns, inasmuch as domestic issues and bread-and-butter questions are of far greater concern to the electorate. Foreign affairs do not serve as a lightning rod for public opinion, barring a major crisis or a perceived threat to national security and territorial integrity.[5] Even so, both countries have seen presidents in recent years who, whatever the relevance for internal politics, have exercised substantial authority and activism internationally. Prime examples in recent years have been Colombian president Belisario Betancur (1982–86) and Venezuela's Carlos Andrés Pérez (1974–79). In this essay, however, attention will be directed toward the Colombian struggle to deal with the security threats mounted by narcotics and by guerrilla insurgents challenging the very survival of the system. For Venezuela, it will assess the impact of border affairs as a source of domestic concern.

Survey data will bring particular insight to the present Venezuelan case, while the Colombian attitudes are ascertainable only in more impressionistic fashion. More important, however, are questions about the impact of bilateral problems on domestic political controversy inside both countries today. These are also linked to an expanding "dirty war" which threatens to grip both nations, and might ultimately pose a challenge to the durability of democracy in Colombia and Venezuela. Our first task will be to sketch the contours of border-related problems, both those of historic character and others which reflect characteristics of contemporary life in Grancolombia. Having done so, we will proceed to examine the political impact and its potential consequences in each country.

BORDER ISSUES AND DIPLOMATIC PROBLEMS

The most fundamental bilateral issue concerns the actual location of the boundary, which remains a source of bilateral disagreement.[6] This in turn has been linked to questions of cattle smuggling, illegal entry and

---

[4] The linkage of foreign policy to domestic affairs is treated in Martz 1984.

[5] For a succinct discussion by a Venezuelan scholar, see Rey 1986.

[6] A recent Colombian foreign minister analyzes matters in Vázquez Carrizosa 1983.

exit, and commercial dealings between citizens of the two countries, not to mention the value of natural resources, either beneath the soil or under the seas, which are not subject to international jurisdiction. The original controversy can be traced back to the winning of independence from Spain, and to much-debated provisions of the 1845 treaty between Madrid and Caracas. Boundary limits were not clearly demarcated, leaving Venezuela with the necessity of negotiating agreements with Colombia, as well as Brazil and British Guiana (Great Britain) elsewhere.

After a half-century of disagreement, in 1881 Bogotá and Caracas called in the Spanish king to arbitrate. Both argued their cases on the principle of *uti possidetus juris*; Columbia claimed the colonial viceroyalty of Santa Fe de Bogotá, while Venezuela sought recognition of the territory of the Caracas Captaincy-General in 1810, when the revolutionary wars broke out. These had produced overlapping claims along the Maracaibo Basin. When the king issued a decision in 1891, it required binational agreement over the source of the Río de Oro. The responsible committee produced findings which Venezuela rejected, and not until the 1930s was there further progress on surveying the frontier. There was still a dispute over portions running along the Guajira Peninsula, one which survives to this day.

This northwestern area was the focus of a 1941 treaty signed by Eduardo Santos for Colombia and Venezuela's General Eleazar López Contreras. The land frontier through the Guajira provided Venezuela a narrow stretch some sixty miles long and less than ten miles in width. Running to the village of Castilletes near the northeasternmost point, it led to Venezuelan claims that Gulf of Venezuela waters from that point of entry to the south lay under their control. Colombia, however, draws its own maritime line from the tip of the peninsula at a different angle. The result of all this is a triangle of overlapping claims off the Guajira coast, the submarine mineral deposits of which are relatively unknown. Given the contradictory interpretations by the two countries, in combination with incompatible agreements and mappings dating from the colonial period, there remains more than ample room for disagreement and misunderstanding.

While problems of smuggling, illegal migration, and related issues have continued to irritate Colombian-Venezuelan border relations, the question of maritime jurisdiction has been, until quite recently, the single source of greatest mutual irritation. Venezuela in particular has tended to view the 1941 accord as having left them shortchanged, with the intensity of sentiment inevitably exacerbated by assumption of large petroleum deposits in the offshore coastal waters.[7] Given the fact that "the continental shelf under the Gulf of Venezuela geologically resem-

---

[7] A characteristic Venezuelan view is that of the respected leftist and former presidential candidate José Vicente Rangel (1980).

bles the oil-rich neighboring Lake Maracaibo, delimiting the territorial waters of the Gulf of Venezuela could constitute one of the most important allocations of strategic resources between any two countries in the twentieth century" (Myers 1985: 17). Petroleum-related interests became more acute in 1966 when Colombia granted new concessions to multinationals in the Gulf of Venezuela. At this juncture, moreover, the fact that Colombia claims nearly two-thirds of territorial seas in the gulf has further "added to Venezuelan concern over . . . issues such as smuggling and illegal immigration into the country" (Ewell 1984: 163).

It was the decade of the 1960s which saw increasingly massive illegal migration of Colombians to Venezuela in search of jobs and higher wages. As Ameringer has written, "Venezuelans resented having to compete for jobs with the illegal immigrants, and Colombians charged that the immigrants were being exploited because of their unprotected status. The number of illegal immigrants was substantial, reportedly around 500,000 during the 1960s" (Herman 1976: 28). This was also a time during which there was an estimated annual flow of 200,000–300,000 head of cattle into Venezuela. But beyond both the illegal immigration and the smuggling of cattle, however, was still "the unresolved question of the Gulf of Venezuela boundary and contiguous offshore oil deposits" (Martz 1977: 183). Bogotá and especially Caracas believed that potential oil riches in the continental shelf rendered the sea frontier especially critical.

Early in the 1970s extended bilateral discussions were held in Rome, but despite efforts to proceed through quiet diplomacy the talks were broken off in 1973. Colombian proposals that the dispute be submitted to international arbitration were unacceptable to Caracas (República de Venezuela 1971: I). Not until the beginning of the next decade were serious efforts renewed to repair the dispute. With the governments in Bogotá and Caracas sharing a deepening concern over Nicaragua's shift to the left, there was a concomitant fear over a recrudescence of Cuban-supported guerrilla insurgency in the Caribbean Basin. If there were to be Colombian-Venezuelan collaboration, clearly the dispute over the Gulf of Venezuela required solution. Intense if quiet diplomatic activity throughout 1980 led to a joint announcement in early 1981 that a provisional draft had been accepted.

Popularly known as the Hypothesis of Caraballeda, it was to prove politically inflammatory in Venezuela. In Colombia the government of Julio César Turbay Ayala did not encounter undue difficulty with an agreement whose details had been masked, and there were indications that Colombia's armed forces would not object strenuously. The preoccupation of the latter was a resolution of the conflict which otherwise, it was felt, would encourage yet additional arms purchases on the part of the Venezuelans. In Caracas, however, the administration of Luis Herrera Campíns found the going anything but smooth. Foreign Minister

José Zambrano Velasco met with a large group of military officers to explain the draft before it was released to the public. The result was strong and vociferous opposition.

At that time Venezuela had three infantry brigades posted along its western border, which included much of its artillery and armed forces (*El Universal* [Caracas], July 15, 1982). There was private uncertainty as to their general state of military readiness, and there was particular concern that any Colombian attack against the Maracaibo Basin oil fields would be especially perilous.[8] The military itself was inclined to the view that it required stronger capabilities along the frontier. This would presumably enhance national security while helping to produce more favorable terms from diplomatic negotiation. The 1981 draft agreement, the military also believed, essentially gave away important national territorial claims. Senior officers therefore prepared to testify against the treaty in hearings before the Senate.

As opposition to the still-unannounced accord spread, the Venezuelan left, spearheaded by the Movimiento al Socialismo (MAS), mounted a public campaign against the proposal. There were public claims that the Hypothesis of Caraballeda would give away more than half of Venezuela's presumed entrance to the Gulf of Venezuela. Heated and highly vocal criticism was directed by the Frente de Defensa de la Integridad Territorial y la Soberanía de Venezuela, which polemicized against the alleged "surrender" to Colombia. In response, Herrera Campíns felt compelled to direct the foreign minister to cease efforts to produce a final draft agreement. Within a few weeks the president told interviewers that any further negotiations on the Gulf of Venezuela would await the inauguration of his successor in January 1984.

With the breakdown of talks, as Myers later wrote, Bogotá and Caracas therefore "found themselves competing with each other for the support of their Caribbean Basin neighbors, including some whose leaders were hostile to the democratic system prevailing in both" (Myers 1985: 18). Furthermore, while the Venezuelans anticipated renewed talks by their next government in 1984, the Colombians felt that they had already made all possible concessions in accepting the 1981 draft treaty (*El Tiempo* [Bogotá], August 13, 1981). Even so, the next initiative came from Bogotá with the August 1982 inauguration of Belisario Betancur. The new foreign minister, Rodrigo Lloreda Caicedo, promptly announced that negotiations remained desirable and carried high priority for Colombia. Moreover, if Venezuela proved intractable, his government was prepared to seek international mediation (*El Tiempo*, August 19, 1982).

The mechanism to be employed would be the Treaty of Non-Aggression, Conciliation, Arbitration, and Judicial Settlement signed on

---

[8]The gulf dispute and its background are outlined in detail in the newsweekly *Resúmen* (Caracas), August 17, 1980.

December 17, 1939, in Bogotá, which had lain quiescent and largely forgotten for some years. Designed originally to assure pacific solution of whatever controversies might arise between the two neighbors, its scope went well beyond frontier questions. Whether or not the International Court of Justice or a specialized ad hoc arbitration commission would be employed was not spelled out. But in any event, Belisario Betancur was far more deeply involved, both personally and politically, in the ongoing Contadora peace process. The Herrera government was meanwhile withdrawing increasingly from foreign affairs, and concerted efforts to renegotiate the gulf conflict did not seem propitious. Entirely aside from the many juridical complexities of the dispute, it was all too evident, as Lloreda Caicedo remarked, that the 1981 failure reflected domestic political problems (FBIS 1982).

THE FRUSTRATIONS OF DIPLOMACY AND POLITICS

Hazleton has written of Colombia and Venezuela that their border controversies "are especially sensitive issues, and diplomatic efforts to resolve them require popular support and a favorable endorsement by the main political parties" (1988: 264). When Jaime Lusinchi became the new Venezuelan president on February 2, 1984, he confronted a disrupted and turbulent economic situation which was of the first order. A program of domestic austerity was instituted, one in which foreign commitments were curtailed. Venezuela was even forced to require full cash payments for oil from Latin American consuming nations (*New York Times*, July 2, 1984). However, the appointment of Isidro Morales Paul as foreign minister underlined Lusinchi's initial intention of reopening negotiations, for Morales was an acknowledged authority on the law of the sea and on international arbitration.

Modest and informal conversations were conducted with Bogotá, where Augusto Ramírez Ocampo became foreign minister later in the year. There was a moment of fresh acrimony in December when Venezuela protested the violation of its territory by three Colombian military helicopters (*El Tiempo*, December 17, 1984). However, there was an apparent desire on both sides to proceed toward fresh negotiations. When Morales Paul was replaced by former foreign minister Simón Alberto Consalvi in March 1985, it was a response to internal government personnel shifts rather than to bilateral problems. Indeed, the Lusinchi government was proceeding to give more urgent attention to the relationship with Colombia, given the growing immediacy of a joint attack on international drug trafficking. For as the magnitude of Colombia's domestic difficulties with the burgeoning industry was becoming dramatically greater, the Venezuelan connection was also assuming larger proportions.

In September 1983 Venezuela had downed a private aircraft carrying 1,467 pounds of cocaine, valued at some U.S. $320 million (*Washington Post*, November 22, 1984). There were further signs that the nation had become a route for international drug shipments. By the following year Caracas estimated that as many as 150,000 Venezuelans were frequent users of cocaine, marijuana, methaqualone, and the cheap but popular semiprocessed cocaine paste known as *bazuka*. Justice Minister José Manzo González proclaimed the Lusinchi government's "war without quarter" against narcotics, while it was also reported that *mafiosi* connections were extending their influence in Venezuela. The result was a modest agreement whereby Venezuela and Colombia jointly decided to coordinate efforts at interdicting drug trade along the border. Bilateral relations were also improved when Presidents Betancur and Lusinchi met at the border to sign a trade agreement on February 23, 1985 (*El Espectador* [Bogotá], February 24, 1985).

The two presidents met again in June 1985, when they signed a joint document which, along with other points, "reiterated the purpose . . . of persevering in efforts to resolve by equitable and just solutions all matters related to the delimitation of marine and submarine areas." Betancur and Lusinchi further pledged themselves "to take a special interest in assuring full success of the negotiations which must be pursued . . . and have therefore resolved to initiate the study of operational means to do so" (Sureda Delgado 1987: 17). However, such exercises in rhetoric and public diplomacy did little to halt the devastating impact of drug trafficking and guerrilla activity, which were linked together in a number of complex institutional and sectoral networks.

Colombian insurgents, including bands from both the M-19 and the pro-Castro Ejército de Liberación Nacional (ELN), intensified their activities on both sides of the frontier. Venezuelan police stations were occasionally raided, whether deliberately or by accident. Added to such irritations were sporadic reports of Colombian fishing boats being seized by Venezuelan naval vessels, as well as Venezuelan troop incursions onto Colombian territory. The possibility of further meaningful talks was also dimmed following the calamitous November 1985 attack on the Justice Building by M-19 guerrillas. The military counterattack and subsequent destruction of the edifice, facing Bogotá's main public plaza, severely undermined both the authority and legitimacy of the Betancur government.

Only following the resounding electoral victory of Virgilio Barco Vivas and his subsequent August 1986 inauguration was the stage set for what proved a more serious effort between Bogotá and Caracas. In December of that year, Simón Alberto Consalvi traveled to Bogotá for a conference with his Colombian counterpart, Julio Londono Paredes.

Appearing to be the most serious undertaking since the mishandled 1981 draft, this was received by Colombia with a combination of enthusiasm and caution. The latter quality proved most appropriate, for Consalvi arrived under the strange injunction from Jaime Lusinchi not to discuss border problems. The Venezuelan foreign minister, who had reportedly urged Lusinchi to permit a diplomatic reopening of the border issue, had little choice but to skirt central questions. The Colombians were angered, and President Barco was privately acerbic in his comments.

Reports of the ill-prepared Consalvi trip and its decidedly unhelpful results produced a spate of criticism in Caracas. The response from a harried President Lusinchi, whose domestic policy was unraveling as oil prices continued to drop, was to convene an emergency meeting at Miraflores Palace with Venezuela's three living former presidents. Rafael Caldera and Luis Herrera Campíns of COPEI, the Social Christian party, gathered with Carlos Andrés Pérez of the social democratic Acción Democrática to review the situation with Lusinchi. Convened without prior preparation or a clear agenda on the part of Jaime Lusinchi, the meeting was wholly unproductive. With both Caldera and Pérez engaged in bitter partisan struggles for their two parties' respective nominations,[9] public attention centered on the interplay of personality and politics. There were no counterproposals to be announced, nor even a clearly enunciated policy on the part of the Venezuelan government.

Persuaded of the necessity for further talks, however, Virgilio Barco soon returned to the initiative with a new proposal drawn from the old 1939 pact. He suggested the creation of a high-level "conciliatory commission," which would include equal numbers of Colombians and Venezuelans while numbering eminent international figures such as former Latin American chiefs of state. It was proposed that such a body might lead in the direction of an agreement to seek arbitration of the frontier dispute by the International Court of Justice. However, on the night of May 12, 1987, Jaime Lusinchi officially rejected the proposal on the grounds that such a panel should not be empowered to pass judgment on matters of vital interest to either country. Despite such diplomatic niceties, however, Venezuela continued to mistrust the notion of third-party mediation. There was a strongly nationalistic insistence that frontier matters be settled by direct bilateral means. Furthermore, there was the practical concern that Venezuelan claims might not be adequately respected by outside parties. For Colombia, of course, its willingness was tied to the belief that its case was more fully defensible than that of its neighbor to the east.

---

[9]Both 1988 presidential nominations were extremely contentious. For COPEI, former president and party founder Rafael Caldera was defeated by his former protégé, Eduardo Fernández. With Acción Democrática, former president Carlos Andrés Pérez won the nomination despite opposition by the bulk of the party leadership, including President Jaime Lusinchi.

The respective positions have been and continue to be both complex and ambiguous. The details have frequently been presented elsewhere, but the political and security aspects remain our major concern here. And despite Colombian frustrations over the general unresponsiveness of the Lusinchi government, Bogotá continued to seek another round of discussions. In Caracas, meanwhile, there was heightened attention in the press to both the unproductive nature of discussions and to the growing "menace," as one put it, of Colombian problems spilling ever more extensively into Venezuela. By June 1987 renewed calls for negotiations were tied to sensationalist headlines about alleged Colombian military intentions. In addition, the nature and frequency of clashes and arguments related to the frontier mounted perceptibly. It would no longer be possible to view the dispute in terms of petroleum, cattle, or migration, for more dangerous forces had come into play.

CONTEMPORARY CHALLENGES TO NATIONAL SECURITY

With the spread of the narcotics industry, frontier problems shifted from precise demarcations and submarine mineral deposits to issues of guerrilla insurgency, threats to public security, and the potential for serious armed conflict. As Venezuela found itself being gradually drawn toward the South American drug empire, the evidence accumulated with disturbing rapidity. The Lusinchi government, despite passage of a major criminal law reform in 1984 and a strong anti-drug stand by the president, found heightened reason for concern. In October 1986, the largest cocaine seizure in the history of the United States took place in Florida with the interception of 6,800 pounds of high-quality cocaine transported from the port of La Guaira. A month later Venezuelan troops patrolling the Sierra de Perija frontier region—directly contiguous to Colombia's most fertile marijuana-growing area—uncovered over twenty-five tons of marijuana neatly packaged in aluminum foil and ready for shipment.

With the pressure against narcotics having mounted in Bolivia and Peru, the Colombian dealers moved to establish new trade routes in Venezuela. Concern also heightened in Venezuela when a congressman was arrested in February 1987 with eleven pounds of cocaine in the trunk of his car. Venezuelan national guardsmen also uncovered large cocaine operations in the Andean border state of Tachira, directly to the south of the Sierra de Perija. As the incidence of such episodes grew in currency, more aggressive action began to be pursued by drug traffickers, by guerrillas in Colombia who sometimes collaborated with them, and by assorted military and security forces. The inevitable blowup came on June 12, 1987, when there was a major clash between Colombian guerrillas and members of an anti-drug unit of the Venezuelan National Guard (Barroeta 1987: 17).

Reports of the fighting were delayed five days, and even then the accounts were at variance with one another. As it developed, however, some two dozen national guardsmen operating out of Maracaibo had been engaged in locating and destroying coca and marijuana plantations. While sleeping, they had been attacked by nearly one hundred irregular "narcoguerrillas," armed with a potent mixture of mortars, grenades, and antitank rockets. At least nine guardsmen were killed and most of the others wounded during the fighting. Their commander, General Marcial Rojas Aguero, vowed that the guard would remain on full alert, while President Lusinchi called upon Colombia to share responsibility for combating the threat. He insisted that Venezuela "cannot permit the extension of violence or narcotrafficking, and cannot serve as a refuge from the exercise of justice. I believe that we should make a joint effort to assure that events of this nature are not repeated" (*El Nacional* [Caracas], June 18, 1987).

While President Barco in turn lamented the events, he was far more preoccupied with the rising level of violence occurring in much of Colombia. Indeed, an attack by members of the communist Fuerzas Armadas Revolucionarias de Colombia (FARC) in southern Colombia took the lives of some thirty Colombian soldiers. As a consequence, there was little meaningful collaboration between respective border and security forces in the next several months, although conditions grew worse. A new problem arose with a wave of kidnapings of wealthy Venezuelan ranchers by Colombian guerrillas, aimed at producing ransom payments. Guerrilla incursions also continued, while the *narcotraficantes* increased the tempo of cocaine transshipments en route to the United States and Western Europe. During a December visit to the troubled region, Lusinchi expressed the growing view that "subversion and narcotics trafficking, which at one time posed separate challenges, now appear to have joined forces and are acting together" (*New York Times*, January 20, 1988).

Although Defense Minister General Eliodoro Guerrero Gómez reiterated Venezuela's determination to adopt more drastic measures, the movement toward joint action did not proceed with alacrity. Only on January 21, 1988, did Colombian Interior Minister César Gaviria Trujillo meet with his opposite number, José Angel Ciliberto, in the mountainous Andean town of San Antonio del Tachira. Two joint measures were announced at the conclusion of the conference. First, there was a very broad and ill-defined pledge on the part of both nations to increase their military presence along the 2,250-kilometer border. Second came the seemingly redundant agreement to renew the 1984 pact allowing the two governments to coordinate efforts in fighting both drug trade and guerrilla activity.

Even as these events were sharpening tensions along the border, the dispute over maritime jurisdiction had resurfaced as the result of a new squabble which broke out in August 1987. It started when the Colombian warship *Arc Caldas* entered waters only three miles off the northern Guajiran shore. On August 13 Caracas formally protested the intrusion and demanded an explanation for this "provocation" (*El Nacional*, August 14, 1987). The next day Virgilio Barco retorted that the message was "unfriendly," with the action an innocent result of unresolved border issues (*El Espectador*, August 15, 1987). Two days later military reinforcements arrived along the border on both sides, while OAS Secretary General João Baena Soares and Argentine President Raúl Alfonsín issued a public call for pacific settlement of the dispute.

Colombia ordered the withdrawal of the *Arc Caldas* and all other warships in the general vicinity and repeated its description of the episode as an accidental consequence of inadequate border demarcation. Jaime Lusinchi then addressed his nation at greater length on August 19, rejecting the Colombian explanation as "slanderous" and reiterating Venezuela's territorial claims over the waters in question. At the same time he expressed a willingness to reopen talks on the border dispute, although adding his distaste for perceptions that talks might be the result of pressures created by the intrusion of the *Arc Caldas*. The Venezuelan chief also took the occasion to repeat once again the view that bilateral agreement was essential, for his country was not amenable to multilateral discussions or to other forms of third-party involvement (*El Nacional*, August 20, 1987).

This was a position, as previously noted, which had been defended by a succession of Venezuelan governments. The apparent inflexibility of attitudes was again underlined in October at a conference on "El Diferendo con Colombia en la Política Exterior Venezolana" convened at Caracas's Universidad Simón Bolívar. Aníbal Romero, adviser to the Venezuelan Chancellery, stated unequivocally that the gulf waters constituted a matter of critical national interest, one which required both military and diplomatic defense as necessary. Colombia's claims were characterized as linked almost exclusively to potential petroleum wealth, and as such constituted the most dangerous source of tension for all of Venezuela's foreign relations. Bogotá, he maintained, would have to withdraw "radically" from its position as enunciated in the Hypothesis of Caraballeda. While confident that the two neighboring democracies could work out their differences, he gave little indication of compromise on Venezuelan claims. Considering broader frontier differences, moreover, he referred to the Venezuelan necessity of strengthening its military capabilities. There was a veiled belligerency to his declaration that, in the light of prevailing conditions, "we cannot permit new aggressions and violations of our sovereignty" (*Diario de Caracas*, October 9, 1987; see also Romero 1986).

With the traditional maritime dispute inflamed by the August episode, Venezuelan sensitivities toward Colombia were increasingly responsive in other areas as well. By 1988, the purported "Colombianization" of Venezuela suddenly leapt to the pages of both the daily press and of newsmagazines.[10] Preoccupation over the impact of the *narcotraficantes* was profound, as was the rising use of drugs among the Venezuelan population. The apparent infiltration of drug-related guerrilla forces added to the concern, while the traditional flow of contraband continued unabated. While Colombians saw these problems with less sense of immediacy—given the general deterioration of security conditions throughout its territory—Venezuelans viewed them with greater urgency. Furthermore, general attitudes toward Colombia were being progressively soured by the course of events. None of this was comforting as the country embarked upon the customarily intense campaigning which would precede the December 1988 general elections.

THE FRONTIER AND PUBLIC OPINION

Extensive political polling in Venezuela was already substantial, given the competitiveness of elections and past utilization of public opinion studies.[11] In addition there were other, narrower issue-oriented studies which also shed light on the attitudes of the Venezuelan public. A poll in December 1987 which concentrated on international affairs proved instructive for our analysis of frontier-related questions.[12] It demonstrated substantial concern over both the drug problem and the question of the border demarcation. Respondents were first asked to indicate which of five foreign relations questions were perceived as most important. The results are presented in table 10.1. As is evident, 41 percent saw the diminution of drug traffic as the highest priority, followed by 27 percent who wanted to avoid the intrusion of Colombian violence into Venezuela. Another 14 percent focused on resolving the gulf conflict. As seen in the table, such attitudes presented a stark picture of national attitudes on foreign policy-related questions. The findings are strong and clear.

Beyond these broad impressionistic views, it also developed—not surprisingly—that public opinion was inclined to adopt a strong and firm position in defense of national interests. While in principle this was to be expected, it took on sharp definition with regard to the border and its problems. First, with regard to methods, 61 percent favored bilateral

---

[10]Characteristic discussions are found in *Auténtico*, *Número*, and *Momento*, all of Caracas. In comparative terms, there is less frequent and less assertive treatment in such Bogotá counterparts as *Semana*, *Guión*, *Nueva Frontera*, and the like.

[11]The most detailed treatment of Venezuelan polling is found in Martz and Baloyra 1976, including pp. 108 and 203ff. The theoretical framework used for this and later campaign studies was set forth in Martz 1971. A detailed treatment for 1978 is O'Connor 1980.

[12]The poll, in the preparation and design of which the author participated, was conducted by the Social Democratic Instituto para la Difusión del Pensamiento Político. A total of 2,156 were interviewed in the nationwide survey.

TABLE 10.1
VENEZUELAN PUBLIC OPINION ON FOREIGN POLICY

Which of the following five problems do you consider most important?	Percent
Diminish drug trafficking	41
Avoid the spread of Colombia violence into Venezuela	27
Resolve the conflict over the gulf	14
Contribute to the establishment of peace in Central America	10
Manage Venezuela's foreign debt	8

negotiation while 29 percent declared that Colombia should accept the Venezuelan position and, if unresponsive, should be faced with military force. Only 10 percent advocated that a third party mediate the conflict. Concerning the substance, moreover, nearly two-thirds (64 percent) wanted total control of the gulf by Venezuela, even if the use of military force were necessary. Those wanting to share the gulf with Colombia (but with Venezuela retaining the greater portion) were 21 percent of the total, leaving 15 percent who said that Venezuela should share the disputed territory equally with Colombia.

Basically, Venezuelans believed by and large that the gulf was theirs, and that military force might be applied if necessary. They were not attracted to negotiation by third-party participation. These and other findings in the poll consistently indicated Venezuelan concern about the potential intrusion of Colombian violence. And while there was some willingness to cooperate with the Colombians, many Venezuelans sought direct and independent action. For example, 49 percent sought coordination with Colombia to combat guerrilla violence, but 45 percent preferred a special command of Venezuelan *cazadores* to deal with violence. This left a bare 6 percent opting for ignoring the problem.

Turning to the fight against drug traffic and its related problems, 47 percent of the national sample supported increased cooperation with the neighboring republic. However, fully 51 percent wanted a strengthening of special Venezuelan police units to deal separately with the conflict. Only 2 percent opposed special efforts. Furthermore, sentiment was even more strongly approving of independent efforts in the fight against contraband. Fully 55 percent advocated the creation of special Venezuelan police units, compared with 44 percent who favored some form of cooperation with the Colombian government. Interestingly enough, a regional breakdown of respondents demonstrated that residents of the populous border state of Zulia were more inclined toward such collaboration than was the national sample. Thus, they chose joint action over unilateral strengthening of police units by a margin of 60–39 percent (compared to the national figure of 47–51 percent). As to the fight against contraband, the *zulianos* living so directly with the problem preferred greater collaboration by 51–49 percent (as against the national figure of 44–55 percent).

A final aspect of the Colombian-Venezuelan border relationship was that of the *indocumentados* crossing from Colombia to seek employment and greater earnings in Venezuela. After long years of this continuing flow of illegals—customarily estimated at upwards of 250,000—Venezuelan public opinion was strikingly adamant. Respondents were given the choice of closing the frontier and deporting the illegals; closing the border but ignoring the *indocumentados* already present; and finally, throwing open the border to all. Table 10.2 summarizes the findings for the nation and by region.

TABLE 10.2
VENEZUELAN ATTITUDES TOWARD ILLEGAL IMMIGRATION

	\multicolumn{4}{c}{Which of the following policies would you prefer concerning illegal immigration into Venezuela?}			
Policy	Zulia	Andes	Guayana	Nat'l
		(percentages)		
Close and deport	36	46	56	63
Close without deporting	56	43	31	31
Open frontier to all	8	11	13	6

Nationally, nearly two-thirds preferred the toughest option, with a bare 6 percent willing to throw open the borders. Sentiment was nearly as strong along the disputed eastern Esequibo boundary with neighboring Guyana, where contraband and illegal crossing were virtually nonexistent. In the Andes and in Zulia, lying along the Colombian border, attitudes were comparatively less harsh—most especially so, of course, with the latter. These regional findings for Zulia were the only exception to the generally unyielding attitude held by Venezuelans on the eve of 1988.

SUMMARY AND CONCLUSIONS

Differences over the maritime demarcation in the waters off the Guajira Peninsula have divided Colombia and Venezuela for generations. Unless or until a solution is reached, it will be difficult for the two neighbors to collaborate in foreign affairs where they might logically find mutual priorities and interests. The more recent flood of immigrants across the frontier has added to the well-established practice of smuggling and contraband in cattle, produce, and a host of diverse goods. To such traditional sources of tension, however, have been added the modern-day advent of drug trafficking and guerrilla insurgents. With such elements having so devastated Colombia internally since the 1970s, Venezuela increasingly faces similarly intimidating pressures. The potential is alarming, and Venezuelan public opinion indicates as much in the desire for strong and adamant actions being reported in nationwide surveys.

The intrusion into domestic politics is especially striking for Venezuela. It is not merely that mounting preoccupations coincided with the timing of a new electoral campaign. Neither was it suggestive of policy differences between the Acción Democrática's Pérez and Eduardo Fernández of COPEI. Rather, the impact came from a rising tide of apprehension over the penetration of drug money and influence into the national body politic. Early in 1988, for example, reports of a special, drug-financed security force responsible to Minister Manzo González ("*manzopol*") led to his resignation from the Lusinchi government. At the same time, charges of drug/mafioso links were spreading, even inducing a congressional skirmish at fisticuffs between two deputies caught up in unsubstantiated charges and allegations (*Zeta* [Caracas], May 24–June 1, 1988). The leadership of both COPEI and Acción Democrática, while unwilling to curb attacks against their opponents, privately lamented both the real and the imagined penetration of drug interests into national life. All of this further inflamed public opinion, while Caracas's open and sensationalist press enjoyed a field day with rumors and gossip.

To the west in Colombia, directly border-related preoccupations were further from the center of political concern, but only as a consequence of deteriorating authority on the part of the Barco administration. Continuing assassinations and kidnapings, coupled with bribery and intimidation, were destroying the judicial system and corrupting the political process. The bloody attack and kidnaping of 1986 Conservative presidential candidate Alvaro Gómez Hurtado in May was but another dramatic testimony to the overreaching power and impact of *narcotraficantes* throughout the nation (*El Siglo* [Bogotá], May 30, 1988). Under these circumstances, concern about the frontier was inclined to turn back upon historic questions of the demarcation, accompanied by seemingly genuine preoccupation about the capability and intentions of the Venezuelan armed forces.

Prevailing attitudes about the boundary itself have been consistent in recent years. Venezuela has felt itself served poorly by past agreements, opposes third-party participation, and mistrusts Colombia. The latter, while accepting outside arbitration in hopes of resolving the matter, felt that its neighbors were unwilling to bargain in good faith. There was even some feeling that the conduct of Venezuelan foreign policy was being handled by, at the least, unskilled diplomats and political leaders. Notwithstanding all these elements, the challenges and potential for serious strife had grown out of the drug industry and its links with guerrilla organizations. Although it would be unduly alarmist to anticipate outright war as a serious threat, the scope and dimensions for renewed clashes and mutual antagonism have been clearly enlarged. Past experience gives little cause to anticipate meaningful negotiation and compromise. Perhaps the urgency of understanding will prove more forceful.

REFERENCES

Ameringer, Charles J. 1986. "Foreign Policy in Democratic Venezuela." In *Venezuela: The Democratic Experience*, edited by John D. Martz and David J. Myers. 2d ed. New York: Praeger.

Barroeta, Elsy. 1987. "Nueva amenaza, la narcoguerrilla," *Visión* (Mexico), July 13.

Ewell, Judith. 1984. *Venezuela; A Century of Change*. Stanford, Calif.: Stanford University Press.

FBIS (Foreign Broadcast Information Service). 1982. *Daily Report: Latin America*, August 19.

Hazleton, William A. 1988. "Colombian and Venezuelan Foreign Policy: Regional Powers in the Caribbean Basin." In *Democracy in Latin America: Colombia and Venezuela*, edited by Donald L. Herman. New York: Praeger.

Herman, Donald L. 1976. "Ideology, Economic Power and Regional Imperialism: The Determinants of Foreign Policy under Venezuela's Christian Democrats." Paper prepared for the Seventeenth Annual Convention of the International Studies Association, Toronto, February 25.

Martz, John D. 1971. "Democratic Political Campaigning in Latin America: A Typological Approach to Cross-Cultural Research," *Journal of Politics* 33:2 (May): 370–99.

———. 1977. "Venezuelan Foreign Policy toward Latin America." In *Contemporary Venezuela and Its Role in International Affairs*, edited by Robert D. Bond. New York: Council on Foreign Relations.

———. 1984. "Venezuelan Foreign Policy and the Role of Political Parties." In *Latin American Nations in World Politics*, edited by Heraldo Muñoz and Joseph S. Tulchin. Boulder, Colo.: Westview.

Martz, John D., and Enrique A. Baloyra. 1976. *Electoral Mobilization and Public Opinion*. Chapel Hill: University of North Carolina Press.

Myers, David J. 1985. *Venezuela's Pursuit of Caribbean Basin Interests: Implications for United States National Security*. Santa Monica, Calif.: Rand.

O'Connor, Robert E. 1980. "The Media and the Campaign." In *Venezuela at the Polls*, edited by Howard R. Penniman. Washington: AEI.

Peeler, John A. 1985. *Latin American Democracies: Colombia, Costa Rica, Venezuela*. Chapel Hill: University of North Carolina Press.

Rangel, José Vicente. 1980. "Problemas fundamentales de seguridad y defensa de Venezuela." In *Seguridad, defensa y democracia en Venezuela*, edited by Aníbal Romero. Caracas: Equinoccio.

República de Venezuela. 1971. *Libro amarillo de la República de Venezuela, 1971*. Caracas: Imprenta Nacional.

Rey, Juan Carlos. 1986. "La democracia, la opinión pública y la política exterior," *Política Internacional*, January–March, pp. 2–6.

Romero, Aníbal. 1986. "La situación estratégica de Venezuela," *Política Internacional*, January–March, pp. 6–15.

Silva Lujan, Gabriel. 1985. *Política exterior: ¿Continuidad o ruptura?* Bogotá: CEREC.

Sureda Delgado, Rafael. 1987. "Negociar, ¿Sí o No?" *Elite* (Caracas), May 26.

Vázquez Carrizosa, Alfredo. 1983. *Las relaciones de Colombia y Venezuela: La historia atormentada de dos naciones*. Bogotá: Ediciones Tercer Mundo.

———. 1986. *Los no alineados: Una estrategia política para la paz en la era atómica*. Bogotá: Carlos Valencia Editores.

11

Pendulum Politics: Paraguay's National Borders, 1940–1975

Melissa H. Birch

When the governments of Paraguay and Brazil signed an agreement in 1973 to construct the Itaipu Dam on the Paraná River, many observers were surprised. Historically Paraguay had maintained much closer relations with Argentina, with whom it shared language, culture, political traditions, and economic ties. In his book on the diplomatic history of Paraguay from 1869 to 1938, in the section on relations in the twentieth century, Salum Flecha devoted eighteen pages to relations with Argentina and two pages to relations with Brazil.[1]

Admittedly, relations between Argentina and Paraguay were not without conflict. The War of the Triple Alliance (1865–70), which pitted Paraguay against Argentina, Brazil, and Uruguay, left Paraguay, one of the richest nations in South America at the beginning of the period, in ruins. In the twentieth century, the Argentine monopoly on shipping along the Paraguay River and its authority over traffic along the Paraná and Río de la Plata river system gave it virtual control over Paraguay's access to the sea. This influence over the economic life of the country combined with substantial Argentine investment in extractive industries and extensive land-holdings in Paraguay to foster a clear resentment of Argentine hegemony.

The Paraguayan Liberal Party, traditionally associated with a pro-Argentine perspective, dominated the political scene until the end of the Chaco War. The party's long-standing friendly relations with Argentina may help to account for Argentina's consistently pro-Paraguay stance at the Chaco peace conferences. The Chaco War and the negotiations leading to its end strengthened Paraguay's existing relations with Argentina.

---

[1] Salum Flecha 1972. The book also devotes fifty-four pages to the Chaco War and relations with Bolivia, a subject which is not covered in this chapter.

Relations with Brazil were not nearly as extensive or well developed—perhaps the result of the physical remoteness of Brazil from the centers of population in Paraguay. While common rivers provided Paraguay and Argentina with natural transportation and communication links, overland travel to Brazil was very difficult. Brazilian population centers could only be reached by a complicated river and rail route or, later, by air. Until the construction of a more direct road and improved rail links in the 1950s and 1960s, most travel and shipping between Asunción and Brazilian cities such as Rio de Janeiro and São Paulo went down the Paraguay and Paraná rivers to Buenos Aires (a distance of about 1,200 miles) and then aboard ocean-going vessels north along the coast of Brazil to Santos or Rio de Janeiro. Railroads connected these coastal cities to other metropolitan centers in the interior. These circumstances help to explain why Brazil had a much lower profile in Paraguay than did Argentina.

Located in the "heart of South America" between these two giants, Paraguay is one of only two landlocked countries in Latin America. This mediterranean location has been a constant theme of Paraguayan public life and letters—crossing party lines and two centuries—and has forced the country to develop policies to deal with its powerful neighbors.[2] Although they have taken many forms, these policies, at least in the twentieth century, have been carefully crafted so as to protect national sovereignty and integrity while promoting advantageous economic relations and access to the sea. The Paraguayan public-policy behavior that has emerged can be described as "pendulum politics."[3]

This chapter traces the development of Paraguay's relations with Argentina and Brazil, focusing on the years between 1940 and 1975. During this period, Paraguay was able to increase its ties with Brazil significantly without excessively antagonizing Argentina and was thus able to break Argentina's hold over the Paraguayan economy, especially with regard to international shipping, while simultaneously expanding economic relations with that country as well. The essay argues that the two sets of bilateral relations composed an important part of Paraguayan public policy during the period regardless of the party in power.[4] One objective of this policy of pendulum politics was the acceleration of

---

[2] Bolivia, which borders Paraguay on the west and north, is also landlocked and has not been economically powerful enough to be of much assistance to Paraguay in its quest for development or an outlet to the sea.

[3] Of course, Paraguay has a full range of diplomatic relations with many members of the international community. There is abundant literature on relations with Bolivia, especially in connection with the Chaco War. In English, see Rout 1970; Zook 1960. For an important analysis of relations with the United States, see Grow 1981.

[4] U.S. foreign aid also played an important role in Paraguayan economic development during the period. U.S.-Paraguay relations during the 1940s are examined in great detail in Grow 1981. U.S. aid has also been important to the Stroessner administration, but a study of those relations is still waiting to be written.

economic growth. Thus, the impact of these policies on growth, trade, and foreign investment is also examined.

BACKGROUND

Pendulum politics, as a coherent public policy, could be said to begin with the administration of Higinio Morinigo, who governed Paraguay between 1940 and 1948. Morinigo's policies, however, were heavily influenced by the political events of the years immediately preceding his rise to power. For Paraguay, the major event of the 1930s was the rising level of hostility along the border with Bolivia. Although the border dispute had been smoldering for years, fighting began in June 1932 when Bolivian forces attacked a Paraguayan military post at Pitiantuta in the northern portion of the Chaco. After three years of fighting and lengthy negotiations, Paraguay was awarded twenty thousand square miles of territory in the Chaco, a prize far more valuable in terms of the vindication it provided the country than for any proven economic value.

The roots of the hostilities, however, can be traced to economic issues and to the landlocked status of the belligerents. This situation was perhaps first recognized by Dr. Eusebio Ayala, the president of Paraguay from 1933 to 1936. Ayala observed that without a river link and close relations with Argentina, Paraguay would be as trapped as Bolivia was. In a letter dated September 14, 1932, to the Paraguayan ambassador in Buenos Aires, Ayala states,

> Until now, they have looked above all at the political, military, and even historic aspects [of the Chaco conflict] and reflecting on the problem, I want to believe . . . that the fundamental factor is economic. Bolivia and Paraguay are both mediterranean republics overpowered in the economic arena by the neighboring states that control our access to the open sea routes (Rivarola 1957: 193).

The letter went on to call for a regional conference of Argentina, Brazil, Chile, and Peru, plus Paraguay and Bolivia, which would have as its objective the signing of agreements on rail, highway, and water transportation to link the belligerents with their larger, bordering countries and would guarantee access to the open seas to both Paraguay and Bolivia on advantageous terms.[5] With such a regional approach, Paraguay hoped to gain an outlet through Brazil, while Bolivia would make a similar arrangement with Argentina.

---

[5] Rivarola 1957: 195. Ayala had met with Saavedra Lamas as president-elect of Paraguay in July 1933. Topics under discussion included the possibility of arranging a new commercial treaty between the two countries.

Ayala's letter was shown to Argentine Foreign Minister Carlos Saavedra Lamas and Argentine president Agustín P. Justo, who were favorably impressed with the ideas.[6] Several months later, Saavedra Lamas met with Chilean Minister of Foreign Relations Miguel Cruchaga Tocornal in the Argentine city of Mendoza to confer on a new Chaco peace initiative. The Acta de Mendoza, signed February 3, 1933, called for an immediate cease-fire and arbitration of the dispute. In addition, the Acta de Mendoza included a provision—using the language of the Ayala letter, which Saavedra Lamas had carried with him—for a regional meeting to address the issue of Paraguay's and Bolivia's landlocked states.

Although nothing came of the peace initiative, the Acta de Mendoza and its call for a regional conference to establish a set of trade, transportation, and communication conventions provided a precedent for such discussions. The economic roots of the war could no longer be ignored, and the amelioration of the problems of the mediterranean state of the belligerents became a clear objective in the peace process. With the Protocol of June 12, 1935, peace in the Chaco was finally achieved. The agreement provided for an immediate cease-fire and arbitration to establish the exact boundaries in the Chaco. In addition, the countries that guaranteed the peace—Argentina, Brazil, Chile, Peru, Uruguay, and the United States—promised to promote arrangements and accords to provide a "system of transit, trade and navigation to ameliorate the geographic situation of the belligerents" and promote their economic development.[7]

The economically costly Chaco War (1932–35) drew resources from the entire nation, but the battles were confined to the sparsely populated western half of Paraguay. Agriculture and industrial production were almost entirely located in the eastern region and suffered only inasmuch as labor and imported inputs were in short supply during the war. Paraguay's productive capacity was left intact and the country was able to replace depleted stocks. When World War II broke out in Europe, Paraguay was able to respond to the increased European demand for foodstuffs and raw materials.

While the impact of the Chaco War on the Paraguayan economy was minimal, it had a marked effect on the political scene. The Liberal Party,

---

[6]H.G. Warren (1949) argues that Argentina found this proposal attractive because it would increase the dependency of both Paraguay and Bolivia on Buenos Aires as their trade along the Río de la Plata increased. It is difficult to imagine Paraguay more dependent on Argentina. From Paraguay's perspective, however, the proposal was attractive because it would at least standardize the arrangements and eliminate some of the vagaries of treatment Paraguayan shipping received at the hands of Argentine firms. At best, the new agreement might open alternative trade routes, especially with Brazil.

[7]Zook 1960: 240. This was not an entirely altruistic offer. In Brazil, M. Travassos published *Projeção Continental do Brasil* (1938), which discussed the usefulness of export corridors for hinterland countries to break the hegemony of Argentina on river shipping and port traffic in Buenos Aires.

which had held power since 1904, was unseated in 1936. Young officers who returned from the war expressed their dissatisfaction with the management of the affairs of state and resolved to create a new, nationalistic political order. Symbolic of this new spirit was a daring young veteran of the Chaco War, Col. Rafael Franco, who came to power by coup in February 1936 espousing a nationalist doctrine that came to be known as Febrerismo.[8] The new government lacked broad-based organizational support, however, and Franco was overthrown six months later in a military coup that returned the Liberal Party to power. In an effort to consolidate their hold on the government, the Liberals chose another Chaco War hero, José Félix Estigarribia, as their candidate for the next elections.

Estigarribia had commanded Paraguayan forces in the Chaco War and then served as Paraguay's ambassador to the United States. He returned to Paraguay when elected president in 1939. Estigarribia was strongly influenced by the younger members of the Liberal Party and the ideas of Febrerismo. His administration represented an increase in state-sponsored economic activity and a decided turn away from the laissez-faire policies of the older Liberals. Before leaving the United States, Estigarribia signed an agreement with Secretary of State Cordell Hull for $3 million for highway construction in Paraguay. On his way back to Paraguay, he stopped in Brazil, where he signed a cultural exchange agreement and an accord for the construction of a spur off the São Paulo-Campo Grande railroad to Ponto Pora on the Paraguayan border (Raine 1956: 253). The projected Concepción-Pedro Juan Caballero rail line in Paraguay, when completed, was intended to connect with this spur and thus link the two nations' rail systems.[9]

Estigarribia served as president for only thirteen months. He was killed in an airplane accident on September 5, 1940, and was succeeded by his minister of defense, Higinio Morinigo.[10] Morinigo ruled without party identification as *jefe supremo del estado* (supreme chief of state) but with the support of the military and, at least in the early years, fascistic elements of the Catholic church.[11] His nationalistic program, which he called the Revolución Nacional Paraguaya, proposed a nonelectoral democracy, because the population was felt to be unprepared to vote

---

[8] For an excellent study of the Febrerista Party, see Lewis 1965.

[9] At the time, the Paraguayan railroad went only south from Asunción to Encarnación, where it was linked to the Argentine system by a ferry that crossed the Paraná River.

[10] Morinigo became president with the support of the Liberal Party, but within a month the Liberals withdrew from the government and two years later Morinigo outlawed the Liberal Party, sending most party leaders into exile.

[11] Known as the Tiempistas, a group of devoutly Catholic, Jesuit-trained professors favored a form of Catholic socialism patterned after the Estado Novo in Portugal and Brazil. These individuals headed the ministries of labor, public works, justice and culture, and economics and acknowledged a "number of points of contact: between their ideology and the totalitarian doctrines popular in Germany and Italy in the 1940s." See Grow 1981: 65.

intelligently. It rejected liberalism and promoted state intervention, especially in the economic sphere. "The inertia of the liberal state should cede its place to the dynamism of the protecting and directing state" (*La Tribuna* [Asunción], December 26, 1940).

BILATERAL AGREEMENTS, 1940–1954

Morinigo, at the head of the "directing state," was not content to leave economic relations with Paraguay's powerful neighbors to the private sector. His international policy had two goals. The first, and more traditional, was to expand Paraguay's role in international affairs, especially within the hemisphere. The second goal was somewhat more unusual but consistent with his activist view of the role of the state. Morinigo planned to:

> win the well-being of the [Paraguayan] people, [by] concluding treaties and agreements that coordinate our economy with that of the other American countries and assure benefits that compensate and attenuate the disadvantages derived from our Mediterranean location" (in Ocampos Caballero 1983: 102–04).

The nature and number of international agreements reached in the following years suggest that this latter goal was an essential component of the Revolución Nacional Paraguaya and that it constituted the basis of public policy in the period.

In June 1941, Morinigo's foreign minister, Dr. Luis Argana, traveled to Brazil to meet with President Getulio Vargas and Brazilian Foreign Minister Osvaldo Aranha. Public statements made during the visit emphasized Latin American solidarity and the necessity of strengthening ties among the American nations in the face of the war in Europe. The previous hostilities between the two countries were described as a spat between two brothers when they are young which is forgotten as they mature and develop strong bonds (*Jornal do Comercio*, June 14, 1941, p. 4).

Argana signed ten agreements with the Brazilians in the areas of commerce, transportation, and cultural relations. Of particular note, however, were the agreements on trade and transportation. A five-man committee was established to study navigational problems on the Paraguay River with an eye toward dredging shallow passages and establishing a binational (Paraguayan-Brazilian) commercial shipping company. The two countries also agreed to put into effect the terms of the 1914 La Plata Basin agreement with respect to border trade and to establish a commission to prepare a new commercial and navigation treaty. Most important of all, the government of Brazil extended free port privileges to Paraguay at the Atlantic port of Santos, near São Paulo (*Jornal do Comercio*, June 18, 1941, p. 1).

At the same time, the two countries signed an accord for the construction and a thirty-year concession for the operation of a railroad between Concepción and Pedro Juan Caballero, two cities in northern Paraguay. On August 11, 1941, the Empresa Ferroviaria Noreste del Brazil, which was building the rail link between São Paulo and Campo Grande as part of a South American transcontinental railway, was given the contract to extend rail lines from the Ponto Pora (Brazil) spur to connect with the Concepción-Pedro Juan Caballero line.[12] Brazil's interest in the project derived from an 1856 treaty that had given Brazil free port rights at Concepción. As Brazil began its westward expansion, an overland route to Concepción that would bypass the swamps of the Pantanal would facilitate the movement of materials into and out of the rapidly growing Brazilian state of Mato Grosso.[13] A direct land route to Concepción would also avoid shipping through Buenos Aires and shorten the distance considerably.

For Paraguay, these agreements opened the way for a variety of alternative shipping arrangements. If a Brazilian-Paraguayan shipping firm were to come into operation, competition on the Paraguay River would increase, and shipping rates would come down. A railroad between Concepción and Pedro Juan Caballero would open up the northern region of the country and provide a land route to the sea. Exports and imports could travel by river to Concepción and then by rail to the Atlantic port of Santos, where they could be shipped to international markets. If such overland links were achieved, Buenos Aires could be bypassed altogether. Paraguay would have an alternative (to the Río de la Plata river system) route to the sea, and Argentina's control over access and shipping on the river would be significantly undermined.

As a further demonstration of the growing ties between Brazil and Paraguay, Getulio Vargas visited Asunción in August 1941, where he inaugurated the first foreign branch office of the Banco do Brasil. In 1942 an economic mission from Paraguay visited Rio de Janeiro,[14] and in 1943 Paraguay signed a treaty with Brazil granting it most favored nation status. Brazil lifted tariffs on *nanduti* (a native lace) and tannin, and

---

[12] The 1939 agreement between Paraguay and Brazil had provided for the construction of the spur from the Campo Grande line south to Ponto Pora. While little was ever done on the Paraguayan side, the Brazilian side was complete by 1954. See Raine 1956: 387.

[13] *Hacienda Pública*, no date, pp. 87–102 in González archives MS-E231. The González Collection is housed in the Kenneth Spencer Research Library, University of Kansas, Lawrence, Kansas. It includes numerous volumes of González's papers and correspondence, generally unnumbered; noted by volume number.

[14] *O Estado de São Paulo*, June 6, 1942. Members of the mission included R. Balmelli, Manuel Galiano, and M. Harmodio González. The exact nature of their work was not reported in the article.

Paraguay removed those on coffee, cacao, and other Brazilian products (C. Warren 1943: 197–98).

In 1942 the Missão Militar Brasileira was established in Paraguay; Brazilian military officers began teaching at the Paraguayan Officers Training School, and Paraguayan officers attended Brazilian military schools on scholarships provided by the Brazilian government. Alfredo Stroessner was one of these scholarship recipients. He attended the Escola das Armas da Vila Militar in Rio de Janeiro in 1943. During the 1940s the Brazilian military and cultural missions in Asunción were the only ones of their kind maintained by the government of Brazil in a foreign country.

Morinigo made an official visit to Brazil in May 1943.[15] He marveled at Brazilian economic development and described his visit as opening "a new era of Paraguayan-Brazilian relations." While in Brazil, Vargas signed a decree that forgave Paraguay's debt to Brazil owed from the War of the Triple Alliance.[16]

In December 1943, on the occasion of Morinigo's state visit to Argentina, and perhaps prompted by the increasing network of trade and transport ties developing between Paraguay and Brazil, Argentine president Pedro Pablo Ramírez granted free port facilities to Paraguay in Buenos Aires and Rosario. The two heads of state also signed a trade and payments treaty that provided numerous trade concessions to Paraguay. The accords included the creation of a commission to study the possibility of establishing a customs union between the two countries.[17] While the idea may have been particularly attractive in the early 1940s, interest in a customs union predates the political concerns of the World War II period. The idea of a customs union as a policy for economic growth was suggested in the early 1930s by Federico Piñedo in Argentina.[18] In the aftermath of World War I and the Great Depression, economic orthodoxy had prevailed in fiscal matters in Argentina. In international trade, the nineteenth-century doctrine of mercantilism was reborn in the form of an economic nationalism that seemed to convey that "to import was a crime and to export was a virtue" (Alemánn 1977:

---

[15] Morinigo also made a state visit to the United States in 1943 and en route made stops in eight other Latin American countries in a gesture of hemispheric solidarity. The eight countries were: Mexico, Panama, Venezuela, Colombia, Ecuador, Peru, Chile, and Bolivia. For details of his visit to the United States, see Grow 1981, especially chapter 6. For details of his visits to the Latin American countries, see Morinigo's own testimony in Ocampos Caballero 1983.

[16] See Ocampos Caballero 1983: 17. Argentina had forgiven Paraguay these debts on August 13, 1942.

[17] According to some scholars, this agreement was part of an unsuccessful Argentine attempt to form an anti-U.S. bloc in Latin America. See, for example, Raine 1956: 266.

[18] Alemánn 1977: 40. Federico Piñedo was an economist and minister of finance in the early 1930s and then again in 1940. His ideas on economic integration are found in *En tiempos de la República*, first published in Buenos Aires in 1946.

39). Tariff barriers were erected to protect the nation and its economy. Piñedo, a staunch advocate of free trade, rejected this approach, arguing that "Argentina could be self-sufficient... but the prospect of a great Argentina would have disappeared" (Alemánn 1977: 42).

In Piñedo's view, national greatness would be achieved only through some sort of economic cooperation. The only recognized form of economic integration at the time was the customs union, patterned after the Zollverein in nineteenth-century Germany, but the model for Piñedo was the economic and trade arrangements between the states of the United States. He recognized the virtue of a market like that of the United States that "offered industry a market compatible with large-scale production, which resulted in lower production costs while paying high wages" (Alemánn 1977: 40). To support his view, he noted the rapid development of the United States in the century and a half after its union, and contrasted this pattern with the disunity and much slower growth experienced in Europe and South America over a comparable period.

Interest in economic integration in the Southern Cone seems to have increased in the 1940s. In strictly economic terms, it offered an opportunity to increase intraregional trade when the war in Europe had interrupted traditional patterns of trade between Europe and South America. This interruption also encouraged domestic production of previously imported goods.

Piñedo became finance minister in Argentina again in 1940, and the Argentine economic reactivation plan, designed by Raúl Prebisch and Piñedo, included—a very novel idea at the time—a provision for the promotion of industry. The industries to be favored were those thought to have a reasonable chance of reaching efficient levels of production. Implicit in this policy was the intention that much of the favored production would be exported.[19] Thus, Piñedo met in 1940 with his Brazilian counterpart, Jose Carlos Macedo Soares, and they proposed to their respective governments the formation of a customs union, open to other South American countries, that would facilitate free trade between the countries (Alemánn 1977: 39–47). Although neither program was adopted, industrial production as a share of Argentine GNP grew more than 4 percent per year between 1933 and 1945. Within a few years, a customs union would be viewed as assuring ready markets for Argentina's increasing industrial production as well as guaranteeing a steady supply of necessary inputs.

In 1946 Paraguay signed transportation agreements with Argentina and Brazil. An agreement to facilitate automobile traffic between the two countries by establishing ferry service at Encarnación and Puerto Pil-

---

[19]The program was "too far reaching for the era" and was rejected by Argentina's Congress. See di Tella 1986: 129.

comayo near Asunción was signed in March. The agreements with Brazil introduced direct air service between Rio de Janeiro and Asunción by the Brazilian airlines PanAir do Brasil. A separate agreement revised the June 1941 accord to allow the Brazilians to build the Pedro Juan Caballero-Concepción railroad.

The superficial political stability of the Morinigo regime began to give way to the underlying rivalries of various political actors by the second half of the 1940s. The fate of the Axis countries in Europe resulted in shifts of power within the Morinigo cabinet. The power of the fascistic members ebbed, while that of more moderate members increased. In July 1946 Morinigo formed a new coalition government in which portfolios were divided evenly between members of the Colorado and Febrerista parties.

As a result of the cabinet changes, Juan Natalicio González, representing the Colorado Party, became finance minister. He served in that position until assuming the presidency in August 1948. A well-known intellectual, author, and political thinker, González espoused a "doctrine of national socialism that was opposed in every respect to the ideas of limited government and laissez-faire economics espoused by the Liberal party" (Lewis 1980: 29).

Shortly after becoming finance minister, González traveled to Buenos Aires, where he met with recently elected Argentine president Juan Domingo Perón and Central Bank president Miguel Miranda. In addition to discussing the reactivation of a lapsed trade and payments agreement between the two countries, González asked for two loans from the central bank, because Argentine promises to encourage Argentine private investment in Paraguay had not yielded much additional capital. The purpose of the loans would be to expand trade between the two countries and develop the Paraguayan market for Argentine exports. González proposed that the two loans, in the amount of 100 million Argentine pesos for the promotion of Paraguayan economic development and 50 million pesos for various public works projects, would be repaid over twenty-five years at the lowest possible interest rate.[20]

Miranda responded favorably that, since the reorganization of the central bank, the policy of the government of Argentina was to promote regional trade. Loans such as those proposed by González were believed to strengthen the economies of neighboring countries and also to benefit Argentina by assuring it a supply of raw materials for its rapidly expanding industry and a market for the output of this industry. According to Miranda, this latter point was especially important because "there is a fear prevalent that within the next few years the

---

[20]González Collection, MS-E198, "Plan de desarrollo económico del Paraguay, 1945–46." Typescript of minutes of meeting between González and Miranda, no date.

disintegration of the British Empire could come about, which would seriously affect Argentine exports."[21]

In response to this meeting, González apparently commissioned a number of studies on the potential impact of expanded trade with Argentina on various sectors of the economy, as well as studies of necessary public works projects and estimates of their respective costs. The reports were produced over the course of the following two years in Paraguay's central bank and finance ministry, often by way of questionnaires and surveys of industry groups. Taken together, they constitute the beginning of economic planning in Paraguay.[22] Progress on reaching a trade agreement with Argentina was interrupted, however, by the political chaos in Paraguay of the late 1940s.

Quarreling among the members of the Paraguayan cabinet resulted in the reorganization of the government and the appointment of an all-military cabinet in January 1947. But the quarreling did not cease; in fact, increased intensity led to a brief civil war between March and August 1947, followed by a month-long reign of terror by the winning faction. In the political struggle that followed, Morinigo came out on top, but he was unable to regain his full political strength. Between June 1948, when the Morinigo government was overthrown, and September 1949, four different Colorado governments took power. Some political calm was restored with the rise to power in 1949 of the leader of the democratic wing of the Colorado Party, Federico Chaves, who remained in office until 1954. The effectiveness of the Chaves government was undermined, however, by vigorous and clandestine dissent from within the Colorado Party led by the followers of former president Natalicio González.[23]

Chaves faced an extremely difficult situation. In the aftermath of civil war, the economy faced shortages of food and other essential items. Rationing and price controls promoted discontent and an active, high-priced black market. Chaves adopted expansionary credit policies in an attempt to encourage production in the private sector. Instead, they

---

[21] González Collection, MS-E198, "Plan de desarrollo económico del Paraguay, 1945–46." This quote and the account of the meeting is taken from a typescript of notes from González's meeting with Miranda. Another benefit of such loans to neighboring countries, according to Miranda, was that increased trade would promote harmonious relations, which would reduce the need for military expenditures. In fact, Miranda said, he was not worried if Paraguay never repaid the loans, because the savings in military expenditures would more than make up for it.

[22] The process was institutionalized during Juan Natalicio González's presidency when the National Council of Economic Coordination was created. See Danco 1963: 43.

[23] González Collection MS-E192, vol. 1. The papers contained in this volume include letters from Víctor Morinigo to González outlining his activities to oust Chaves and pamphlets that he (or they) wrote referring to the Chaves government as a "communist element" that had infiltrated the Colorado Party. These pamphlets were apparently distributed clandestinely in Asunción between 1950 and 1951.

fueled a speculative boom that resulted in inflation and a drain on foreign exchange.[24]

In 1952 the Comisión Mixta Brasileña-Paraguaya (Brazil-Paraguay Joint Commission on Roads) was established. The commission was to direct the continuation of the road east across Paraguay from Asunción to the Paraná River, the border with Brazil. A road from Asunción east to Brazil was proposed as part of the Pan American highway program, and Estigarribia had obtained some financing from the United States in 1939 for the road. Exploratory studies to establish the appropriate route had begun in the mid-1940s but were halted within seventy kilometers of the Paraná because of dense jungle and difficult terrain. The remaining distance was surveyed by air using Brazilian military aircraft. In the early 1950s, progress on the road link to Brazil was "being held in abeyance until other more urgently needed roads can be built. Instead of carrying the Marshall Estigarribia highway across the country, through the sparsely populated eastern region, construction was halted at Col. Oviedo and continued southward to Villarica" (Raine 1956: 386–87). Such a road would connect with the Paraguayan railroad, which was linked to the Argentine system at Encarnación.

In December 1949 a new trade and payments agreement had been signed, but it was soon overshadowed by plans for a more wide-ranging agreement. National commissions in each country began to study the potential impact of a Paraguay-Argentina pact similar to the one Argentina had signed with Chile earlier in the year. On August 14, 1953, Paraguay joined the Argentine-Chilean Union. The treaty provided for a three-year agreement, to be renewed annually thereafter unless one party advised, with three months notice, that it wished to end the agreement. The countries agreed to coordinate economic policies and planning in such a way as to expand production and trade, and assure the stability of supplies. Special facilities for investment between the two countries (read, Argentine investment in Paraguay) were to be created, and mineral and oil exploration activities were to be extended. The trade component of the accord provided for the elimination of tariffs on trade between the two countries and for a minimum of $15,000 of merchandise from each country to be traded. The list of products that would compose this $15,000 minimum reveals that the arrangement was overwhelmingly conceived of as a swap of Paraguayan timber ($11,000) for Argen-

---

[24]Costanzo 1961: 46. Some scholars have attributed the rapid expansion of credit to political largess to Chaves's supporters. This idea may have originated with Juan Natalicio González and is found in the vitriolic attacks on Chaves written by Víctor Morinigo. The volume "Latrocinios Chavista" in the González Collection purports to document how Chaves's cronies stole millions from the Central Bank. But on close scrutiny the evidence is not compelling. Since the public-sector budget was virtually in balance and the United States was pushing private sector-led economic development, it appears possible that the credit expansion was part of an attempt at expansionary monetary policy to promote growth.

tine wheat ($10,000). Following the theme of the Acta de Mendoza, the agreement also called for the "systematization, integration, and further development of highways, railroads, air transport, river and ocean shipping." The statement also added oil and gas pipelines and aqueducts to the list of integrating links to be established between the two countries (Republic of Argentina 1953: 11).

This treaty was viewed with alarm by some in Paraguay, who believed that it reflected a "selling-out" to the Argentines. Chaves was overthrown before the treaty could be ratified, however, and Perón was overthrown before he could woo Chaves's successor into the fold. Thus the treaty merely represents another attempt at regional economic cooperation, integration of transportation systems, and expanded trade.

As a result of this agreement, the Chaves government was perceived as "pro-Argentine" or "pro-Perón." It should be noted, however, that during the same period, the Chaves government was also increasing its ties with the United States and seeking technical assistance from the newly formed development agencies of the United Nations and the World Bank. These ties also seem to have created some resentment. In a letter to Juan Natalicio González, Víctor Morinigo notes that he was told that:

> [D]on Federico [Chaves] has not hesitated one second in opting for a policy of cooperation with the United States. And I would tell them: eat, without even manioc, and feed the people with it. Paraguay is not in the Caribbean and its geographic location imposes on it a certain policy with its great neighbor to the South.[25]

STROESSNER AND THE MARCH TO THE EAST

The coup that ended the Chaves government and brought Alfredo Stroessner to the presidency in August 1954 also brought about a resurgence of activities with Brazil. Although Stroessner and González shared a dislike for the Chaves government, Stroessner did not seem to share González's sense of the innate nature of relations between Paraguay and Argentina.

In August 1954 Brazilian president Getulio Vargas approved the construction of the road east from Col. Oviedo to the Paraná River. In a treaty signed in Rio de Janeiro on January 20, 1956, financing for the road was secured. The Rio de Janeiro agreement seems to have made official something that already had been decided. The peculiar financing arrangement, based on the reactivation of an old loan made by the government of Brazil to the government of Paraguay in 1942, had been

---

[25]González Collection, MS-E192. Letter dated May 3, 1952.

approved by Vargas shortly before his death in 1954.[26] His successor, João Cafe Filho, agreed to continue the project but insisted that the arrangement be approved by Congress. By 1955 approval was obtained and preliminary work begun (*O Globo*, November 12, 1955).

The January 1956 agreement signaled the reestablishment of relations between Paraguay and Brazil and, like the Argana-Aranha accords of 1941, it would set the stage for a series of future accords and stronger links between the two countries. Under the agreement, Paraguay renewed Brazil's free port privileges at Concepción and Brazil gave Paraguay privileges at Paranágua, a port on the Atlantic south of Santos and directly east of Asunción. Thus, the road east from Asunción to the Paraná could connect with the expanding Brazilian highway system to carry goods to the new facilities at Paranágua.[27] At the time of the signing, traffic across the Paraná was minimal and carried out by small boats traveling between Pto. Pres. Franco in Paraguay and Foz de Iguaçú in Brazil. Thus the Brazilians agreed to finance the construction of a bridge across the Paraná.

An additional accord signed at the January 1956 meeting provided for Brazil to finance and conduct studies of the hydroelectric potential of two tributaries to the Paraná River, the Acaray and Monday rivers, in the area near the proposed bridge. The Brazilian government also committed to co-sign whatever loans were necessary for the construction of a hydroelectric facility and to buy 20 percent of the energy produced. Paraguay's ambassador to Brazil and soon-to-become minister of foreign relations, Raúl Sapena Pastor, commenting on these developments, noted that relations between the two countries had "advanced fifty years in one." Brazil was giving Paraguay a "window on the Atlantic" and helping Paraguay achieve "economic independence." Sapena Pastor noted that, while Brazil asked little in return, Paraguay was

> doing everything to be useful to Brazil and one example of that is the recent pact that permits the construction by Brazil of hydroelectric facilities on the Acaray and Monday rivers in [Paraguayan] territory so that a great

---

[26] Brazil had loaned Paraguay 100 million cruzeiros (equivalent to U.S. $6 million) on June 6, 1942, forgiven the loan and accrued interest in August 1955, and now reissued the funds (112,254,777 cruzeiros) payable over a twenty-year period at 4 percent interest. The purpose of the original loan was the construction of the route to the Paraná, but disbursements had been terminated in 1948. See Miranda 1980: 66.

[27] The missing link within Brazil in this network was the Foz-to-Curitiba portion of the road, and Brazil promised to complete this portion of its highway system so as to connect with the road coming from Paraguay. This Curitiba-Foz road had been included in the National Highway Plan of 1942, but little or no progress had been made. Rail or river service was adequate to meet the needs of isolated communities in this part of Brazil. Sizable immigration into the area did not take place until this road was built in the late 1950s, opening the eastern portion of the state of Paraná and facilitating Brazilian westward expansion.

part of the [Brazilian] state of Paraná can have progress based on electric power.[28]

The presidents of Paraguay and Brazil met in Foz de Iguaçú in October 1956 to lay the cornerstone for the bridge and sign accords establishing a joint commission to study a highway from Concepción to Pedro Juan Caballero.[29] Also signed in October was a General Treaty on Trade and Investment. Its most notable feature seems to have been Article 8, which provided that payment for goods traded would be made in cruzeiros (up to 250 million in each direction). The list of goods covered by the treaty that Paraguay might export to Brazil included cattle, foodstuffs, tobacco, cement, essential oils, wood, hides, and handicrafts items such as *nanduti* and *aho poi*. The list of Brazilian exports covered by the treaty was some six times as long as that of Paraguay; processed raw materials and capital goods played the largest part. Imports would be exempt from all foreign exchange taxes, licenses, or fees, and exports free of all bonuses or subsidies. The cruzeiro operations in Brazil would be authorized without previous deposit requirements (*cobertura cambial*) and in Paraguay would be transacted in the free market. Requests for permission to export or import between the two countries would be granted automatically by the appropriate agency in each country. In effect, the treaty allowed trade between the two countries to take place outside all the existing regulations for foreign trade in each country.[30] A second important feature of the treaty was its treatment of capital. Brazilian firms and individuals wishing to invest in Paraguay would receive the same treatment as national domestic investors. The purpose was to encourage the establishment of small industries in Paraguay to transform raw materials and increase the value added of Paraguayan exports.

In February 1957 an accord was signed to begin construction of the Concepción-Pedro Juan Caballero road, and in September, when Stroessner traveled to Rio de Janeiro for Brazilian independence day celebrations, he signed an accord for the construction of a hydroelectric project on the Acaray River. Later that month construction of the international bridge

---

[28] *O Estado de São Paulo*, May 29, 1956, p. 42. The speech was given on the occasion of Sapena Pastor's departure from Brazil and the signing of further agreements on the construction of the international bridge over the Paraná.

[29] Work on the road was begun again in 1948 after the end of the civil war by the Brazilian Battalion Z4, using equipment from Mate Larangeira. Brazilian investors were beginning to establish large coffee plantations in the area near Pedro Juan Caballero, and the region was of increasing interest to the Brazilian government. In March 1955 the rail spur to Ponto Pora was completed, and the government donated some of the equipment used in its construction to the government of Paraguay to speed progress on the Paraguayan side.

[30] While not a primary purpose, the hope was that such measures would reduce the illegal trade taking place in border areas. Contraband along the border with Mato Grosso was estimated at 70 to 80 million cruzeiros in the mid-1950s. *O Estado de São Paulo*, January 11, 1956.

began. During this time, construction of the road east from Col. Oviedo was progressing. Construction was carried out by the joint commission itself and by Brazilian and Paraguayan firms.[31] It was completed in 1959 at an average cost of 900,000 guaranies per kilometer.[32]

As the decade ended, Paraguay accorded Brazil free port privileges at Encarnación, and the joint commission for the Concepción-Pedro Juan Caballero road turned in its final report. The report endorsed the construction of the road, noting its potential positive impact on economic activity in the northeastern region of Paraguay, especially with respect to the commercialization and export of yerba mate and coffee. The report also noted that the road would be a singular example of the Pan American spirit, as it would connect Paraguay with the Brazilian highway system and the transcontinental railroad running from Santos on the Atlantic to Arica (Chile) on the Pacific. The Brazilian author of the report went on to note, however,

> the most significant aspect of these undertakings, as Foreign Minister Macedo Soares has said, is not the construction to be carried out but the complete demonstration that Brazil wishes to cordially extend its loyal hands to Paraguay, giving the technical assistance to realize all the necessary studies and providing the financial assistance required to cover the cost of carrying out these studies. Once the studies are completed, I am convinced that the good relations between Paraguay and Brazil will permit the execution of this project if it should be the case that financing were necessary.[33]

While bilateral relations with Brazil were expanding at a rapid pace, Argentina was not ignored. In 1958, an Argentina-Paraguay accord was signed to form a joint technical commission to study the hydroelectric potential of the Yacyreta-Apipé rapids on the lower Paraná River where it forms the border between the two countries. The joint commission prepared a feasibility study identifying two alternative dam sites and submitted their report in 1964. Further study was required, and activities of the commission progressed slowly throughout the 1960s.

---

[31] Beginning in August 1956 the Brazilian firm Th. Marinho de Andrade worked on kilometers 135–195. The Paraguayan firm Barrail Hnos. built some 163 meters of bridges along the route. Robert Both Cia. constructed culverts along the first 23 kilometers of the route. González Collection, MS-E231, report of the Joint Commission on the Col. Oviedo-Pto. Pte. Stroessner Highway, no date on document but signed January 1959 by Indalecio Colman, head of the Paraguayan portion of the commission.

[32] Depending on the exchange rate used, this is equal to U.S. $20,000 to $60,000.

[33] González Collection, MS-E231. Report by Col. Elysio Carlos Dale Coutinho of the Joint Commission on the Concepción-Pedro Juan Caballero road as reprinted in *Hacienda Pública*, no date, pp. 87–102.

The Argentine-Paraguayan project on the lower Paraná River, however, was soon overshadowed by events upstream. In January 1961 Presidents Stroessner and Juscelino Kubitschek met to inaugurate the bridge linking Paraguay and Brazil at the town of Puerto Presidente Stroessner. The bridge was not yet complete, but Kubitschek was about to leave office, and the meeting was a high-profile public relations event. During the ceremonies, Kubitschek presented Stroessner with the plans for the Acaray-Monday hydroelectric project. The dams would produce some 400,000 kilowatts of power, and with the plans in hand, Paraguay hoped to obtain the needed $15 million financing from one of the recently formed multilateral development banks. Stroessner presented Kubitschek with a key to the city of Asunción and a piece of property in the newly created city of Puerto Presidente Stroessner on the Paraguayan side of the bridge. Stroessner took the occasion to say that, "if with this bridge and its land Brazil has opened for us the doors to overcome our mediterranean state in order to move us closer to the Atlantic, then Paraguay has opened its heart to Brazil forever" (*Patria*, January 28, 1961).

Over the next few years, relations between the two countries prospered. The two signed an accord for the peaceful uses of nuclear energy in 1961. When the Paraguayan national airlines, LAP, began service in 1963, its first flight was the Asunción-São Paulo-Rio de Janeiro route. In 1964 the National University's School of Philosophy, built with a grant from Brazil, was inaugurated, and the bridge across the Paraná was finally fully completed and inaugurated again—this time with Stroessner and Brazilian President Humberto de Alencar Castello Branco in attendance.

Meanwhile, as Paraguay moved ahead slowly on the Acaray project,[34] Brazil began studies for a very large dam on the Paraná at the Guairá Falls (or Sete Quedas in Brazil). Brazilian president Janio Quadros commissioned the first full study of the energy potential of the Guairá Falls in 1961. The design of the hydroelectric project was commissioned to a Brazilian engineer, Octayio Marcondes Ferraz, who had been involved in the Paulo Afonso project in the Brazilian northeast. His design called for the dam to be built at the point on the Paraná where the river turns south and falls more than fifty meters. It would possess an installed capacity of ten million kilowatts for an estimated cost of $1.015 billion in 1963.

Actual construction of the dam could not begin, however, until a long-standing boundary dispute between Paraguay and Brazil was settled. The commission established to demarcate the northeastern boundary after the War of the Triple Alliance (1865–1870) had not been able to come to agreement on the exact national boundaries in the area

---

[34]For a full discussion of this process, see Birch 1984.

of the Guairá Falls. According to the Brazilian interpretation of the boundary decision, the western edge of the proposed Sete Quedas Dam would lie in Brazilian territory. The Paraguayans disputed this interpretation. In June 1965 Brazil moved troops into the area and Paraguay protested.

Relations between the two countries deteriorated until a diplomatic solution was finally found. On June 22, 1966, Paraguay and Brazil signed the Acta Final, which constitutes the foundation of the Itaipu Treaty. The Acta Final established that the

> electric energy eventually produced by the variation in elevation of the Paraná River from and including Saltos de Guairá or the Salto Grande de las Siete Caídas to the mouth of the Iguaçú River will be divided in equal parts between the two countries.

The negotiations that led to the Acta Final were conducted in utmost secrecy. In fact, the text of the agreement was not made public until June 21, 1973. Marcondes Ferraz, designer of the discarded Sete Quedas project and president of the Brazilian national electric power company, Eletrobras, was completely unaware of the negotiations when the Acta Final was signed. He describes the Acta Final as something that "came out of Itamaraty [the Ministry of Foreign Relations]."[35] The Acta Final is perhaps the crowning touch to decades of a growing alliance. As a result of the Acta Final, a joint commission was formed, preliminary studies were conducted, and the Itaipu Treaty was signed on April 26, 1973. Construction of the dam began in 1975.

In December 1973, Paraguay signed the Yacyreta Treaty with Argentina for the construction of a dam on the Paraná River at the Apipé rapids downstream from Itaipu near the city of Encarnación. Progress on the construction of the dam has been slow, with much time spent negotiating minor differences and fighting accusations of corruption in the adjudication of contracts. The contract for civil works was awarded in 1983 and it is estimated that Yacyreta will begin generating electricity in 1993.

Paraguay experienced rapid economic growth in the late 1970s as a result of the construction of the Itaipu Dam. During the same period, international commodity prices rose; agricultural production in the eastern region expanded rapidly and was exported through Paranágua using the fully completed highway links through Brazil. The economic growth was possible as a result of the series of international accords outlined above. Thus, we turn our attention to the economic impact of pendulum politics.

---

[35] Interview with Octavio Marcondes Ferraz, São Paulo, Brazil, June 21, 1983.

Pendulum Politics and Economic Development

As described in the opening section of this chapter, Paraguay's strongest international relations were with Argentina. With the end of the Liberal era in 1936, however, and the rise of a new party and a more statist political spirit in Paraguay, the door was open for the development of a new set of international relationships. Estigarribia, who had traveled widely and had served as ambassador in the United States, indicated his larger perspective through the accords he signed with Argentina, Brazil, and the United States on his way back to Paraguay to assume the presidency. Morinigo made this international perspective explicit in his conception of the Revolución Nacional Paraguaya. He actively sought international accords with neighboring countries to promote Paraguay's economic growth. The Argana-Aranha accords of 1941 were the first concrete step toward breaking the hegemony of Argentina over Paraguayan trade, and they set in motion a chain of events that would create conditions to favor Paraguayan economic growth and development over the next forty years.

The success of Morinigo's strategy was largely the result of the political climate of the period. His proposals were positively received by neighboring governments because his views with regard to the important role of the state in the economy were consistent with ideas popular in those countries as well—especially in Brazil after the creation of the Estado Novo in 1937.[36] Spurred by the Chaco War and the increasing role of the military in national government, Brazil's traditional rivalry with Argentina intensified and Paraguay was a strategic target (see Levine 1970: 157).

Estimating the effect of Morinigo's policy on economic development, however, is difficult. The first systematic attempt to estimate the size and composition of the Paraguayan economy was not undertaken until the mid-1940s (published in 1948 by Soler and Cirovic). This study notes that during 1938–46 the volume of production of basic goods remained quite stagnant, while the volume of production of those goods more typical of urban consumption increased. Imports of such goods also rose. Between 1938 and 1941, increasing urbanization (largely the result of returning veterans who stayed in Asunción) and rising incomes put upward pressure on domestic prices. After 1941, however, rising international prices are thought to have been the cause of the rising price level in Paraguay. The study argues that, while domestic prices rose, the guarani remained stable in its relation to gold and the U.S. dollar, which implies that the increase in the value of gross domestic production reflects rising real income rather than inflation. The report estimates the total value of

---

[36]In Argentina, the change came later, during the mid-1940s, as Perón became more influential.

GNP in 1946 at 450 million guaranies ($150 million) for a per capita income of $125.[37]

As in other Latin American countries, Paraguayan exports rose rapidly between 1940 and 1946, about 150 percent in volume terms and 315 percent in value. The import bill rose 214 percent between 1941 and 1946; volume was quite erratic but showed a general tendency to decline.[38]

Despite increasing relations with Brazil, Paraguayan trade remained focused on Argentina. Exports to Argentina accounted for about 20 percent of all Paraguayan exports between 1940 and 1946, and imports from Argentina represented 47 percent of Paraguay's imports. The share of Paraguayan exports going to Brazil was 0.3 percent during the same period; imports from Brazil, predominantly cotton and cotton textiles, amounted to about 16 percent of all imports.[39] In addition, a large portion of Paraguay's export income was derived from Argentine firms operating in Paraguay, principally in ranching and forest industries.

Argentine investment in Paraguay in 1948 amounted to about $15 million, or about one-fourth of all foreign investment in Paraguay. Brazilian investment in the country was confined to the banking industry and amounted to $0.8 million, or about 1 percent of the total (table 11.1). Thus improved relations with Brazil seem to have had little immediate effect on the Paraguayan economy. Real improvement in transportation facilities between the two countries was needed to transform the words of the accords into concrete economic effects.

Of course, during the early 1940s, World War II dominated the scene. Even the United States, which did not regard Morinigo's state-interventionist economic policies favorably, was willing to overlook them in its effort to win the cooperation of the Latin American nations for the Allied cause. During the war years, Paraguay probably prospered more from increased aid than from increased exports. As World War II ended, U.S. policy in Latin America changed markedly. The emphasis shifted from foreign aid designed to acquire goodwill and allegiance to the promotion of economic and political philosophies conducive to the expansion of U.S. private business interests abroad. Morinigo's national-

---

[37] These calculations differ from an Argentine estimate reported in the same study that placed total GNP at $56 million (170 million guaranies) and per capita income at $55. The Soler and Cirovic (1948) estimates appear consistent with subsequent data.

[38] Soler and Cirovic 1948: 32. The International Monetary Fund reports slightly different statistics: between 1938 and 1946, export growth of 300 percent and import growth of 240 percent. However, 1938 exports seem unusually low, amounting to only 60 percent of exports in 1928. The IMF reports no data for 1940. See *International Financial Statistics*, 1949, p. 18.

[39] There was undoubtedly some quantity of unregistered trade across the border with Argentina and Brazil. Since there are no reliable estimates of the size of this trade, no attempt is made to include it here. We rely on the published statistics.

TABLE 11.1
PARAGUAY'S FOREIGN INVESTMENT

	1948	1950	1952–60	1974–80
	(percentage of total investment)			
Argentina	25.3	42.7	32.4	12.7
Brazil	1.2	1.5	6.4	27.2
United States	25.0	25.3	38.9	15.8

Sources: Ministry of Economy, *Paraguay Industrial y Comercial,* Asunción, July 1949; U.S. Embassy estimate, Danco 1963: 137; Baer and Birch 1987.

ism was no longer ignored; U.S. aid to Paraguay quickly declined. At about the same time, a resurgence of economic liberalism in Brazil came with the end of the Vargas era. These factors, combined with the rivalries within the Morinigo administration, brought the Revolución Nacional Paraguaya to an end.

Although the 1947 civil war was brief, the political and economic turmoil left in its wake endured for many years and wreaked havoc on the Paraguayan economy. The four presidents who held office in the next five years were all Colorados but their administrations were characterized by a renewed focus on Argentina. Beginning with the return in 1946 of Juan Natalicio González to the political arena in Paraguay, the themes of the 1930s—of Piñedo and the Acta de Mendoza—were revived. However, initiatives begun while González was finance minister were not formalized until the economic union was signed by Chaves. Political and economic instability prevented any proposals for increased trade and economic growth from being implemented.

As a whole, the period between 1947 and 1953 shows little economic progress. Exports dropped in 1947, while imports rose—giving Paraguay its first balance of trade deficit since the Chaco War period. Agricultural production stagnated. Industrial production fell by 7 percent between 1946 and 1949 and then rose slowly until 1953 when it regained its 1946 level (see Danco 1963: 130). Real economic growth was slight (table 11.2) and inflation soared.

TABLE 11.2
PARAGUAY'S REAL GNP GROWTH, 1938–75

1938–46	1946–52	1954–65	1965–75
	(Annual average)		
4.83%	2.7%	3.61%	5.88%

Sources: Ugarte Centurion 1983; Central Bank of Paraguay.

Exports to Argentina increased as a share of total exports to almost 30 percent, while those to Brazil dropped slightly. Paraguay's imports from Brazil and Argentina both declined as a share of total imports as trade with Europe resumed. According to data from 1950, Argentine investment in Paraguay increased to almost 43 percent of total investment, while Brazilian investment remained roughly constant, limited to the banking operations of the Banco do Brasil.

With the fall from power of Chaves and Perón and the rise of the former Brazilian *becario* (scholarship recipient) Alfredo Stroessner to the presidency of Paraguay, the pendulum began to swing back toward Brazil. Fortuitously, by the mid-1950s, as Paraguay attempted to pick up the pieces and revive the failing economy, Vargas had returned to power in Brazil and adopted an aggressive development policy that called for a billion dollars of investment in transportation, energy, and basic industries over a five-year period. Known as the Lafer Plan, it marked the beginning of a developmentalist attitude and coincided with a policy of cooperation with the international financial system (see Skidmore 1967: 95). Although Vargas remained in power this time for little more than three years, succeeding Brazilian administrations, most notably that of Kubitschek (1954–59), found Paraguay's aspirations consistent with their own national goals and encouraged the development of ties with Paraguay.

Brazilian cooperation was too extensive and too expensive to be attributed to a lavish gesture of friendship. The portion of the Asunción-Paranágua highway in Paraguay alone cost some $1.4 million, the studies for the Acaray-Monday hydroelectric projects cost nearly $1 million, and the bridge across the Paraná River cost some 200 billion cruzeiros. At least some portion of the highway funds were loans, but the bridge and the feasibility studies were outright gifts. The likely explanation is that Brazil saw short-term and long-term benefits to be derived from these projects. They were all carried out by Brazilian firms and/or government agencies and involved little or no foreign exchange while employing domestic resources and developing technical capabilities in Brazil.

In the long run, Brazil stood to gain from improved relations with Paraguay. In the mid-1950s, Paraguay was an unknown market for Brazilian entrepreneurs; thus the importance of the 1956 General Treaty on Commerce and Investment required some explanation. In January, Foreign Minister Jose Carlos Macedo Soares met with business leaders in São Paulo to explain the treaty, its benefits, and its place in Brazilian foreign policy. While acknowledging that Paraguay was a small and poor country, he explained the long-run outlook as follows:

> It is the intention of our country to contribute to the awakening and economic independence of Paraguay,

providing favorable conditions for development, incentives for investment, and industrialization within the country in order that, in the possibly near future, it may constitute a real market for our products (*O Estado de São Paulo*, January 11, 1956).

As a way of increasing trade between the two countries, the 1956 Treaty on Trade and Investment seems to have been quite effective. In 1955 Paraguay exported to Brazil products valued at $0.2 million and imported from Brazil goods of approximately the same value. Five years later the board of directors of the Federation and Center of Industries of São Paulo (CIESP-FIESP) met to discuss the "delicate situation" of the trade agreement: Brazilian exports to Paraguay had reached $1.1 million in 1960 but imports from Paraguay amounted to only $0.5 million. Worse yet, there was little hope that imports from Paraguay could be increased, since markets in Brazil had a surplus of many of those products Paraguay was in a position to supply. The organizations called for further study of the problem because Paraguay "represented a large market of consumers of Brazilian products." In fact, in 1958 Paraguay had been the largest single buyer of Brazilian textiles.[40]

This trend continued throughout the 1960s and during the 1970s. The bridge across the Paraná was finally completed in 1965, and during the following decade imports from Brazil rose to an average of 8 percent of all Paraguayan imports. Exports to Brazil, although still a small fraction of total exports, tripled. By the Itaipu period (roughly 1975–80), imports from Brazil were exceeding those from Argentina as a share of all imports. As a result of expanded agricultural production made possible by the new road and the construction of Itaipu, Paraguay experienced dramatic rates of growth during the second half of the 1970s (see Baer and Birch 1984).

CONCLUSIONS

Some have suggested that Paraguay's ties with Brazil that were so evident in the 1970s are a product of the Stroessner regime and that they represent the Colorado Party's response to the Liberal-Argentina alliance: a Colorado-Brazil alliance. This chapter would argue that such is not the case. Public policy in Paraguay did not switch in conformity with the party in power in Paraguay, but more in response to the economic conditions and public policies of neighboring countries. To preserve its own sovereignty, Paraguay needs to be able to swing between the two countries, and it goes wherever it gets more favorable treatment. The strong Brazilian presence seen in Paraguay during the Stroessner ad-

---

[40]*Diario de São Paulo*, February 10, 1961. Dollar values of trade taken from *Direction of International Trade* 10 (1958): 91 and 13 (February–June 1962): 23.

ministration is the result of a long process with its roots in the 1930s and a traceable path back to the 1941 Argana-Aranha accords.

Nations began to see in the 1940s a bigger role for the State in economic and social affairs, and the State assumed more responsibility for direction of the economy. The Paraguayan state was faced with a small country, dependent on trade but with no direct outlet on the sea and no obvious mineral or cash crop to exploit. Neighboring countries were more economically advanced but were experiencing the same transformation of political ideas. As the state assumed a more active role in the economy it seems quite natural that it would play off its traditional strengths: legal structures and international relations. Thus new constitutions, new laws regarding land tenure, banking and investment, and finally direct production of goods by firms owned by the state appeared in the 1940s. The ideas of the U.N. Economic Commission on Latin America (ECLA) in the 1950s created a favorable climate for such constructs, and with the growth of development agencies in the 1960s, government planning and government-designed strategies for development became the norm. For Paraguay, all these developments helped to promote the strong state and state-led international relations as development policy.

That the swing of the pendulum toward Brazil has been of such duration is more a reflection on the contrasting state of political and economic affairs in Argentina and Brazil than it is a product of the length of the Stroessner presidency. Between 1960 and 1980, economic growth in Argentina averaged about 2 percent per year, while in Brazil it averaged more than 5 percent. During the same period, Argentina experienced at least twelve changes of government; Brazil had only eight.

At some point, bilateral policies become integration policies. For Paraguay, Argentina, and Brazil, the development of the two gigantic hydroelectric projects, Itaipu and Yacyreta, may well be that point. The joint administration of a strategic resource like energy may signify the end of national borders as the boundary of a decision-making unit. Paraguay is now in a position to interrupt the supply of electric power to Brazil and, if Yacyreta reaches completion, to Argentina. If Yacyreta is not brought on line, Paraguay could be subject to the same treatment from Brazil, while if Yacyreta is completed, Paraguay would always have an alternative source of power. Thus Yacyreta, which is superfluous in terms of Paraguay's energy needs, becomes critical to Paraguay's strategy of pendulum politics. The two projects, which far outstrip Paraguay's economic need for electric energy, are required for the protection of national sovereignty in the game of pendulum politics.

If Argentina and Brazil were to end their traditional rivalry, Paraguay's strategy would become less effective. The Argentine-Brazilian integration agreement signed in July 1986 may signal just such a change in relations between those two countries. If the agreement prospers and the rivalry ends, Paraguay will have to find a new strategy for dealing with its larger and more powerful neighbors.

REFERENCES

Alemánn, Roberto T. 1977. "Sobre uniones aduaneras y áreas de libre cambio." In *La Argentina: Su posición y rango en el mundo por Federico Piñedo y ensayos en su honor*. Buenos Aires: Editorial Sudamericana.

Baer, Werner, and Melissa H. Birch. 1984. "Expansion of the Economic Frontier: Paraguayan Growth in the 1970s," *World Development* 12:783–98.

Birch, Melissa H. 1984. "Public Enterprise and Economic Development: The Case of ANDE in Paraguay." Ph.D. diss., University of Illinois, Champaign.

Costanzo, G.A. 1961. *Programas de estabilización económica en América Latina*. Mexico City: Centro de Estudios Monetarios Latinoamericano.

Danco, Leon A. 1963. "A Review of Some Factors Influencing the Economic Development of Paraguay, 1954–59." Ph.D. diss., Western Reserve University.

Di Tella, Guido. 1986. "Economic Controversies in Argentina from the 1920s to the 1940s." In *The Political Economy of Argentina 1880–1946*, edited by Guido di Tella and D.C.M. Platt. London: Macmillan.

Grow, Michael. 1981. *The Good Neighbor Policy and Authoritarianism in Paraguay: United States Economic Expansion and Great-Power Rivalry in Latin America during World War II*. Lawrence: The Regents Press of Kansas.

Levine, Robert M. 1970. *The Vargas Regime*. New York: Columbia University Press.

Lewis, Paul H. 1965. *The Politics of Exile*. Chapel Hill: University of North Carolina Press.

———. 1980. *Paraguay under Stroessner*. Chapel Hill: University of North Carolina Press.

Miranda, Aníbal. 1980. *Apuntes sobre el desarrollo paraguayo, 1940–73*. Asunción: El Gráfico.

Ocampos Caballero, Augusto. 1983. *Testimonios de un presidente: Entrevista al Gral. Higinio Morinigo*. Asunción: El Lector.

Raine, Philip. 1956. *Paraguay*. New Brunswick, N.J.: Scarecrow.

Republic of Argentina. 1953. *Unión Económica Argentino Paraguaya: Afirmación de un destino común*. Buenos Aires: Ministerio de Relaciones Exteriores y Culto.

Rivarola, Vicente. 1957. *Memorias Diplomáticas*. Buenos Aires: Editorial Ayacucho.

Rout, Leslie B., Jr. 1970. *Politics of the Chaco Peace Conference, 1935–39*. Austin: University of Texas Press.

Salum Flecha, Antonio. 1972. *Historia diplomática del Paraguay de 1869 a 1938*. Asunción: Emasa.

Skidmore, Thomas E. 1967. *Politics in Brazil, 1930–1964*. New York: Oxford University Press.

Soler, Carlos A., and Milán Cirovic. 1948. *La producción total del Paraguay en 1946 y su valor neto: Ensayo sobre la renta nacional*. Asunción: La Colmena.

Travassos, Mario. 1938. *Projeção continental de Brasil*. São Paulo: Companhia Editora Nacional.

Ugarte Centurión, Delfín. 1983. *La evolución histórica de la economía paraguaya*. Asunción: Editorial Graphis.

Warren, Carlos. 1943. *Emancipación económica americana*. Montevideo: Editorial Ceibo.

Warren, Harris Gaylord. 1949. *An Informal History of Paraguay*. Norman: University of Oklahoma Press.

Zook, David H., Jr. 1960. *The Conduct of the Chaco War*. New Haven, Conn.: Bookman.

12

National Borders and Foreign Policy: The Case of Argentina

Freeman J. Wright

This study explores several ways in which a South American nation is influenced by its bordering countries. The episodes and data to be presented concern Argentina and its five neighbors—Bolivia, Brazil, Chile, Paraguay, and Uruguay. The areas of interaction include a territorial dispute, trade, migration, and economic cooperation.

Virtually any consideration of interactions among bordering nations can benefit students of Latin America. Policy analyses have tended to focus on internal domestic factors or on external influences associated with North-South relationships. Interactions among neighbors have traditionally been given secondary levels of importance—buried within such concepts as the "international environment" approach to political development or the "core-periphery" relationship in dependency theory. Studies of Latin America from the perspective of U.S. or Soviet foreign policy also have relegated relations among bordering nations to more or less incidental concern.

On a positive note, renewed interest in Latin American geopolitics has begun to focus attention on relationships among bordering nations. Perhaps the most influential work has been Child's *Geopolitics and Conflict in South America*, which contains a typology of potential conflict situations, including territory, resources, migration, ideology, and influence (1985: 14–15). Other writers assess the United States and Canada with results that suggest the usefulness of exploring the pertinence of these topics to other hemispheric neighbors (Keohane and Nye 1977: 167–78). And while Ferguson's book on economic cooperation in Latin America does not give extensive consideration to programs among neighbors, it does clearly establish their importance (Ferguson 1984).

The information and analysis to follow are intended to enlarge the perspectives held by scholars interested in the influence of bordering nations on one another. When the range and variety of such influences are more fully appreciated, analysts can better address many questions usually ignored or slighted in the study of Latin American politics. Some of these include: To what extent can domestic political elites make policy without consideration of bordering states? Are relations with neighbors used by manipulative national decision makers as rationale for measures which otherwise would not be popular or feasible? How do patterns of trade and migration between bordering countries compare or contrast with those articulated in theories of political development and dependency? For example, do the more influential South American nations interact with poorer, weaker neighbors in ways similar to those between so-called "developed" or "core" nations and their "underdeveloped" or "peripheral" neighbors? Finally, how well can bordering states cooperate?

BORDER CONFLICT AND TERRITORIAL DISAGREEMENT

Latin American nations have had their share of border disputes and territorial disagreements, and Argentina is no exception. Border conflicts have been especially important to Chile, Bolivia, and Peru; Bolivia, and Paraguay; Peru and Ecuador; Venezuela and Colombia; Costa Rica and Nicaragua; and El Salvador and Honduras.

Argentina's most notorious territorial conflict has been the Malvinas War of 1982 with Great Britain, but more pertinent in the present context is the Beagle Island dispute of 1977–1985 with Chile. The Beagle affair exemplifies well how boundary disagreements can plague relations between two neighbors and also how unpopular autocratic regimes may attempt to exploit such tensions for domestic political advantage.

The eastern entrance to the Beagle Channel lies in Tierra del Fuego at the southern tip of South America. The channel's southern coast is Chilean; its northern shore is Argentine. At its entrance are three small islands whose sovereignty had never been resolved to both nations' satisfaction, despite many attempts at negotiation. A 1902 treaty had assigned Great Britain the role of arbiter of any future disputes, but Argentina never gained confidence in British motives in the South Atlantic and ultimately secured instead an arbitration by the International Court of Justice (ICJ), which was released (and ratified by the British Parliament) in 1977. The ICJ awarded the channel islands of Picton, Lennox, and Nueva to Chile.[1]

Chile announced forthwith its willingness to comply with the award, but a disappointed Argentina refused to accede and instead sought bilateral negotiations. The Argentines demanded at least one

---

[1] For the background in international law, see F.V. 1977.

island and wanted Chile to accept only a twelve-mile limit (instead of the standard two hundred) around its territory. When the Chileans resisted all such overtures, the Argentine generals tried a show of force by violating Chilean air and sea space. Chile protested, but Argentina continued to keep the pressure on with the support of most of its national press.[2]

The two nations' dictators, Jorge Videla of Argentina and Augusto Pinochet of Chile, met unsuccessfully in Mendoza, Argentina, in January 1978 in an effort to reduce tensions, but Argentina continued to reject the award's legitimacy and restated its complex legal claims to the territory. Chile indicated a willingness to negotiate the extent of the maritime boundaries surrounding the islands but not the grant of territory. Videla and Pinochet met again, this time in Chile, and established a binational commission to continue consideration of the problem. When in November 1978 this commission's report showed scant progress, the Argentine military regime made some more bellicose noises and raised the number of Chileans expelled from southern Argentina to about three thousand.

This new crisis generated diplomatic efforts for resolution by the Organization of American States and the United Nations, but it was the offer of Vatican mediation in late December 1978 that ultimately proved productive. After a key meeting in Uruguay, some shuttle diplomacy, and the continued failure of Chile and Argentina to resolve anything on their own, Pope John Paul II proposed yet another approach. According to the papal plan, Chile would own the three small islands in question but its maritime limit would extend only a limited distance. Chile expressed some reservations but nonetheless quickly endorsed the approach; Argentina neither explicitly accepted nor rejected it and continued to temporize through the entire duration of the military government, a period which included, of course, the war with Great Britain in the Malvinas.

Argentina evinced interest in settlement of the Beagle conflict only after the restoration of civilian government through the elections of October 1983. Indeed, the new president, Raúl Alfonsín, gave the matter extremely high priority, even though during the campaign he had not indicated the full extent to which he would expand negotiable points, probably out of a fear of provoking military intervention. Three months after the elections, Argentina and Chile signed a Treaty of Peace and Friendship recommitting themselves to meaningful negotiations. In another nine months, a protocol was ready, and in November 1984 Alfonsín put this accord before the Argentine electorate, who endorsed it by a margin of nearly three to one.

---

[2]Thorough accounts of Beagle Channel negotiations and their impact on domestic politics include Garrett 1985 and Fraga 1985.

The public dialogue revealed some divisions of opinion in Argentina. Shortly after Alfonsín was elected, several dozen leading military officers and nationalistic civilian diplomats of the Videla and Galtiera regimes signed a public proclamation urging the continued protection of national interests in the Beagle Channel. About a year later, just prior to the electoral consultation (Alfonsín would not call the November 1984 vote a binding referendum), the opposition to the protocol intensified and widened to include Peronistas. In defending the accord, Alfonsín argued that, in addition to permitting Argentina to work with Chile constructively in such areas as binational development projects, it would allow his administration to spend more time redressing the Malvinas question. Even with the aforementioned strong display of popular support by direct vote and subsequent approval by a fifty-vote margin in the Chamber of Deputies, the treaty was ratified in the Senate, where the Peronistas were stronger, by only one vote before finally being signed in April 1985.

Acceptance of the treaty required concessions from both nations, though more came from Argentina than from Chile. It was not as beneficial to the Chileans as the 1977 International Court of Justice's award had been, but Chile nonetheless obtained the three channel islands, because they fell on its side of a boundary drawn in the treaty to determine areas of sovereignty; however, Argentina had to respect only a three-mile maritime limit around the islands and thus had full navigational rights to its side of the channel boundary. Moreover, the outcome did not threaten Argentina's position in the Antarctic. It was clear to all, however, that the more powerful of two nations had not prevailed in the dispute.

In sum, the Beagle affair provided an issue which fanned nationalistic flames in Argentina, but not to the point of buttressing the deteriorating position of the military government or of causing political damage to the democratic Alfonsín administration. Recent Peronista victories in provincial, congressional, and presidential elections have not been attributed to reconsideration of how the Beagle Channel conflict was settled, but rather to economic issues and government handling of crimes committed by military officers during the Dirty War. Through the 1984 "consultative" election, the Argentine public demonstrated a preference for peaceful conflict resolution stronger than that of the military rulers and many of the civilian politicians who succeeded them in office. There is no apparent reason for the Beagle Island episode to encourage Carlos Menem's regime to exploit tensions with Chile for domestic political advantage.

ECONOMIC INTERDEPENDENCE AND COOPERATION

The economic interdependence of nations has long been recognized and in recent years has been given steadily increasing attention, although the question has not commonly been addressed in the context of bordering less-industrialized nations. This section examines the issues of trade, migratory labor, and joint economic development between Argentina and its neighbors. A variety of information sources is considered, including recent statistics on the flow and structure of international trade, migratory labor data, studies of Bolivian and Paraguayan migrants in Argentina, and information on power projects involving Argentina with Paraguay and Brazil.

Further study in these topic areas would greatly assist understanding of the full impact of borders on national policy in Latin America. In nations with small domestic markets, increased trade with neighbors becomes especially important, and Latin America's efforts to develop regional trading associations attest to this. Because some Latin American nations are far more industrialized than others, a fruitful question for further analysis would be whether these differing levels of industrialization could lead to patterns of economic dominance by the more advanced neighbor. Pertinent examples of labor migrating across borders exist throughout the hemisphere. One study of international labor patterns lists several:

> The United States is certainly not unique in its use of foreign labor, although it rarely shares the limelight with other migrant economies. For years, Mexican coffee plantations have employed Guatemalan workers. The Dominican cane fields are filled with Haitian migrants. And the Venezuelan countryside draws Colombian workers across the frontier dividing those two countries (Sanderson 1985: 3).

Although Argentina's international power agreements are not its only examples of cooperation (see Rudolph 1985: 269; Selcher 1985), they illustrate well how domestic politics and nationalism influence collaboration.

INTERNATIONAL TRADE

In 1986 Argentina conducted a larger share of its international trade with bordering nations than did most South American countries (see table 12.1). Argentine exports and imports amounted to $12.5 billion, of which trade with Bolivia, Brazil, Chile, Paraguay, and Uruguay constituted $2.3 billion, or 18.5 percent of Argentina's total international trade. Among the more geographically isolated northern and western nations of South America, only Peru conducted a modestly significant share of its trade (7.9 percent) with its neighbors. For Chile, Colombia, Venezuela, and Ecuador, the figure was less than 1.0 percent. Brazil's trade with its seven bordering South American nations made up only 8.6

percent of its international trade; but due to a high world total of almost $41 billion, this amounted to a significant $3.5 billion. Percentages of total trade conducted with neighbors were higher than Argentina's in Bolivia (59.6 percent), Paraguay (48.0 percent), and Uruguay (19.6 percent), but Argentina's dollar amount of $2.3 billion was second only to Brazil's.

TABLE 12.1
SOUTH AMERICAN NATIONS RANKED BY THE PERCENTAGE OF
TOTAL TRADE CONDUCTED WITH BORDERING NATIONS, 1986

Nations	Percentage of Total Trade with Neighbors	Absolute Value of Goods Traded in Millions of U.S. Dollars		Number of Neighbors	Geographic Region
		with all Nations	with Neighbors		
Bolivia	59.6	1,342	800	5	Center
Paraguay	48.0	743	357	3	Southeastern
Uruguay	19.6	2,013	395	2	Southeastern
Argentina	18.5	12,544	2,318	5	Southeastern
Brazil	8.6	40,941	3,528	7	Eastern
Peru	7.9	4,245	337	4	Western
Chile	.6	7,327	406	3	Western
Colombia	.5	9,251	437	3	Northern
Venezuela	.4	16,074	598	2	Northern
Ecuador	.2	5,031	92	2	Western

Source: Compiled from Wilkie, Lurey, and Ochoa 1988: 540–605.

Argentina's bordering nations vary substantially in importance as trading partners. The dollar amounts of total trade (exports plus imports) for each year from 1980 through 1986 appear in table 12.2. Calculations from these figures reveal that during this period 53.4 percent of Argentina's trade with its neighbors was with Brazil; the other bordering national trading partners were led by Bolivia (18.4 percent), followed by Chile (12.7 percent), Uruguay (8.6 percent), and Paraguay (6.8 percent). This ranking prevailed in five of the seven years, and the percentages seldom varied substantially from one year to the next. The most significant change over the period was Bolivia's growth in comparative importance; its percentage of Argentina's trade with bordering nations rose from under 12 percent in 1980 and 1981 to an average of about 21 percent for the final five years.

Further perspective on the importance of Argentina's trade with its neighbors can be gained by comparing it with trade with the United

TABLE 12.2
COMPARISON OF TRADE BETWEEN ARGENTINA, BORDERING NATIONS,
THE UNITED STATES, AND THE WORLD, 1980–1986
TOTAL TRADE (ABSOLUTE VALUE OF GOODS)
IN MILLIONS OF U.S. DOLLARS

Trading Partners	1980	1981	1982	1983	1984	1985	1986	Total
Bordering Nations								
Brazil	1,837	1,488	1,255	1,024	1,309	1,098	1,276	9,287
Bolivia	385	470	510	451	480	452	449	3,197
Chile	472	379	311	305	269	196	285	2,217
Uruguay	333	249	206	166	181	165	197	1,497
Paraguay	274	261	195	126	144	95	111	1,204
Total	3,301	2,847	2,477	2,072	2,383	2,006	2,318	17,402
United States	3,098	2,957	2,199	1,761	1,543	1,723	1,628	14,909
World	18,566	18,577	12,964	12,340	12,692	12,210	12,544	99,893

Source: Wilkie, Lurey, and Ochoa 1988: 540, 542.

States and total world trade. Except for 1981, Argentina's combined trade with Brazil, Bolivia, Chile, Uruguay, and Paraguay exceeded trade with Argentina's largest single trading partner, the United States (table 12.2). Moreover, the gap tended to widen as the decade progressed, reaching a peak of $840 million in 1984 and a second high of $680 million in 1986. The seven-year totals were $17.4 billion in trade with the bordering nations, $2.5 billion more than the $14.9 billion worth of goods exchanged with the United States. Calculations from table 12.2 show that Argentina's trade with its five neighbors also constituted a significant percentage of its world commerce throughout the period, ranging from a low of 15.3 percent in 1981 to a high of 19.1 percent in 1982, with a seven-year average of 17.4 percent.

Other data for 1986 further clarify the significance of the trade between Argentina and its bordering nations. Although Argentina accounted for a mere 4.0 percent of Brazil's trade and was far down its giant neighbor's ranking of trading partners, Brazil was third on Argentina's list, after the United States and Canada. Conversely, Bolivia ranked only eighth among Argentina's partners, while Argentina led Bolivia's list, accounting for 35.0 percent of its northern neighbor's total trade, as opposed to shares of 24.1 percent for the United States and 20.2 percent for Brazil. On the other hand, Chile, Uruguay, and Paraguay did not rank among Argentina's top ten trading partners, nor was Argentina close to the top of these nation's lists (Wilkie, Lurey, and Ochoa 1988: 540–603).

A breakdown of Argentina's trade with Brazil, Bolivia, Chile, and Uruguay by exports and imports appears in table 12.3. In every year from 1980 through 1986, Argentina imported more from its neighbors than it exported to them. The seven-year totals were $7.3 billion in exports, $2.8 billion less than the $10.1 billion in imports, for an average yearly deficit of $400 million.

TABLE 12.3
ABSOLUTE VALUE OF GOODS TRADED BETWEEN ARGENTINA AND ITS BORDERING NATIONS, 1980–1986 (IN MILLIONS OF U.S. DOLLARS)

Trading Partner	1980	1981	1982	1983	1984	1985	1986	Total
Exports								
Brazil	765	595	567	358	478	496	575	3,834
Chile	218	189	164	189	150	111	127	1,148
Paraguay	189	169	146	87	94	73	68	826
Uruguay	185	128	116	77	83	99	121	809
Bolivia	133	126	114	56	88	69	70	656
Export Total	1,490	1,207	1,107	767	893	848	961	7,273
Imports								
Brazil	1,072	893	688	666	831	612	701	5,463
Bolivia	252	344	396	395	392	383	378	2,540
Chile	254	190	147	116	119	85	158	1,069
Uruguay	148	121	90	89	98	66	76	688
Paraguay	85	95	49	59	50	20	43	398
Import Total	1,811	1,643	1,370	1,325	1,490	1,166	1,356	10,158

Source: Wilkie, Lurey, and Ochoa 1988: 542.

Only Bolivia and Brazil contributed to Argentina's unfavorable balance of trade with its neighbors. From 1980 through 1986, Bolivian exports to Argentina exceeded $2.5 billion, while its imports reached only $656 million. Brazil exported almost $5.5 billion in goods to Argentina and imported over $3.8 billion. Argentina's total deficits with the two neighbors were approximately the same—about $1.88 billion with Bolivia and $1.63 billion with Brazil. But the far lower volume of trade with Bolivia made its export-import ratio to Argentina nearly 4 to 1, as opposed to Brazil's 1.5 to 1. Over the seven-year period, Argentina counted slightly favorable trade totals with Chile ($79 million) and Uruguay ($121 million). Argentina's $428 million surplus with Paraguay reflected an export-import ratio of nearly 2.7 to 1, but it also was generated by a low volume of trade which averaged only $175 million per year.

Despite a negative balance of trade with its neighbors, Argentina maintained a world surplus for the last five years of the period. After total trade deficits in 1980 ($2.5 billion) and 1981 ($2.3 billion), Argentina realized favorable balances in 1982 ($2.3 billion), 1983 ($3.3 billion), 1984 ($3.5 billion), 1985 ($4.6 billion), and 1986 ($2.4 billion) (Wilkie, Lurey, and Ochoa 1988: 540). The 1985 figure was a record for Argentina. Even though its world trade surplus dropped to $400 million in 1987 (USITA 1988: 6), the decade's positive balance of trade provided Argentina with money to use for payments on its massive external debt. The point of this discussion is, however, that this happened in spite of the trade deficit with bordering countries that averaged $400 million per year.

Data in table 12.4 permit analysis of Argentina's 1986 commerce with Brazil, Bolivia, Chile, Uruguay, and Paraguay by category of goods traded. These data show that Argentina traded manufacturing products with its neighbors more than it exchanged agricultural products or mineral fuels and crude materials. Consisting of chemicals, basic manufactures, machines, transport equipment, and miscellaneous items, manufactured products constituted 48.2 percent of the imports and 46.8 percent of the exports. Crude materials and mineral fuels were imported more than exported by a margin of about four to one (40.0 percent to 9.8 percent). Nearly the reverse ratio existed for the agriculturally related products—food and live animals, beverages and tobacco, animal and vegetable oils, and fats. These commodities made up a substantial 43.4 percent of the exports and merely 11.9 percent of the imports. The largest trade surplus by single commodity and nation was a positive $290 million in agricultural products exchanged with Brazil; the principal contributor to the trade imbalance between Argentina and its neighbors was a negative $348 million in crude materials and mineral fuel with Bolivia.

TABLE 12.4
ARGENTINE TRADE WITH NEIGHBORING NATIONS
BY TYPE OF COMMODITY, 1986
(MILLIONS OF U.S. DOLLARS)

Trading Partner	Agricultural Products		Mineral Fuels, Crude Materials		Manufactured Products	
	Imports	Exports	Imports	Exports	Imports	Exports
Brazil	111.6	402.1	123.1	40.3	456.6	255.7
Bolivia	.2	13.8	350.0	2.1	2.5	44.6
Chile	17.9	31.1	27.3	9.8	103.3	95.9
Uruguay	10.6	16.6	3.8	22.5	78.5	90.2
Paraguay	17.7	10.3	28.7	32.7	1.1	24.4
Total	158.0	473.9	532.9	107.4	642.0	510.8

Source: Compiled from USITA 1988.

Argentina's strong position in Bolivia's export market for crude materials and mineral fuels might imply a core-periphery relationship between the two nations, but other components of dependency are absent. It is true that Bolivia sent 60 percent of all its exports to Argentina and virtually all of these were in the mineral fuel and crude material category, but Bolivia purchased only $45 million worth of manufactured products from Argentina. A full dependency relationship also would have had to include the significant presence of Argentine corporations and capital investment in Bolivia, foreign aid, and concomitant political influence.

MIGRATORY LABOR

Migrants from Bolivia, Paraguay, and Chile have influenced Argentina's labor force, social structure, and public policy. The following discussion considers the number, type, and location of these migrants; their patterns of assimilation; Argentine policy responses; and the migration's impact on one of the bordering nations.

Table 12.5 displays the number and distribution of migrants from all five neighboring countries as counted in the last four Argentine censuses (Villar 1984). The data reveal a doubling of migrants between 1947 and 1980 and average annual rates of increase of 3.8 percent from 1947 to 1960, 2.5 percent from 1960 to 1970, and 1.6 percent from 1970 to 1980. It is believed that the decline in growth rate during the 1970s was due in part to decreases in the purchasing power of salaries and stricter immigration controls during the later years of the decade.

TABLE 12.5
DISTRIBUTION OF FOREIGNERS FROM BORDERING COUNTRIES
BY ARGENTINE REGION, 1960–1980[a]

Region	1947	1960	1970	1980
Metropolitan	122,070[b]	121,420	249,860	304,670
Pampeana		5,370	58,300	81,245
Northeast	100,160	126,090	116,660	101,557
Northwest	46,950	74,720	52,470	47,395
Cuyana	9,390	23,350	23,320	33,852
Patagonia	34,430	70,050	87,450	108,326
Total	313,000	421,000	588,060	677,045

[a]Regions are defined as follows. Metropolitan: the Federal Capital and greater Buenos Aires. Pampeana: the remainder of the province of Buenos Aires, Santa Fe, Entre Ríos, Córdoba, and La Pampa. Northeast: Chaco, Formosa, Corrientes, and Misiones. Northwest: Salta, Jujuy, Tucumán, Santiago del Estero, La Rioja, and Catamarca. Cuyana: Mendoza, San Juan, and San Luis. Patagonia: Neuquén, Río Negro, Chubut, Santa Cruz, and Tierra del Fuego.

[b]The 1947 data from the metropolitan and Pampeana regions were not differentiated.

The changing geographical distribution of these migrants reflects several important trends, including urbanization. The metropolitan region's share of migrants from bordering nations grew from 26 percent in 1960 to 45 percent in 1980. Table 12.6, which differentiates by nationality of the migrants, reveals that by 1970, 136,369 Paraguayans had located in the city and province of Buenos Aires, compared to 41,702 Chileans and 37,943 Bolivians in the same area. All studies agree that Paraguayans also have remained the principal foreign-born group in the northeast, while Bolivians occupy this position in the northwest, and Chileans in Patagonia. The census data in table 12.5 reflect almost no migrant increase in the two northern regions between 1947 and 1980, while in Patagonia this population tripled during the same period to place the south second behind the metropolitan region in the total number of people born in neighboring countries.

TABLE 12.6
ARGENTINES BORN IN BOLIVIA, CHILE, AND PARAGUAY
BY PROVINCE OF RESIDENCE

Nationality	Residence	1947	1960	1970
Bolivians	Buenos Aires[a]	3,502	12,250	37,943
	Jujuy, Salta	41,917	68,480	47,486
	Others	2,355	8,425	18,171
Total		47,774	89,155	103,600
Chileans	Buenos Aires	8,508	30,072	41,702
	South[b]	33,140	68,913	53,149
	Others	9,915	19,180	50,049
Total		51,563	118,165	144,900
Paraguayans	Buenos Aires	12,383	45,975	136,369
	Formosa, Misiones	58,205	85,071	72,945
	Others	22,660	24,223	24,036
Total		93,248	155,269	233,350

[a]Includes the city and province of Buenos Aires.
[b]Includes the provinces of Chubut, Neuquén, Río Negro, Santa Cruz, and Tierra del Fuego.
Source: Adapted from Carrón 1979: 476.

Citizens of bordering nations originally came to Argentina to work in agriculture (Villar 1984: 453–55). Paraguayans were first attracted to the timber industry in the northeast and later to cotton and tea production in the same region. Bolivians came to work in the sugar industry and tobacco fields of the northwest and the grape fields of Cuyana. Chileans in Patagonia have been involved in fruit production, mineral extraction, timber, and, given the sparse population in this developing region, general economic activities. Paraguayans and Bolivians—more than Chileans—have moved to regional urban centers as well as to the Buenos Aires area to work at unskilled labor and domestic service. Skilled workers and professionals do not typically select a neighboring developing country as a destination. Although the political troubles of the 1970s in Chile and Uruguay caused many people to flee repressive regimes, Argentina's political climate did not offer an attractive alternative.

The Paraguayan sociologist Juan M. Carrón used census data from 1947, 1960, and 1970 to place immigrants from neighboring countries by Argentine residence and to determine their sector of employment (Carrón 1979). In 1970, there were 58,500 Uruguayan-born migrants, 79 percent of whom lived in the city and province of Buenos Aires, and 49,050 Brazilians, about half of whom lived in the northeast province of Misiones and another 30 percent in the Buenos Aires area.

Carrón's census data (table 12.6) locate the 103,700 Bolivians, 144,900 Chileans, and 233,350 Paraguayans counted in 1970. Of the Bolivian migrants, 45.8 percent were found in the northwest (Salta and Jujuy) and 36.6 percent in the city and province of Buenos Aires. Of the Paraguayans, who almost equaled the combined number of Bolivians and Chileans, 58.4 percent were found in the city and province of Buenos Aires and 31.2 percent in the two northeastern provinces of Formosa and Misiones.

Occupational data correlate well with the urbanization trend. In 1960, 34.3 percent of all workers born in neighboring nations were employed in agriculture; by 1970, this figure had dropped to 21.7 percent. During the same decade, the percentage of migrants from bordering nations in manufacturing jobs dropped slightly (from 26.4 to 24.4 percent), but sizable increases marked employment in such other urban sectors as construction (from 9.8 to 20.9 percent) and personal services (from 8.4 to 13.5 percent) (Carrón 1979: 484).

Another scholar considered the impact of workers from bordering countries in Argentina's metropolitan labor market of the 1960s. Adriana Marshall (1979) estimated that such migrants accounted for approximately 20 percent of the decade's rise in the greater Buenos Aires work force, as opposed to 14 percent of the national labor force's increase. Compared to native workers, recent migrants from bordering nations were younger, more likely to be unemployed, and, if employed, more apt to be wage earners, especially in unskilled construction and industrial work (if they were males) and domestic service (females). Within the manufacturing sector, the shoe and plastics industries were common employers. The still greater likelihood of employment in construction is partly due to the cost advantages of using temporary labor and avoiding payment of social benefits. The floating reserve of foreign labor helped keep Argentine construction labor intensive. The native work force was freed up for movement into more skilled, steadier jobs. The influx of foreign women to domestic service had a lesser displacement effect, but it permitted more native families to enjoy servants. Like their male counterparts, immigrant women were less deterred by lower wages, less security, and fewer social benefits.

Despite urbanization trends among migrants from neighboring nations, more than 125,000 such foreign-born laborers were shown by the 1970 census still to be working in agriculture. Undoubtedly, many other temporary rural workers did not appear in the official count. Scott Whiteford, a North American anthropologist, portrays the life of a major group of these workers in a study of Bolivians who came to toil in the sugar plantations of Argentina's northwest (Whiteford 1981).

Bolivian workers once were obtained primarily through coercive methods. For many years, most returned home annually from the plantations of Jujuy and Salta. Over the course of time, however, an increasing number opted to stay on in Argentina beyond the five months of steady employment in the sugar industry, often to work in different agricultural harvests. Other survival tactics for those who stayed on included marketing, short-term jobs, and operating stores for fellow migrants. Many moved to the city of Salta, but Whiteford cautions against perceiving them as urbanites; instead, they remained part of a labor reserve which transcended country-city distinctions. The operational economic unit was the family, and different members pursued different strategies for economic security and to take advantage of Argentina's educational and social service systems. Still, many Bolivian migrants came to regard life in Salta as preferable to a wholly rural existence because it afforded better opportunities for social organization, jobs, housing, and cheaper food. Low-income neighborhoods of Bolivians grew in the city of Salta and increasingly have become integrated into the Argentine socioeconomic benefit system.

Another perspective on immigration to Argentina from bordering nations considers the topic from the viewpoint of a contributing neighbor (Gillespie and Browning 1979). While the estimated 470,000 Paraguayans living in Argentina in 1973 constituted only about 2 percent of the host country's population, their numbers compared to about 20 percent of Paraguay's 2,400,000 inhabitants. Many Paraguayans enter Argentina as tourists or temporary workers and are given visas. It is not known how many simply stay on after visa expiration, but the number of illegal immigrants from all bordering nations (and Paraguayans were the largest single national grouping) did reach such proportions that in 1973 President Juan Perón granted amnesty to an estimated 350,000 such migrants on the condition that they seek legal status.

To put the number of Paraguayans entering Argentina into a perspective familiar to North Americans, it has forced an assimilation comparable in scope to the United States accommodating several million immigrants over a few decades. The 1950–1972 period counted 230,000 migrants, including about 50,000 females of childbearing age (Gillespie and Browning 1979: 506, 508). No comparable figures are available since 1972, but it can be safely assumed that migrant Paraguayans and their offspring born in Argentina have accounted for much of one of Latin America's lowest population growth rates.

To summarize, migrants to Argentina from Paraguay, Bolivia, Chile, and to a lesser extent from Brazil and Uruguay, have increased in number and significance over the past several decades. They caused laws, decrees, and regulations to be issued in 1951, 1958, 1965, 1971, and 1981; Juan Manuel Villar, who has detailed this public policy, gives us this perspective:

> To this day, European-born aliens still comprise the bulk of foreigners in Argentina but the relative importance of this group has been decreasing rapidly. Conversely, the migratory flows from neighboring countries constitute critical movements . . . attracting considerable official attention (Villar 1984: 455; see also pp. 459–64).

ECONOMIC COOPERATION

The Paraná River Basin, which is one of the world's largest water systems, has been the main locale for important examples of cooperation among Argentina, Brazil, and Paraguay. The goal has been to develop joint hydroelectric power, particularly in portions of the basin that Paraguay happens to share with its two larger, more ambitious neighbors. As of mid-1983, optimism was high. The Itaipu dam, an outcome of Brazilian-Paraguayan cooperation, was scheduled to begin operations within a year, while two downstream projects involving Argentina and Paraguay (Yacyreta and Corpus) were in development and planning stages. It was estimated that the total annual power production of the three dams eventually could exceed 100 trillion kilowatt hours (Da Rosa 1983).

The treaty through which Argentina and Paraguay reached agreement on the Yacyreta dam was signed in 1973 under Juan Perón, an advocate of regional economic cooperation. It was modeled after Brazil's Itaipu treaty of the same year and was negotiated as a means of checking Brazilian hydroelectric aggrandizement as well as a way of providing Argentina with a vast source of cheap power. Both treaties recognized the Paraná water as a "common pool" resource to be used in an interdependent fashion through binational partnership arrangements. The treaties created separate binational public corporations for each dam which would be equally owned and jointly administered by Paraguay and Brazil (for Itaipu) and Paraguay and Argentina (for Yacyreta). These binational entities were to sell power back to the national power agencies in each country—ANDE in Paraguay, ELETROBRAS in Brazil, and Agua y Energías in Argentina.

Although treaty provisions attempted to promote equity, critics in each nation found real or imagined inequities. Some Paraguayans believed that their nation might never receive its share of the power and thus should receive greater payments from its wealthier neighbors. Some Brazilians thought Paraguay would be receiving more than its fair share of benefits simply by being able to buy Itaipu electricity at the cost of production. Some Argentines urged renegotiation of the Yacyreta treaty, and a few called for withdrawal from the project on the grounds that their nation's terms were less favorable than those obtained by Brazil. Another Argentine complaint was that the Itaipu project would threaten downstream use of the Paraná.

Of more practical concern to Argentina was the delay in construction at Yacyreta. By 1983, $2 billion had been spent on the project, but the main engineering work had not yet been started. Lack of policy continuity in the military regimes, the Malvinas war, domestic political crises, and recommendations for renegotiation from international funding sources all had frustrated progress.

Delays in building Yacyreta persisted under Alfonsín. Contributing problems in 1985 included a dispute with Paraguay over exchange rates, budget cuts in Argentina, and a disagreement over the value of some additional Paraguayan land needed for the project. In 1987, relations between the two nations suffered from Paraguay's refusal to extradite two couples who allegedly fled Argentina with children of young parents killed by the military in the Dirty War. Predictions for Yacyreta finally coming on stream had been moved back to the mid-1990s (*Kiesings Record of World Events* 32:34418, 34:35888).

Nuclear power, an area of modest cooperation between Argentina and Brazil, has also been characterized by individual efforts and competition, in part due to military implications. Argentina's nuclear power quest has been endorsed by all significant national elites except the hydroelectric power lobby, and it also has enjoyed mass appeal. Its nuclear programs suffered from budget cuts in the mid-1980s, but they also have realized significant advances. Due to Brazil's late start, lower levels of political consensus, and the lack of an effective agency to provide bureaucratic leadership, it has trailed Argentina in the nuclear field. In fact, Argentina's comparative advantage has spurred interest in Brazil, where military possibilities have received more overt attention (Adler 1988: 71–87).

Examples of nuclear collaboration between the two nations have been several in number and potentially significant. On the production side, Argentina and Brazil signed a "1980 agreement for exchange of nuclear know-how and materials . . . followed in 1986 by an economic integration treaty that includes joint nuclear development (Adler 1988: 82). On a national security note, they signed a 1985 pact "to reassure each other that no weapons programs were underway," and in 1986 went on to sign a protocol "providing for the prompt notification of any nuclear mishaps, and to discuss electronic monitoring of each other's nuclear facilities" (Poneman 1987: 186). Formal pacts may not lead to a joint nuclear program, but they reflect awareness of the need for some collaboration.

CONCLUSION

As promised at the outset, this discussion of several areas in which bordering nations have had a recent impact on Argentina has been preliminary, rather than conclusive. Boundary disputes, international trade, migratory labor, and economic cooperation do not tell the whole story, and each of these areas could profit from further research and analysis.[3]

What we now know, however, already shows that Argentina's neighbors exert important impacts on its political, economic, and social systems. A democratic regime successfully resolved a long-standing border dispute with Chile and was able to do so with popular support after military rulers had tried to incite public sentiment against settlement. Argentina's trade with its neighbors almost always has exceeded its trade with the United States or any other individual nation. At the same time, Argentina's imports from Bolivia as well as both its imports from and exports to Brazil proved to be very significant components of its overall trade structure. Migrants from bordering nations—especially Paraguay, Bolivia, and Chile—were shown to be of substantial and increasing importance to Argentina's economic production, employment patterns, and hence to its public policy. Finally, the promise of hydroelectric power cooperation with Paraguay and Brazil and nuclear power collaboration with Brazil has truly major economic and political implications which, though fraught with difficulties and uncertainties, might serve as models for other nations.

REFERENCES

Adler, Emanuel. 1988. "State Institutions, Ideology, and Autonomous Technological Development: Computers and Nuclear Energy in Argentina and Brazil," *Latin American Research Review* 23:59–90.

---

[3]One very fruitful area for additional research is the role of migrants in Argentina's informal economy. According to Hernando de Soto (1989), poor Peruvians operate largely outside of time-consuming, expensive formal governmental economic regulations and do so in an effective entrepreneurial style. Migrants might be proportionately more active in Argentina's informal economy than are native-born citizens for at least two reasons. Migrants could face additional red tape, and they probably would have comparatively fewer resources to cope with it.

Carrón, Juan M. 1979. "Shifting Patterns in Migration from Bordering Countries to Argentina," *International Migration Review* 13:475–87.

Child, Jack. 1985. *Geopolitics and Conflict in South America*. New York: Praeger.

Da Rosa, J. Eliseo. 1983. "Economics, Politics, and Hydroelectric Power," *Latin American Research Review* 18:77–107.

De Soto, Hernando. 1989. *The Other Path: The Invisible Revolution in the Third World*. New York: Harper and Row.

F. V. 1977. "The Beagle Channel Affair," *American Journal of International Law* 71:73–107.

Ferguson, Yale. 1984. "Cooperation in Latin America: The Politics of Regional Integration." In *The Dynamics of Latin American Foreign Policy: Challenges for the 1980's*, edited by Jennie K. Lincoln and Elizabeth G. Ferris. Boulder, Colo.: Westview.

Fraga, J.A. 1985. *Ensayos de geopolítica*. Buenos Aires: Instituto de Publicaciones Navales.

Garrett, James L. 1985. "Beagle Channel: Confrontation and Negotiation in the Southern Cone," *Journal of Interamerican Studies and World Affairs* 7:93–104.

Gillespie, Francis, and Harley Browning. 1979. "The Effect of Emigration upon Socioeconomic Structure: The Case of Paraguay," *International Migration Review* 13:502–18.

Keohane, Robert O., and Joseph S. Nye. 1977. *Power and Interdependence: World Politics in Transition*. Boston: Little, Brown, and Co.

Marshall, Adriana. 1979. "Immigrant Workers in the Buenos Aires Labor Market," *International Migration Review* 13:488–501.

Poneman, Daniel. 1987. *Argentina: Democracy on Trial*. New York: Paragon House.

Rudolph, James D., ed. 1985. *Argentina: A Country Study*. Area Handbook Series. Washington, D.C.: United States Government.

Sanderson, Steven E., ed. 1985. *The Americas in the International Division of Labor*. New York: Holmes and Meier.

Selcher, Wayne A. 1985. "Brazilian-Argentine Relations in the 1980's: From Wary Rivalry to Friendly Competition," *Journal of Interamerican Studies and World Affairs* 27:25–53.

USITA (United States International Trade Administration). 1988. *Latin American Trade Review, 1987: A U.S. Perspective*. Washington, D.C.: U.S. Department of Commerce, International Trade Administration, March.

Villar, José Manuel. 1984. "Argentine Experience in the Field of Illegal Immigration," *International Migration Review* 18:453–67.

Whiteford, Scott. 1981. *Workers from the North: Plantations, Bolivian Labor, and the City in Northwest Argentina*. Austin: University of Texas Press.

Wilkie, James W., David Lurey, and Enrique Ochoa, eds. 1988. *Statistical Abstracts of Latin America*, vol. 26. Los Angeles: Latin American Center, University of California, Los Angeles.

About the Contributors

C. Richard Bath is Professor of Political Science and former Director of the Center for Inter-American and Border Studies at the University of Texas, El Paso. Bath specializes in inter-American relations, border studies, and environmental/resource issues in U.S.-Mexican relations. He has published four books and over thirty-five articles in journals and edited volumes, and is co-editor of *Air Pollution along the United States-Mexico Border* (Texas Western, 1974).

Melissa H. Birch is Associate Professor in the Darden Graduate School of Business Administration, University of Virginia. She has served as a Fulbright Scholar in Paraguay, an Organization of American States Fellow in Paraguay and Brazil, and a Tinker Foundation Fellow. Her research has focused on multinational development and Paraguay.

William H. Bolin, currently Senior Research Fellow at the University of California, Los Angeles, is retired Vice Chairman of Bank of America. He has held various positions in the International Banking Division of Bank of America, working primarily with developing countries, and was Executive Officer of Bank of America's World Banking Division from 1981 to 1984. He has served as Director or Trustee of the Overseas Development Council, the Council of the Americas, the Near East Foundation, and the Pan American Development Foundation.

Ricardo Córdova Macías is a Ph.D. student in Political Science at the University of Pittsburgh. He has previously served as a Consultant and Fellow of the United Nations University, a Research Scholar at the Center for Interdisciplinary Humanities Research at Mexico's National University (UNAM), and research assistant at the Center for Latin American Studies, UNAM. He has written a number of articles and monographs on Latin America, including chapters in *El Estado en América Latina* and *América Latina, Hoy*, both published by Siglo XXI.

Rodolfo O. de la Garza is Professor of Government at the University of Texas at Austin. He is recognized for his research on Chicano voting attitudes and behavior, U.S.-Mexican relations, and the Mexican political system. He recently edited *Ignored Voices: Public Opinion Polls and the Latino Community* (Center for Mexican American Studies, University of Texas, 1987).

Lawrence A. Herzog is Professor, Department of Mexican American Studies, San Diego State University, San Diego, California. He specializes in urban design and planning in the U.S.-Mexico border and in Latin America. He is the author of many articles on the subject and two books: *Where North Meets South: Cities, Space and Politics on the U.S.-Mexico Border* (Center for Mexican American Studies/University of Texas Press, 1990) and *Planning the International Border Metropolis* (edited, Center for U.S.-Mexican Studies, University of California, San Diego, 1986).

John D. Martz is Professor of Political Science at Pennsylvania State University and is currently editor of the journal *Studies in Comparative International Development*. Martz has written or edited sixteen books and numerous articles on the foreign and domestic policies of Colombia, Venezuela, and Ecuador. His most recent book is *U.S. Policy in Latin America: A Quarter Century of Crisis and Challenge* (University of Nebraska Press, 1988).

Rebecca Morales is a Visiting Fellow at the Center for U.S.-Mexican Studies, University of California, San Diego. She previously taught urban planning in the School of Architecture and Urban Planning, UCLA, and also served as Associate Director of the Latin American Center. Her current research looks at the changing relationship between industrialization and regional growth. Her forthcoming book, *Flexible Production: Restructuring of the International Automobile Industry*, focuses on contemporary industrial processes in Asia, Latin America, North America, and Europe.

Stephen P. Mumme is Associate Professor of Political Science at Colorado State University. His research focuses on environmental policy and politics along the United States-Mexico border. He is co-author of *Statecraft, Domestic Politics, and Foreign Policy Making: The El Chamizal Dispute* (Westview, 1988) and author of *Apportioning Groundwater beneath the U.S.-Mexico Border* (Center for U.S.-Mexican Studies, University of California, San Diego, 1988), as well as numerous journal articles.

Mitchell A. Seligson is Professor of Political Science and Director of the Center for Latin American Studies at the University of Pittsburgh. His books on Central America include *Peasants of Costa Rica and the Development of Agrarian Capitalism* (University of Wisconsin Press, 1980) and

Elections and Democracy in Central America (co-edited, University of North Carolina Press, 1989).

Leslie Sklair is Senior Lecturer in Sociology at the London School of Economics and Political Science, England. He has written two books and numerous articles on the sociology of knowledge and the sociology of development. His recent work has addressed the maquila industry and the U.S.-Mexico border, including the books *Assembling for Development: The Maquila Industry in Mexico and the United States* (Westview, 1989) and *Annotated Bibliography and Research Guide to Mexico's In-Bond Industry, 1980–1988* (Center for U.S.-Mexican Studies, University of California, San Diego, 1988). He also authored *Sociology of the Global System* (Johns Hopkins University Press, 1990).

Richard W. Slatta is Associate Professor of History at North Carolina State University. His first book, *Gauchos and the Vanishing Frontier* (University of Nebraska Press, 1983), won the annual Hubert Herring Prize from the Pacific Coast Council on Latin American Studies as the best book on a Latin American topic. Slatta also edited the book *Bandidos: The Varieties of Latin American Banditry* (Greenwood, 1987) and is author of *Cowboys of the Americas* (Yale University Press, 1990).

Jesús Tamayo-Sánchez holds degrees in Architecture and Urban Planning. For twelve years he practiced and taught architecture in Mexico. Since 1978, he has been a Research Scholar at the Center for Economics Research and Teaching (CIDE) in Mexico City. Tamayo is co-author of *Zonas fronterizas, México-Estados Unidos* (CIDE, 1983) and co-editor of *México en el Siglo XX* (UNAM, 1975).

Claudio Vargas is a Researcher at the Center for Latin American Studies at the University of Guadalajara, Mexico.

Freeman J. Wright is Professor of Political Science at California State University, Fresno, and has studied Latin American politics for over twenty-five years. His publications include *Latin American Politics: A Developmental Approach* (co-authored, Mayfield, 1975), two monographs, and a number of scholarly articles. He has been an Organization of American States Fellow in Chile, a member of the faculty at the Central University of Ecuador, and Senior Fulbright-Hays Lecturer in Argentina.

CENTER FOR U.S.-MEXICAN STUDIES, UCSD

ACADEMIC STAFF
Wayne A. Cornelius, Director
Cathryn L. Thorup, Director of Studies and Programs

PUBLICATIONS PROGRAM
EDITORIAL ADVISORY BOARD

Kevin J. Middlebrook, Co-chairman
Indiana University at Bloomington

Peter H. Smith, Co-chairman
University of California, San Diego

María Amparo Casar
Centro de Investigación y Docencia Económicas

Romana Falcón
El Colegio de México

Joe Foweraker
University of Essex

Mercedes González de la Rocha
CIESAS Occidente

Merilee Grindle
Harvard Institute for International Development

Soledad Loaeza
El Colegio de México

Abraham Lowenthal
University of Southern California

Nora Lustig
Brookings Institution

Lorenzo Meyer
El Colegio de México

Richard Newfarmer
World Bank

Juan Pérez Escamilla
Consultores en Decisiones Gubernamentales

Eric Van Young
University of California, San Diego

Mónica Verea
Universidad Nacional Autónoma de México

Laurence Whitehead
Oxford University

Sandra del Castillo, Managing Editor

Publication and dissemination of important new research on Mexico and U.S.-Mexican relations is a major activity of the Center for U.S.-Mexican Studies. Statements of fact and opinion appearing in Center publications are the responsibility of the authors alone and do not imply endorsement by the Center for U.S.-Mexican Studies, the Editorial Advisory Board, or the University of California.

ORDERS: For a complete list of Center publications and ordering information, please contact:

Publications Distributor
Center for U.S.-Mexican Studies, 0510
University of California, San Diego
9500 Gilman Drive
La Jolla, CA 92093-0510

Phone: (619) 534-1160 FAX: (619) 534-6447